To the memory of F. P. Ramsey
whose work I should most like to be able to
emulate.

Contents

Preface

This book derives originally from talks on time broadcast by the
Australian Broadcasting Commission in 1975 and later, revised, by
the BBC; so I would thank Julie Anne Ford of the ABC and Fraser
Steel of the BBC for encouraging me to write the talks, thereby
setting me off on the book. I was in Australia in 1975 as a Visiting
Fellow in the Philosophy Department of the Research School of
Social Sciences at the Australian National University, to whom
I am much obliged for enabling me to go there and discuss all sorts
of things, including time. To many philosophers and others whom
I met in Canberra, Sydney, Melbourne, Adelaide and Brisbane, I
owe the great pleasure and mental profit of my visit. In Canberra
I was pleasantly and profitably provoked by a class on time run by
Genny Lloyd and Bill Godfrey-Smith, whose intense and ingenious
devotion to real tenses made me think the tenseless truth could still
do with some help from its friends, and so decided me to write a
book about it. Of philosophers elsewhere in Australia, Graham
Nerlich and Jack Smart have most influenced my thinking about
time.

   Since 1975 I have developed the ideas in this book through many
discussions and lectures at Cambridge and elsewhere, and learned a
lot from comments made on those occasions by colleagues and
students. In particular, my reconstruction in chapter 6 of
McTaggart's argument against real tenses owes much to sugges-
tions and corrections made by Timothy Smiley. Besides that, my
views on time have been most affected – one way or another – by
the graduate research I have been privileged to supervise of Bill
Godfrey-Smith, Huw Price and Jeremy Butterfield. Jeremy Butterfield, especially, now a Cambridge colleague and a close friend,
has taught me more than anyone else about the relevance of physics
and the semantics of tense.

   Outside Cambridge, two recent discussions of my work on time
have been exceptionally valuable to me. One was at a meeting in

March 1979 of the Thyssen United Kingdom Philosophy Group which discussed *inter alia* a first draft of my 'McTaggart, fixity and coming true', referred to below. (I have also had helpful comment on that work from David Lewis and John Mackie, and at a seminar at the University of Arizona in early 1979, arranged by Wesley Salmon.) The other was in a class on time I gave at Stanford University in 1978, which I am indebted to Nancy Cartwright for arranging and examining as well as contributing to. To John Perry, then Head of the Philosophy Department there, I owe thanks for its hospitality as well as for ideas on indexicals freely appropriated in chapter 5.

The Stanford class was part of a six-month visit to the USA from October 1978, when I lived in Berkeley and was, through the good offices of Barry Stroud, allowed to use the Library and other facilities of U.C. Berkeley's Philosophy Department, and so given the chance of pertinent and useful conversations with its students and faculty. My work on time in the USA was also furthered by the help and friendship of Ian Hacking and Nancy Cartwright, John and Sue Shively, Isaac and Judy Levi and, above all, Edwin Almirol. The visit itself came at the start of my two-year Radcliffe Fellowship, during which the book was virtually done and without which it would not have been. So I must here render especial thanks to the Radcliffe Trustees and their advisers for awarding me the Fellowship, and to my Cambridge colleagues for granting me exceptional leave to take it up. My American excursion during it was made possible by a much appreciated Overseas Visiting Fellowship from the British Academy.

I am grateful also for two other contributions made by the British Academy to this book. They made me their Henriette Hertz Lecturer for 1979, which provided an occasion to develop and try out most of the material of chapter 10 as 'The possibility of prediction', read to the Academy on 3 May 1979; and in 1977 they gave money for compiling an annotated bibliography of recent work on time and other metaphysical matters. It was the basis of the bibliography at the end of this book, to which I owe much more than (for reasons given in the Introduction) I acknowledge in the text. I am correspondingly indebted to those who compiled and annotated it for me: David West, John Dupré, Peter Smith and Jeremy Butterfield.

The actual writing of the book was kept going by encouragement, not to say pressure, from Jeremy Mynott and Jonathan

Sinclair-Wilson of the University Press, whose philosophical and commercial judgment will I hope not thereby be impugned, and from Penny Thomson, who typed and subedited it. Now it is done, I am grateful to them, as I am to Anmol Vellani for indexing it, and to the designer and printers for making a handsome volume of it. The object depicted on the jacket was, I should record, given to me by Bill Godfrey-Smith, for whom its changelessness embodies all that is wrong with tenseless views of time.

In the course of the book I have reused, with permission where necessary, material contained in the following: 'In defence of dispositions', *Philosophical Review* **83** (1974); 'Special relativity and present truth', *Analysis* **34** (1974); 'The possibility of prediction', *Proceedings of the British Academy* **65** (1979) (also available as an offprint); 'Consciousness and degrees of belief', *Prospects for Pragmatism*, ed. D. H. Mellor (1980), Cambridge; 'The self from time to time', *Analysis* **40** (1980); 'On things and causes in spacetime', *British Journal for the Philosophy of Science* **31** (1980); 'McTaggart, fixity and coming true', *Reduction, Time and Reality*, ed. R. Healey (1981), Cambridge; 'Thank goodness that's over', *Ratio* **23** (1981); 'The reduction of society', *Philosophy* **57** (1982).

Cambridge
February 1981

Since the original publication the treatment of Prior's 'Thank goodness that's over' in chapter 3 has been superseded by Murray MacBeath's 'Mellor's Emeritus headache', *Ratio* **25** (1983), 81–8. This improves my tenseless account of the apparent presence of experience: see my 'MacBeath's soluble aspirin', *Ratio* **25** (1983), 89–92.

Since 1981 I have also come to think, *pace* Davidson, that facts, not events, are the primary causes and effects. This does not in fact affect the treatment of change in chapter 7, the discussion of events, causes, things and parts in chapter 8, the derivation of temporal from causal order in chapter 9, or the argument against backward causation in chapter 10. See my 'Fixed past, unfixed future', *Contributions to Philosophy: Michael Dunnett*, ed. B. Taylor (1985), Nijhoff.

Cambridge
October 1984

Introduction and summary

This book is about such of the metaphysics of time as follows from settling the significance of tense, i.e. of the distinctions we draw between past, present and future. One way and another, tense covers most of time's metaphysics, for its status is itself the main and most contentious metaphysical question about time, and on it depends much else besides: what makes tensed statements true or false; our need for, and the nature of, tensed thought and speech; the fact that all our thought, action and experience takes place in the present; our sense of time passing; how we perceive the temporal order of things and events; our inability to perceive the future or affect the past; time's intimate connection with change; how time differs in this and other ways from space; how things differ from events; why causes generally precede their effects and whether some might succeed them; the direction of time and of its passing from future to past; whether time travel is possible; the peculiarly temporal character of prediction. All these matters will be settled in the course, or in consequence, of settling the status of tense.

Four metaphysical questions about time I shall not discuss: whether time is continuous, dense or discrete; what makes different intervals of time the same or different in extent; whether time is something over and above what happens in it; whether time has a beginning or an end. These questions are too independent of tense, and too considerable, to be tackled with it in this book. The third and fourth turn too much on theoretical physics and cosmology, the second on how much the measurement of time depends on conventions, and the first and fourth on the logic of infinity.

Some philosophers think abstruse and debatable theories of physics or of meaning are also needed to solve the problems I shall tackle. I disagree, but instead of arguing my case abstractly, I would rather prove it *passim* by doing without them. I shall take note *en passant* of some seemingly relevant bits of physics and semantics, but only to show that they are either irrelevant or indisputable. It is for instance debatable whether, and if so when, statements about the past or future can be true or false; and in general how far saying in what conditions a statement would be true gives its meaning. But I need not take sides in either debate (although I shall incidentally settle the first). I need only the undoubted fact that whenever statements about the past or future *are* true or false, their truth or falsity is fixed, given their meaning, by how much earlier or later they are made than whatever they are about. (If 'It will rain tomorrow' is ever true, it is true the day before it rains.) It may similarly be debatable in relativistic physics whether causes always precede their effects absolutely, i.e. in all reference frames; but my proof that they do, while consistent with relativity, does not invoke it and is impervious to controversy about it. Generally, indeed, I refer to physics chiefly to dispel misapprehensions of its authority: over the direction of time, for example, or the distinctions I need to draw between time and space and between things and events in order *inter alia* to account for change.

It is somewhat unfashionable nowadays to do metaphysics in English without relying on physics or the philosophy of language, and although I forgo the fashion, I am not trying to change it. Maybe metaphysics does mostly depend on physics and philosophy of language. But the metaphysics of time mostly does not; and that being so, there is value in tackling it my way. Steering clear of scientific and semantic debates makes my course not only safer but easier to follow, since I thereby avoid much needless technicality and jargon. That will help, I hope, to make time's metaphysics more accessible to students and to the public, without burking any material difficulty in it: a desirable end, given the importance of time and the fascination it holds for most people. It is not an easy subject, but nor is it the preserve of physicists or purveyors of theories of meaning.

I am of course in debt to much philosophical writing, old and new, about time and related matters. Among writers of this century, McTaggart, Russell, Einstein, Minkowski, Weyl, Broad, Braithwaite, Ayer, Quine, Popper, Reichenbach, Smart, Grünbaum, Putnam, Earman, Swinburne, Lucas, Nerlich, Quinton, Davidson, Prior, Geach, Gale, Mackie, Dummett, Lewis, Jeffrey, Sklar, Godfrey-Smith, Newton-Smith, Thalberg and Perry have all supplied or provoked more or less important parts of my argument. But although I list relevant works by these and other authors at the end of the book, I shall refer very little to them in the text. That is partly for the sake of readers unread in all this literature, and partly because its bulk, and the variety of its idioms, prevent my doing it justice succinctly and without obscuring the gist of the book. I must emphasise therefore that the fewness of my references is not meant as a sign of originality. On the contrary, its excuse is that my main points, albeit disputed, are so common in the literature as to be by now public property. So I trust no offence will be taken for or by authors whose work I use without acknowledgment.

One author, however, I will acknowledge: J. E. McTaggart, who proved the unreality of tense and of the flow of time. Although well known to philosophers, his proof has rarely had its due, and since it is the lynchpin of my book, I wish to make amends for that explicitly.

This book in short is a self-contained, argued exposition of a view of time quite familiar to philosophers. It is not itself very original, nor is it a guide to what is. Its aim is simply to expound the view in plain terms, showing by consecutive argument how ramified its consequences are. There, if anywhere, lies its claim to be read; so, to fortify the claim, I will now outline the argument, whose structure might otherwise be veiled by the detail of ensuing chapters. But being more digest than preamble, what follows may be too condensed for readers new to the subject: if so, they should skip it now and return to it later.

Everyone distinguishes past, present and future, and applies the distinction to everything that is in time at all: to people, animals and plants, to experiences, thoughts and actions, to inanimate things, events and processes, to dated facts about all these, and to dates themselves. We and contemporary animals, our and their activities and experiences, and the plants and other natural objects, happenings, facts and artefacts of our time were once future, will all eventually be past and are now present; whereas our remote ancestors and their times, once future and then present, are now past, while our remote descendants, who will in time become present and then past, are as yet still only future.

The present, and temporal distances from it, past and future, I follow custom and call tenses. This sense of 'tense' relates of course to verbal tense, but the two must not be confounded. What I call tense need not be marked by modifying verbs. Not all languages use verbs to mark tenses, and even English verbs only differentiate past, present and future qualitatively, finer distinctions of tense being made by adverbs and phrases like 'ten minutes ago', 'today' and 'next year'. To me it makes no odds how tenses are marked, so by 'tensed' statements and sentences I shall mean those that say, by verbal tense or otherwise, how near or far from the present, past or future, something is. By 'tense' I shall not mean verbal tense unless I say so.

Distinctions and transitions of tense, between what has been, is and will be past, present and future, divide philosophers into two fundamentally opposed camps. The one, "tensed", camp takes these distinctions to reflect real nonrelational differences between past, present and future things (events, facts, etc.). By 'non-relational' I mean that an event's being present when it occurs, its previously being future, and subsequently past, are supposed to be more than the unchanging relations all events always have to earlier, simultaneous and later times, viz. the tenseless relations respectively of being later, simultaneous and earlier than them. Futurity, temporal presence and pastness are all supposed to be real nonrelational properties which everything in time successively possesses, changing objectively as it exchanges each of these properties for the next.

Tenses, in short, are supposed to be much like (e.g.) temperatures; and just as temperature differences make things differ in other ways, so for the tensed camp other differences depend on differences of tense. The camp is not indeed united on what else depends on tense. Some think existence does, so that only what is present exists, or only what is past or present, what is still only future being as yet non-existent. Others admit the future's existence, but allow objectively possible alternatives to it which they deny to the present and the past, these being fixed and settled in some way that the future is not. But all such doctrines require real nonrelational differences between past, present and future for these other differences to depend on; and that is what we in the "tenseless" camp deny.

The tenseless camp often offers only weak inducements to join it: the relative simplicity of tenseless logic, for example, or its consonance with relativity's unification of space and time. But tenseless time needs a stronger sales pitch than that. Tense is so striking an aspect of reality that only the most compelling argument justifies denying it: namely, that the tensed view of time is self-contradictory and so cannot be true. McTaggart showed that in 1908, while trying to show time itself to be unreal. Time, however, is not unreal: the rest of McTaggart's argument is wrong. But the incredibility of his conclusion has unfortunately also infected his disproof of tense, which is why the tensed camp still has members and needs a new presentation of McTaggart's argument to empty it for good.

By showing how time can be real though tense is not, I hope to escape the incredulity McTaggart met. And even about the unreality of tense I must enter a caveat. I am not saying that tense is subjective: for example, that to be present is to be present to consciousness or in some other such way without the scope of physics. Past, present and future tense statements – e.g. a clock saying (in effect) 'It is now two o'clock' by chiming twice – are objectively true or false quite independently of consciousness or of anything else subjective. Physical facts alone suffice to make them true or false. What makes a clock's chiming two true, if it is, is its chiming two at two o'clock; and there is nothing subjective or psychological about that.

But nor is there anything tensed about it. Like other specimens or "tokens" of present tense sentences, the chime is true if and only if it occurs at the same time as it asserts to be present, in this case two o'clock, whether that is now the present time or not. Similarly for tokens of future tense sentences, which are true if and only if suitably earlier than their subject matter: e.g. 'The train will arrive in ten minutes' is true just in case it is said ten minutes before the train arrives. Similarly for past tense tokens, true if and only if suitably later than their subject matter: 'Today is the Queen's fiftieth birthday' is true if said fifty years after her birth and false otherwise. So far as time goes, in short, the truth of a tensed statement depends only on how much earlier or later it is made than whatever it is about. Whether its subject matter is also past, present or future is irrelevant to its truth; so such statements can quite well be objectively true or false even though nothing in reality is past, present or future at all.

The above means that I subscribe to the so-called "token-reflexive" account of what makes tensed statements true or false, an account which lets me keep objective tensed truths and falsehoods while rejecting objectively tensed things, events and facts. But the tensed camp deny that this can be all there is to tense, and in particular to our experience of tense. All the double chimes of an accurate clock, for example, are equally true because they occur at some two o'clock or other. But as we hear it chime, we know also that just one of these two o'clocks really is present, which none of the others is. Hearing the chime tells us that, because it is a fact of experience that all experience takes place in the present. This curious phenomenon, the experienced temporal presence of experience, is the crux of the tensed view of time, and the tenseless camp must somehow explain it away. I do so here by exploiting the token-reflexive account of what would make a simultaneous thought, 'This experience is present', true.

Although I put the token-reflexive account of tensed truth to these tenseless uses, I have a caveat to enter about it too. I am not trying to give tenseless – i.e. non-token-reflexive – translations of tensed statements. That is easily shown to be impossible. Nor could we dispense with the states of tensed belief which they express, because to get what we want we have to act at more or less specific times. To catch the six o'clock news, for example, I must turn on the radio then, which in practice means that I turn it on when I believe it is six o'clock *now*. We need, that is, to act on beliefs true only at some times and not at others, i.e. on beliefs expressed by temporally token-reflexive and therefore tensed statements. Tenseless beliefs, true always if at all, could neither cause nor explain the timeliness of our actions unless accompanied by appropriately tensed beliefs.

By showing how temporally token-reflexive thought and speech is both untranslatable and indispensable, I show why there are inescapable objective truths about what is past, present and future, even though nothing really is past, present or future in itself. Although tense is not an aspect of reality, to us who act in time it is an inescapable mode of perceiving, thinking and speaking about reality.

But what then distinguishes temporal from spatial token-reflexives? The thought or statement 'Cambridge is here', true only in Cambridge, is as token-reflexive as 'It is now two o'clock', as indispensable in its place, and as untranslatable into non-token-reflexive terms. What makes 'It is now two o'clock' tensed is not just that it is token-reflexive, but that to be true it needs to be thought or said neither *earlier* nor *later* than two o'clock, whereas 'Cambridge is here' needs to be said within the *spatial* bounds of Cambridge. But what makes *earlier* and *later* temporal as opposed to spatial relations? Or, to put the question another way: how does time differ from a dimension of space?

The obvious answer is that time is the dimension of change. Motion, for example, is change of spatial location, i.e. being in different places at different times; and change in general is things having different properties from time to time. But things spread out in space can also have properties varying from place to place. A poker, for instance, can as readily be at once hot one end and cold the other as it can be all hot one day and all cold the next. Why is variation of its temperature across space not change when its variation through time is? It will not do to *define* change as variation through time, if time itself can only be defined as the dimension of change.

Real tense provides an easy way out of this vicious circle. The tenses of things, events and facts, i.e. how far future, present or past they are, are constantly changing. This is the familiar flow or passage of time, and it is what distinguishes tenses from dates. A thing's dates are permanent, its tenses are not: that is the obvious – and, as we shall see, the only – difference between them. Now, nobody believes in "spatial tenses", i.e. in any spatial "hereness" or "thereness" of places besides the token-reflexive facts which make 'Cambridge is here' true in Cambridge and false elsewhere. Consequently there is no spatial analogue of the passage of time, the ever-changing tense of things, events and facts moving inexorably from the far future through the present to the remote past. So if only this movement existed, it could be used to distinguish time from space, so that change could be defined as the temporal variation of a thing's properties without begging the question against its spatial counterparts.

But McTaggart has proved the passage of time impossible, so that account of change will not do. The way tenses would have to keep changing, to accommodate the token-reflexive facts that make tensed statements true or false, is what prevents them existing in reality at all. So how, if not by its passage, may time be distinguished from space as the dimension of change? McTaggart thought it couldn't be, and hence that change, and therefore time itself, were unreal. And much of the tenseless camp concurs with him in substance, citing in support of time's spacelikeness the spacetime of relativity, whose spatial and temporal components can be identified only arbitrarily. (It is no accident that relativity's spacetime manifold is often taken to imply a changeless universe.)

In fact relativity gives no reason to think time spacelike or the world devoid of change. On the contrary, it invokes in causation the very means we need to distinguish tenseless time from space. If one event affects another, it is absolutely earlier, i.e. earlier in all reference frames. Causal order fixes temporal order and thereby distinguishes it from spatial order. But can we say why without again invoking tenses?

The answer lies in how temporal order is perceived. Suppose for example I see one event e precede another, $e^\star$. I must first see e and then $e^\star$, my seeing of e being somehow recollected in my seeing of $e^\star$. That is, my seeing of e affects my seeing of $e^\star$: this is what makes me – rightly or wrongly – see e precede $e^\star$ rather than the other way round. But seeing e precede $e^\star$ means seeing e first. So the causal order of my perceptions of these events, by fixing the temporal order I perceive them to have, fixes the temporal order of the perceptions themselves. And from this modest observation I can derive the universal dependence of temporal on causal order.

This may seem in summary a devious and unlikely derivation, although I hope it will not seem so when carried out. But the striking fact it rests on should be noticed, namely that perceptions of temporal order need temporally ordered perceptions. No other property or relation has to be thus embodied in perceptions of it: perceptions of shape and colour, for example, need not themselves be correspondingly shaped or coloured. This sharing by a perception of the property thereby perceived is peculiar to time, and fundamental enough in my view to define it.

With tenseless time thus defined by means of causation, change can now be defined as variation through time. But not all variation through time is change, and to say what is and what is not, I must explain and exploit a familiar distinction. The distinction is between events on the one hand, and things, such as people, animals, plants and ordinary material objects, on the other. The explanation is that whereas both things and events may be extended in time as well as space, only events have temporal parts; things do not. It was not just a temporal part of Everest that temporal parts of Hilary and

Tenzing first climbed: both men and mountain were wholly present throughout all the temporal parts of that historic event.

Change may now be defined as a variation in a real property of something, provided the variation does not reduce to a difference between different parts of it. Things therefore may change, but not events, since events' properties varying through time always do reduce to different temporal parts having different properties. A concert, for instance, which starts quietly and gets louder simply has more or less loud temporal parts. But although events do not change, they may of course *be* changes, namely changes in things.

This definition of change has obvious virtues, once we admit that change cannot really be different things and events successively becoming present and then past. The first is that it fits usage: we think of people, animals, plants and material objects as changeable; but not events, and in particular not changes. More important, it is intrinsically plausible. Two entities differing in their properties do not in general constitute change, because they supply no one entity that changes. Why make an exception just when one is later than the other and both are parts of something else (which, as a whole, has neither property)? Most important of all, the definition associates change exclusively with time. Spatial variation is not change, because things and events whose properties vary simultaneously from place to place always have corresponding spatial parts to whose different properties the spatial variation reduces. A poker hot one day and cold the next thereby changes, because it is wholly present on each day; but a poker at once hot at one end and cold at the other is not wholly present at each end. Only parts of it are; the poker as a whole is therefore neither hot nor cold, and *a fortiori* does not change in that respect.

Despite its manifest virtues, there are objections to this definition. On it, changes do not change, which McTaggart thought they had to do in order to be changes. But why must changes change? The idea is a *non sequitur*, and I just deny it. Some tidy-minded philosophers have also claimed (apropos especially of relativity) that things are really sequences of events, which for me would mean there is no change. But I see no reason to believe this claim – certainly relativity gives none – and good reasons not to, if only because it groundlessly flouts usage and precludes the only tenable account of tenseless change.

More interestingly, I must also deny the converse reduction, of events to changes in things. This could not be right anyway, because some events, especially in microphysics, are obviously not changes in any thing. But even if they were, the reduction would not do. It would mean defining events as changes in real properties of things, and saying therefore why, e.g. being forty or famous is not a real property, since variation in those respects need not be a change at all. I need not change in any tenseless way on my fortieth birthday, nor when I unwittingly hit the headlines. And the reason is that these alterations in me need not be real events, i.e. need not have immediate effects in my vicinity. In short, for my definition of change to be credible, changes must be restricted to events, independently understood as producers of immediate contiguous effects, and not the other way round.

So much for change through tenseless time; now for its direction. Being tenseless, its direction is not the difference between past and future, but that between earlier and later, which we have seen to be the temporal difference between cause and effect. That explains at once why we can affect some future events, i.e. events later than our actions. Moreover, since to see or otherwise perceive something is *inter alia* to be affected by it – e.g. by photons reflected from it to the eye – it also explains our ability to perceive some past things and events, i.e. events earlier than our perceptions of them. But our sense of the flow of time, from events being affectable to their being perceptible, remains to be explained, and so does our complete inability to perceive the future or affect the past.

The flow of time is relatively straightforward. It turns out to be in reality no more than an accumulation of successive memories. That is, first I have an experience, then I remember having it, then I remember remembering it, and so on. Now memory is like perception in that a memory is an effect, direct or indirect, of what is remembered, and hence is always later in time. These successive memories of memories can therefore only accumulate at successively later, not earlier, times, and this is why our sense of the flow of time has the direction it has.

It is harder to say why we cannot perceive the future or affect the past. What this comes to on my view is that we cannot affect what we have already perceived, i.e. one event cannot both affect and be affected by another. The question therefore is: why can causes and effects not form a closed loop in and via which each event indirectly affects itself? Only if this were possible could we affect the past (or perceive the future – it comes to the same thing), for example by travelling back in time, or could the whole universe form a complete temporal cycle, with all events both earlier and later than each other.

That all this is impossible can be shown by extending an argument of Professor Dummett's. The extended argument exploits the fact that causation is by definition the mechanism *inter alia* of both action and perception, but uses only the weakest possible assumption about it: namely, that a cause makes its effects more probable than in the circumstance they would otherwise have been. This must be so, for it would otherwise make no sense to perform an action for the sake of its effects, since performing it would not increase their probability; while if I would be just as likely to see something even if it never happened, my seeing it would be no evidence for its happening: and both these consequences are self-evidently absurd.

From this undeniable assumption about causation it follows that enough similar causes will almost certainly produce a statistically significant correlation with their effects; conversely, that if there certainly is no such correlation, there is no causation either. Suppose we use this to test the idea of a closed causal loop, taking the loop to include an action, an effect of the action, and the perception of that effect. (This restriction is only to make it easier to visualise the experiment: it is not essential.) We consider therefore many such loops, trying to get the action performed in just half the cases where the effect has been perceived. If we succeed, there will be no correlation between the action and its supposed effect, and so no causation between them. We can only fail, however, if either the effect increases the probability of the action, in which case the causation is the wrong way round, or some of our perceptions turn out to have been wrong, i.e. some of the effects cannot really be perceived until after the corresponding actions have been done. But real events, it has already been remarked, all have contiguous effects, by which they could always be perceived somehow at the time. The only way an effect can be by no means perceptible before its cause is by not after all preceding it – but then there will again be no closed timelike, i.e. causal, loop from action to effect to perception and back to the action. So whatever happens the causes and effects will form no such loop; and that will be so whether they include actions and perceptions or not, since the argument depends essentially only on the statistics. The correlation which causation needs cannot be attributed to it all the way round a closed chain of events. That is why we cannot affect the past or perceive the future, why backward time travel is impossible, and why neither the whole universe nor any part of it can form a closed temporal cycle.

I do not expect the summary of the last few pages, and perhaps especially of the last argument, to be immediately convincing on its own. (If it were, the rest of the book would be superfluous.) But that is not its function, which is to be part trailer, part summary of what follows. For the full truth about time and tense, now read on.

1   *Dates and tenses*

The great problem about time is tense: how does the present differ from the future and the past? The differences are at first sight striking and profound. In the past lies everything we have observed and brought about; in the future everything yet to be and to be done, which we cannot yet observe; while the present contains our experiences, our thoughts and our actions. We plan for the future because we can affect it, whereas the past is beyond our reach. It is sensible to ponder what to do tomorrow, but not what to have done yesterday: the time to ponder that was the day before, when what is now yesterday was still future. And having pondered what to do, the time to do it is always now: only in the present can we act to give effect to our decisions. While the time for action remains future we can only await it; and when it is past it is too late. After the event, we can only see and hear what has been done: to think then of perhaps not doing it is but waste of thought.

These ideas about past, present and future lie at the heart of our concept of time. But although they are evident, they are not self-evident. They want explanation, and while they lack it they will not want for sceptics. Modern physics especially has already so altered our views of space and time that many would set no metaphysical bounds to it. Though none now look to square the circle, some now think we might affect the past. Such fantasies will not be dispelled until we see more clearly what time and especially what tense is. To make that clear is the prime object of this book.

To show what time is, I must assume something about it: metaphysical bricks cannot be made without factual straw. Not all my assumptions will survive, of course, and some will do so only in eccentric senses. But some will stay intact, and on their credibility my case will eventually depend. Naturally I shall recommend them as I go, but I will not try to show in any general way that the facts and arguments I adduce are necessary or beyond all possible dispute. My object is simply to tell the truth about time, and necessity interests me only as a source of truth. What I say may of course be mistaken, as anything may, but that modest platitude is not the end of metaphysics. I am not claiming infallibility, and I shall waste no time answering merely possible or pretended objections to what follows. Doubt and disbelief are not worth dispelling unless they are real. So long as what I say about time is actually believed, I shall be well satisfied.

Tense

I start with some obvious facts about tense. Past and future admit of degrees: future events are not all equally future, nor are past events all equally past. What differentiates them is the order in which they become or became present. Eighteenth-century events were present before nineteenth-century ones, and that makes them now more past. Thirtieth-century events will become present only after twenty-ninth-century ones, and that makes them now more future. The world's happenings seem generally to be arranged in a temporal series according to the order in which they become present, a series which the metaphysician J. E. McTaggart called the "*A* series". The *A* series of temporal positions runs from the remotest past, through the present, to the remotest future, and at any time all events are located somewhere definite within it. Ideas of past, present and future are best understood and developed in terms of the *A* series, which I shall now set out in the detail we shall need. How we know *A* series facts is a question we can postpone for the time being.

The *A* series is more than the order events become present in. We know also how far events are, past or future, from the present. Last Monday's events not only precede next Monday's, they do so by a week, i.e. by as much as those precede the events of the Monday after. Positions in the *A* series have a quantitative measure which tells us how rapidly events succeed each other in the present, as well as the order they come in.

The *A* series measures how long events last as well as how far they are apart. Few events are instantaneous: World War II, for example, lasted six years. That is, it stretches over six years of the past portion of the *A* series. Shorter events can be given more precise *A* series positions. A wedding, for example, is over in a day, so one can say it took place *last week* or *ten days ago*, though not give its A series position to the nearest second. In short, the positions of events in the A series are not points – i.e. instantaneous moments of past, present or future time – but intervals of such moments, stretching (at least) from the start of the events to their end.

An event has any A series position which spans the whole event. An event that took place *ninety-one years ago* also happened *last century*, and in *the present millennium*. When I talk of "the" A series position of an event, however, what I mean is the shortest of these intervals, i.e. the one that just contains the first and last moments in which the event is present.

In calling A series positions intervals of moments, I should emphasise that I make no great claims for moments, except as ways of summarising A series facts about events. Whether time exists independently of events is a serious question: whether, for example, there would be any time in a world in which nothing ever happened. But in talking of moments I take no sides in that dispute. Moments can be thought of as depending on events: the present moment, for example, on our experience of seeing and hearing things. I do not say that this is so, but nor do I deny it: I claim nothing either way.

Nor do I say that all intervals of time divide into shorter intervals. Whether there is a smallest interval of time is a question for physics and metaphysics. I will not beg it here by building its existence (or non-existence) into my terminology.

Besides these negative reasons, physics provides positive reasons not to take moments too literally, since it shows spatial and temporal distances between events to be not completely independent. There are definite spacetime distances between events, but they do not divide uniquely into spatial and temporal components. There are many equally good answers to the question what celestial events are simultaneous with a given terrestrial event. There are many alternative present moments, therefore, since to be present is to be simultaneous with the present moment here on earth. So "the" present, as a unique moment of time stretching across the whole universe, depends partly on a more or less arbitrary choice of so-called "reference frame".

We shall have to discuss all this more fully in chapter 4, in order to distinguish time from space: all it means here is that there are several A series. Since different reference frames make given celestial events simultaneous with different terrestrial ones, they *ipso facto* give them different tenses. On one frame, an explosion in a nearby galaxy will come out present, while on others, equally good, it will come out centuries past or centuries future. Different reference frames distribute the world's events differently among the various *A* series positions, thus generating different *A* series. But all the series behave in the same way, and each of them contains somewhere within it everything that happens in the world. So for the time being we can afford to select one of them and neglect the others.

With these cautions and qualifications, I will refer to *an A* series, of intervals of moments more or less distant, past or future, from the present. For these *A* series positions I need a generic name, which I will follow philosophical custom and call "tenses". In this sense, *last century* and *last week* are tenses, and so are *this month*, *tomorrow* and *next year*. This use of the word 'tense' is a not unnatural extension of its traditional use, since simple verbal tenses – past, present and future – specify *A* series positions. But a caveat must be entered when extending the idea of tense in this way: tense, in the sense of *A* series positions, has nothing especially to do with verbs. In its original linguistic sense, a tense is a way of modifying a verb on the basis of the *A* series position of whatever it refers to. In 'Jane arrived yesterday' the past tense of the verb has to be used because the event referred to, Jane's arrival, occurs in the past. That is implicit in the adverb 'yesterday', which thus demands the past tense of the verb. By the same token, however, the adverb makes the verbal tense redundant. 'Yesterday' would convey pastness perfectly well even if 'to arrive' had no special past tense form. In short, though verbal tense is sometimes used to give an event's *A* series position, it never need be used for that purpose. The job can always be done by adverbs and phrases like 'yesterday', 'this minute' and 'next week', which will be needed anyway whenever *A* series positions have to be given at all precisely. Now what matters here is the information conveyed, not the means used to convey it. So in talking of tenses in what follows I shall normally mean *A* series positions, not special forms or modifications of verbs (unless I explicitly say so).

The unqualified past tense is the interval of moments open all the way from the remotest past up to, but not including, the present moment. A more precise tense is a past tense if it is included in that interval. Thus *yesterday* and *last week* are past tenses, and so are *last century* and *a minute ago*. They are past because all the moments in them are past; and any event whose A series position is a past tense is a past event.

Similarly for the future. The unqualified future is the interval of A series moments open all the way to the remotest future and back to, but not including, the present moment. More precise future tenses are any intervals included in the unqualified future, such as *tomorrow*, *next week* and *three centuries hence*; and any event with such a tense as its A series position is a future event.

The present is different. *Prima facie*, the present tense should be the present moment, since past, present and future are incompatible. On the other hand, most events last some time and could never be contained in a momentary present; yet we should not say that they are never present. This dilemma has led to the doctrine of the so-called "specious present", in which the present is allowed to encroach somewhat on the future and the past. The question is, how much: how long must the specious present be – a minute, a second, a millisecond? – and what marks it off from the past and future proper? But in fact, the question and the doctrine are what is specious, not the present. It is present events that extend into the past and the future, not the present itself.

If present events take time, they will generally have some parts earlier than the present moment and some later, i.e. some past parts and some future ones. In 1943, for example, World War II had parts stretching four years into the past and two years into the future. It was nevertheless a very present event, as any combatant would then have testified. So the right way to construe a present tense is as *any* interval of A series moments, however long, that contains the present moment. *This millennium* is as much a present tense as *this minute* or *this week*, because any thousand-year-long event whose A series position it was would be as much a present event as is your reading of this sentence.

Some may jib at this definition of the present tense, on the grounds that events which have past or future parts should not be let into the present at all. Now we should indeed distinguish here between events, which do have temporal parts, and what I shall call "things", which do not. I shall need the distinction in chapter 7 in order to account for change, and will develop and defend it further in chapter 8; here, I will only use it to show briefly how present things are wholly present in a way that present events are not.

People, for instance, are things in this sense; and anyone who is presently alive is wholly present, not just partly so. The reason is that present people have no past or future parts, as events are apt to do, to detract from the temporal presence of the whole person. Now this distinction between things and events may well make one doubt whether events are ever really present, or perhaps ever really exist, on a par with people and other things. This doubt seems to me misguided, and perhaps a spatial analogy will help to dispel it. There are senses of 'present' and 'exists' in which a town exists and is spatially present at any point within it, even though the town has many parts which do not contain that point. These are precisely the senses in which World War II was present and existed all the time it went on, despite almost always having wholly past or wholly future parts. They are perfectly good senses, especially the sense of 'present', since it is the only sense in which events or towns are ever present anywhere. It seems to me a virtue, therefore, that my definition of present tenses captures this sense. Nor of course does it in so doing exclude things and people: they too are present just when their *A* series positions contain the present moment. By letting both things and events be present, the definition avoids begging the question as to which is the more fundamental kind of entity.

On this definition, present tenses overlap with and include past and future ones. In June of any given year, the present tense *this year* includes both past tenses such as *last month* (May) and future tenses such as *next month* (July). But despite these overlaps and inclusions, past, present and future remain incompatible attributes both of tenses and events. No single tense can be both present and past, nor can it be present and future, since present tenses by definition contain the present moment, and past and future tenses do not. And therefore no event, and no thing or person, is at once both present and past or present and future. Either its *A* series position contains the present moment, in which case it is present, or it does not, in which case it is past or future. As temporal attributes, therefore, pastness, presence and futurity remain incompatible: nothing can have more than one of them at once. (I scout the idea, which I shall disprove in chapter 10, that time goes round in a circle, so that what is future is also past.) And everything that is in time at all has each of these attributes in succession, being first future, then present and then past. That remains the essential, and the problematic, feature of tense, which any account of time must explain.

Dates

To explain tense, and especially how things and events move inexorably from future to past, we also need the familiar notion of dates. Dates are an alternative way of saying when events occur. In 1985, for example, we can say that World War II ended *forty years ago*, which gives its temporal location as an *A* series position. We can also say that it ended in 1945, which gives its location as a date. Dates are clearly not tenses; indeed they are quite independent of tenses, in the sense that any date can be anywhere in the *A* series. The year 1985, like the events in it, was once in the remote future, will eventually be in the remote past, and is at some time everywhere in between. Giving the date of an event – an eclipse, say – as 1985 says nothing at all about its pastness, presence or futurity. The verbal tense I give a date with may of course show if it is past or future: 'The eclipse will happen in 1985' implies that it, and 1985, are somewhere in the future, while 'The eclipse happened in 1985' implies that they are somewhere in the past. But this extra information about the eclipse's tense is quite gratuitous. It could easily be suppressed by adopting or inventing some standard form of verb that does not vary with *A* series position; and sticking to such tenseless verbs would in no way lessen our ability to date events.

Dates form a series of positions in time, therefore, which is not the *A* series. McTaggart called it the "*B* series", in which positions are distinguished simply by how much later or earlier events are than each other. Dating an event as occurring in 1800, for example, puts it a hundred years later in the *B* series than any event dated 1700, regardless of how far into the past those events may be. Nevertheless, although the *A* and *B* series are not the same, they are very similar, and intimately related. Thus events with earlier dates are always either less future or more past than events with later dates. However far past the events of 1800 may become, those of 1700 will always be a hundred years more past – because it will always be the case that the events of 1700 became present a century before those of 1800. The order in which the *A* and *B* series arrange events is exactly the same, and so is the measure of temporal distance and duration in the two series. Events whose date is a century earlier than the present date are *ipso facto* a century away in the past, i.e. they became present a hundred years ago.

It is of course no coincidence that the *A* and the *B* series use the same measure of time and order events in the same way. Both use the same relations between events to fix their relative positions in the series – namely, the relations of being simultaneous with some events, and more or less earlier or later than others. These relations are not peculiar to the *B* series: *yesterday* is earlier than *today* in exactly the same sense in which 8 August is earlier than 9 August. Having the same tense is being simultaneous in exactly the same sense as having the same date is.

Why then, since the *A* and *B* series are so alike, do we distinguish them? And how exactly do they differ? Before answering these questions I need to bring out their extraordinary similarity in more detail. And in order to do that, I will use the word 'date' henceforth to apply to any *B* series position, just as I use 'tense' of any *A* series one. In what follows, dates will not be restricted to periods of a day or a year. The whole period BC is a date; so is *the nineteenth century*; and so is *the last millisecond of 1985*.

Dates so understood are, like tenses, intervals of moments or instants of time. Only, dates are intervals of *B* series moments, not *A* series ones, the difference being that *B* series moments are not defined by how far they are from the present moment. *B* series moments are such times as *midnight on 31 December 1899*, the moment that divides the nineteenth century from the twentieth. These moments, like their *A* series counterparts, must not be taken too seriously. All the cautionary remarks made above about *A* series moments apply to *B* series ones. So I neither claim nor deny that *B* series moments are independent of events, like the birth of Christ, which are used to fix our scale of dates, or that they could exist without such events. I say nothing, *pro* or *con*, as to the infinite divisibility of *B* series time. And most importantly, though I shall ignore it for the time being, I do not deny the existence of alternative *B* series.

There are many *B* series, corresponding to the different reference frames that make different celestial events simultaneous with the events of any given earthly date. But for my present purposes any one *B* series will do. The question here is how *A* and *B* series are related to each other, and the answer to that is the same for all series. To every *B* series there corresponds a unique *A* series and *vice versa*. Suppose for example that different reference frames make different events in Andromeda simultaneous with the terrestrial events of 10 March 1993, thus filling that *B* series position quite differently. The same will go for the *A* series: whatever celestial events get that terrestrial date will *ipso facto* count on that date as being present. Any one reference frame classifies the world's events in the same way in both series, so for comparative purposes it does not matter which pair of series we consider. By "the" *A* and *B* series I mean any relativistically acceptable *B* series and the *A* series corresponding to it.

Spatially remote events get different dates in different *B* series, and the choice of a *B* series is more or less arbitrary. But once chosen, there is nothing arbitrary about the dates events have in the *B* series. Given a particular reference frame, it is as plain a matter of fact what happens in Andromeda on 10 March 1993 as it is what happens in St Andrews. Even within one *B* series, however, an event has many dates, just as it has many tenses in the corresponding *A* series. Queen Elizabeth's Coronation took place on a day in 1953, and that day is one of its dates. But it also has the dates 1953, the *nineteen-fifties* and *the twentieth century*. "The" date of an event, like "the" tense, is the shortest of all its dates: the interval bounded by the *B* series moments at which it starts and ends. *The date of World War II* is the interval bounded by the moment of September 1939 when war was declared and by the moment of final surrender in 1945. My date is the interval bounded on the one side by the *B* series moment of my death and on the other by whatever *B* series moment I acquired my identity at. (With dates, as with tenses, there may be doubt as to what something's first or last moment is, and therefore doubt as to its exact date; but only because there is no doubt about how the one depends on the other.)

Having settled these – largely terminological – matters, we can now see how alike the *A* and *B* series are. Once we specify which *B* series moment is the *A* series present moment, either series is immediately and completely definable in terms of the other. To every *A* series position there then corresponds a unique *B* series position, and *vice versa*. If, for example, the present moment were now noon precisely on 8 August 1962, 10 a.m. would be *two hours past*, 18 August *ten days hence*, and *the next decade* would be *the nineteen-seventies*. Every thing and event that has those dates then had those tenses, and similarly for all other dates and tenses. (The *A* and *B* series can of course be fixed by dating any *A* series moment: it need not be the present moment.) Now this is clearly no coincidence, nor even a merely contingent law of nature. To be so similar, and so closely related, the two series must be different ways of looking at the same thing, namely how things and events occur in time. But how then *do* the *A* and *B* series differ – and which is the more fundamental of the two?

Dates versus tenses

The difference between *A* and *B* series is this: dates are fixed and tenses are not. By this I mean that an event's (or a thing's) tenses vary with time, and its dates do not. Suppose it is now May 1984 and the Queen is fifty-eight. That is, the Queen will then have been born fifty-eight years ago: i.e. the event of her birth has the tense *fifty-eight years past*. But if the Queen is fifty-eight in 1984, she must have been forty-eight in 1974, and unless she dies first, she will be sixty-eight in 1994. The past tense of her birth is increasing all the time.

This variation of tense does not arise only because I am using dates to specify times. Tense varies just the same when times are specified by means of tenses. If the Queen is fifty-eight *this year*, she was forty-eight *ten years ago* and she will, if she lives, be sixty-eight *ten years hence*. Now ageing is by no means a Royal prerogative: all ages increase, because all past tenses do. The *A* series position of everything varies with time in this way, however the time is specified. When it is specified in terms of tense, the way tense varies with it has become the topic of an academic industry known as "tense logic". The topic is called "logic" because the tenses of events of all kinds vary with time in the same way, so tense logic is as general in its application as ordinary logic is. It is, we might say, in the nature of tense itself to vary with time as it does.

It is likewise in the nature of dates not to vary with time. If the Queen was born on 21 April 1926, then that always was and always will be the date of her birth. *Last year*, her birth had that date, and it will have the same date *next year* and at every other position in the *A* series. The date of the Queen's birth is – tenselessly – 21 April 1926, regardless of where the event now happens to be in the *A* series. Similarly with all events and things. Everything always keeps its date regardless of what its tense is.

Events and things also keep their dates regardless of what the date is. By this I mean that if in 1985 (say) the date of the Queen's birth is 21 April 1926, that will be true at all other dates as well. Some philosophers indeed believe that before 1926, when the event was still future, it did not – yet – exist and so had no date at all. But no one thinks it ever had, or ever will have, any date other than 21 April 1926. Everyone agrees that all existing events and things keep the same dates at all times, whether those times be identified as positions in the *A* or the *B* series. Either way the tense of an event or thing will be different at different times, but its date will not.

This is why there is no "date logic" analogous to tense logic: the constancy of dates makes their logic too simple. What makes tense logic worth studying is the way adding more tenses to a tensed statement can turn truths into falsehoods and *vice versa*. If 'Jane arrived yesterday' is true, 'Tomorrow, Jane arrived yesterday' will be false. To recover the original truth, the original tense must be modified: 'Tomorrow, Jane will have arrived two days ago'. And the same goes for any event: '*e* occurred yesterday' always implies 'Tomorrow, *e* will have occurred two days ago' (provided of course the universe continues to exist tomorrow). The reason there is no serious date logic is that there are no analogous facts about dates for a date logic to express. The dates of events do not change with time, so adding another date to a "dated" statement never makes a false statement true or a true one false. Indeed, the point-lessness of adding dates is so obvious that it sounds very odd to do it at all: to say, for example, 'On February 2, Jane arrives (tenselessly) on February 1'. If this says anything, it says the same as 'Jane arrives (tenselessly) on February 1'. Either both statements are true or both are false. That is all there is to the logic of dates: adding dates to dated statements makes no difference to their truth or falsity.

Dates, in short, are temporally unqualified attributes of events and things, and tenses are not. That is the essential difference between the *B* series and the *A*, indeed the only difference. I talked of linking the *A* and the *B* series by specifying a precise date for an *A* series moment, but that was a misleadingly weak way of putting it. It suggests that we have some choice of which *B* series moment to specify as the present or other *A* series moment, whereas there is no choice in the matter at all. At midday on 9 August 1962, that *B* series moment just *is* the present moment. Moreover, these *A* and *B* series moments are not merely correlated at that time, they are absolutely indistinguishable; as, at that moment, are all the corresponding positions in the two series. Then, August 8 *is* today, tomorrow *is* August 9, last month *is* July, and so on. All these pairs of tenses and dates are ordered in the same way by the same temporal relations, and each tense contains exactly the same things and events as its corresponding date. Temporally, there is no difference whatever, on 8 August 1962, between that date and the tense *today*. If the tenses of events did not change, i.e. if the same *B* series moment were to remain the present moment, there never would be anything to choose between them. The *A* and the *B* series would be the same.

The *A* and *B* series differ *only* because tenses change with time and dates do not, a difference that reduces to the way *B* series moments become successively present. Given the inexorable movement of the present along the *B* series, either series could be defined in terms of the other. But how should we interpret that fact? There seem to be three alternatives. The first is that the world is intrinsically tensed – things and events really are present, and more and less past and future – only we for some reason choose to redescribe these *A* series facts in terms of a *B* series. The second is that the world is intrinsically dated, not tensed, and it is *B* series facts which for some reason we redescribe in *A* series terms. And the third is that both series are equally real: events are intrinsically dated, but there is also an extra, independent fact about the world, namely that it contains a moving present.

I shall argue for the second of these alternatives. The world, I believe, is intrinsically tenseless: events and things are not in themselves either past, present or future. Tense is only a way we have of looking at them; a compelling way, admittedly, which we could not do without, but not the way that in reality they are. The argument for this view, and the account of time in terms of it, is the main burden of this book. But before shouldering it, there is one fundamental objection I must deal with at once. This is that tenses, especially present tenses, are properties we can directly observe events to have. If that were true, it would dispose of the second alternative immediately: as a good empiricist, I will not waste time arguing against the deliverances of my senses. Fortunately, it is not true; but it is quite easy in this case to mistake the import of what we see and hear, and a little argument is needed straightaway to prevent the mistake.

Seeing tenses and seeing dates

Whether we can observe events, and what we can observe of them, does indeed depend on their tenses. I remarked on page 13 that we cannot observe future events. I cannot yet see or hear any of the events that will happen tomorrow. I shall of course be able to see and hear some of them when tomorrow comes; but then they will be present or past. While events are future, they cannot be observed, and this seems itself to be an observable fact about them. But if it is, how could that be unless events really are either past, present or future and we can tell by observation which are which? Yet more tempting is the thought that all observation, of all events, itself occurs in the present. That is, our own experiences, of seeing and hearing things, are given to us in experience as being present tense events. Even our knowledge of past events seems to be given to us by our present tense experiences. In the simplest case, we know about past events because we now remember having seen or heard them happen. Our present memory tells us that the experience of seeing or hearing them, when they were present, is itself a past event. And that, directly or by remembering hearing other people's reports, or seeing photographs or other traces of past events, is ultimately how we get all our knowledge of past events.

So, the objection will run, experience tells us the tenses of events, not their dates. Our knowledge of events' dates is something we work out from what we know of their tenses. Suppose for example it is 1985, i.e. we know that Christ was born *1985 years ago*. We also know then that World War II ended *thirty years ago*. In other words, the *A* series position of the latter event is 1945 years later than that of the former. So (by definition) we assign it a date 1945 years later than the date we assign to Christ's birth; hence, on the Christian scale of dates, we say that World War II ended in AD 1945. And this in general is how we assign dates to events: by comparing their tenses with the tense of some arbitrarily selected event such as the birth of Christ.

Not only, the objection will continue, do we derive dates from knowledge of tenses, that in the end is all we use them to convey. The only reason we refer to dates is that their constancy makes them a handy means of saying when events occur. That is why 'Back at two o'clock' is a better notice to pin to my door than 'Back in two hours' is. For the latter to stay true, the tense in it would have to alter all the time – e.g. by being shown on a clock set to run down to zero by the time I expect to return. By giving instead the constant date of my return, I avoid that complication. But a reader of my notice will want to know, not the date but the future tense of my return, i.e. how soon I am coming back. To work that out from my notice he will need to consult his watch, to see what the time is *now* and hence what *A* series position two o'clock now has. Whereas my clock would have told him directly what he wanted to know, without reference to dates at all.

It is tempting to infer from all this that the *B* series is only a device for presenting information about tenses in a conveniently permanent form; that the temporal reality we observe, and in which we are really interested, is tensed, not dated. The temptation should be resisted. Our temporal interest in reality is indeed tensed; but as we shall see, the tense attaches to our interest, not to the reality. Nor do we really observe the tense of events. The idea that we do comes from confusing the events we observe with the experience of observing them. Suppose I am looking through a telescope at events far off in outer space. I observe a number of events, and I observe the temporal order in which they occur: which is earlier, which later. I do *not* observe their tense. What I see through the telescope does not tell me how long ago those events occurred. That is a question for whatever theory tells me how far off the events are and how long it takes light to travel that distance. We used to think celestial events much closer to the earth, and concluded that they were much more recent than we now think them to be. So, depending on our theory, we might place the events we see anywhere in the *A* series from a few minutes ago to millions of years ago. Yet they would *look* exactly the same. What we see tells us nothing about the *A* series positions of these events. It does not even tell us that the events are past rather than future. Someone who claims to see the future in a crystal ball cannot be refuted by pointing to some visible trace of pastness in the image. Our reason for thinking that we cannot observe the future rests on theory, not on observation.

But what about the temporal presence of experience itself? These events at least, our own seeings and hearings, we surely observe to be present? To that rhetorical question I can so far only produce the paradoxical reply that, although we observe our experience to be present, it really isn't. I shall try to make good that reply, and remove its air of paradox, in chapter 3. But for the present I can afford to overlook this peculiar category of events. All I need here is that we can observe the temporal relations of events other than our own experiences without observing their tenses. Their being more or less past is not something we observe: it is inferred from their having been observed, an inference mediated by the theories that tell us how our senses work.

This is enough to set up the *B* series on its own. First, we observe temporal relations between events, e.g. that one event is more or less later than another. This is not in general a matter of theory, let alone of a theory of tense. Nothing is more observable than temporal order. We see it for example whenever we see something move. Suppose I see the second hand of a watch going round clockwise. That means I see the event of it passing the numeral '1' occur just earlier, not just later, than the event of it passing the numeral '2'. To see the hand go round anti-clockwise would be to see these events occurring the other way round in time: the hand passing '1' after it passes '2'. To see any kind of change occur in a definite direction is to see that one event is earlier than another rather than later than it.

Of course we cannot observe all cases of events being earlier or later than other events. Some events are not easily observed at all. Others follow on too quickly or too slowly for the human eye to catch. Just as we need microscopes to see the shapes and colours of very small things, so we need "action replays" to render rapid changes visible. Nor of course are our observations of temporal order infallible, or uninfluenced by physical theory. Just as we learn that in certain lights we are apt to misjudge colours, so we learn that we are apt to misjudge the temporal order of some events. Having learned, for example, how much faster light travels than sound, we learn to discount the earlier appearance of lightning, and no longer conclude that it occurs before the thunder we hear later.

But often we see how much later or earlier events are than each other just as we see colours. Physical theories and instruments may extend our ability to see these temporal relations, and occasionally correct our unaided observation of them; but in the end they too depend on what we can see with the naked eye. And these observations, extended and corrected by physical theory, place events directly in a *B* series. They do so because *B* series positions, unlike *A* series ones, do not change with time. An event's date is a matter simply of how much earlier or later it is than other events. On the Christian scale, as we have seen, an event's date is given (in principle) by how much later it is than the birth of Christ, and this is independent of the tense of either event. Beings remote in space could date all our earthly events on the Christian calendar without having any idea of how long light took to reach them, or even that backwards causation is impossible. They could know enough to set up the terrestrial *B* series, without having a clue where in the *A* series the events in it were. The *B* series can be defined directly in terms of observable and tenseless temporal relations between events, without referring to the *A* series at all.

The converse is not true. The *A* series can only be defined by reference to the *B* series. Tenses have to satisfy the temporal relations that hold between dates. When one event is observed to be earlier than another, i.e. to have an earlier date, it must follow that it is also that much more past. Past, present and future depend on distinguishing dates as dates do not depend on distinguishing past, present and future.

This is not yet to say that the *A* series can be dispensed with, or reduced altogether to the *B* series. Relations between tenses do indeed reduce to those we observe to hold between events and therefore between dates, and that reduces the difference between the *A* and *B* series to the ever-changing present moment. But it may still be an extra fact about the world, over and above all dates, that one moment in this system of dates is present. Imagine for instance another world identical in all its history to ours except that it is now the eighteenth century instead of the twentieth. Surely that is a real difference between such a world and ours? It is no mean task to show that it is not; and unless I do, I cannot deny that the *A* series describes a real aspect of the world that the *B* series fails to capture. But I do deny this; and so in the next two chapters I shall attempt that very task.

2   Tense and token-reflexives

If it were now the eighteenth century, how different would the world be? First of all, obviously, the tense of everything would be different. Everything would be two centuries less past or more future than it now is, i.e. it would be shifted forward two hundred years in the *A* series.

What other differences would there be? I think none, but that is because I think differences of tense are not real, and that has yet to be shown. To show it, I shall need to credit both worlds with the same tenseless facts, even though some – e.g. facts about nineteenth-century events – are facts about the future in the eighteenth-century world and about the past in ours. But some believers in real tense maintain that differences of tense generate differences of tenseless fact as well. If I just deny that, I shall beg the question against them. So I must show that even real differences of tense between the two worlds would not deprive me of the shared tenseless facts I mean to invoke against them.

I need not dispute everything that has been thought to follow from differences of tense. I need not for instance dispute differences of possibility or necessity. Many believe in only one (actual) past, which somehow has to be the way it is, but in many equally possible futures. But even then, of course, there may still be only one *actual* future, just as there is only one actual past. And everyone agrees that the actual future (if any) will be the same in all tenseless respects as what will later be corresponding stretches of the past. The eighteenth-century's actual nineteenth-century future will be identical in all tenseless respects (for example, who lost at Waterloo and in the Crimea) with our own nineteenth-century past. Napoleon cannot actually have lost at Waterloo in our past and have won in the eighteenth-century's actual future; even if he won in some possible eighteenth-century future that is not for us a possible past. And that is good enough for me. I do not mind the two worlds differing in possibilities, so long as they share the same tenseless actualities. That is all I shall need for disposing of tense – and hence of the possibilities and necessities which supposedly depend on it.

So, does tense affect actual tenseless facts? On some views it does, for example the view I mentioned in chapter 1 (p. 23) that only what is past or present is real. The same goes obviously for the even more extreme view that only what is present is real. In these views, incidentally, existence must of course be conceived tenselessly: if 'exists' *meant* 'exists now', it would be the merest tautology that only the present exists. So existence must not here be conceived in a present tense way: proponents of these views are not just peddling tautologies. They are saying, for example, that before nineteenth-century things and events were present, they had no reality at all, i.e. there were not even any tenseless facts about them. And if that were so, the eighteenth-century world would indeed differ drastically from ours. Whereas our world would still, on one of these views, include in its past all nineteenth-century things and events, the eighteenth-century world would include in its future only such nineteenth-century things and events as already existed in the eighteenth century. While on the other view, that only the present exists, our two worlds would differ even more, sharing only things and events that have existed throughout the last two hundred years: the earth, for example, and England. But not Czechoslovakia, which did not exist in the eighteenth century, and not the Holy Roman Empire, which does not exist now. Nor indeed most of the animate inhabitants of our common planet, because their lifetimes are too short to span the gap of time between the two worlds. No people, therefore, and no ordinary animals; only some trees, and perhaps a few giant tortoises.

These views seem to me absurd, and getting rid of them will be an agreeable corollary of getting rid of tense. But first I must wring from them the tenseless facts necessary to do that, and fortunately this can be done quite easily. The reason, roughly, is that the tenseless facts I require need not be facts about what now exists. They need only be consistent with such facts.

No one, I trust, will seriously deny me this modest assumption, even though inconsistency is a commonplace in science fiction, especially about time travel. If a time traveller from the future were to disrupt my present typing, for instance, that tenseless fact about his future behaviour would indeed be inconsistent with the tenseless fact that my present (April 1980) typing is not being disrupted.

This sort of thing is always threatening to happen in time travel fiction, where it is usually avoided by time travellers being very careful, or by invoking different possible universes coming in and out of existence along some further dimension of time. I propose to ignore this sort of nonsense: no one would seriously defend the possibility of time travel by such means. Either the traveller disrupts my April 1980 typing or he doesn't, and that's all there is to it. My typing cannot be both at one time disrupted in April 1980 and at another time not. At all events, the philosophical views I am trying (temporarily) to accommodate make no such foolish suppositions. They do not fill in the eighteenth-century's future differently from the corresponding stretches of our past, they simply leave it blank.

So rather than try to refute these views directly, I can simply fill in the future for them, and the past too if need be. To the admitted (because present) tenseless contents of the eighteenth-century world I can without inconsistency add all the tenseless facts about what happened beforehand and what happened afterwards. Those who deny that at the time there were such facts may conceive them hypothetically: what the tenseless facts about earlier and later happenings would be, or would have been, if only they had been present. And conceived like that, no one can deny them. Even if there is no real future and no real past, the present has certainly changed, and will continue to change – and I am simply saying how. All I am doing is distinguishing the world's actual history from merely possible variants of it: in tensed terms, what is present at some time or other from what never was and never will be present.

There is one objection to this ploy that I must try to meet at once, although a full reply to it will have to wait for chapter 10. The objection is that if the eighteenth-century world contains even hypothetical facts about wholly future things and events, eighteenth-century people should in theory have been able to refer to those things and events, and that seems incredible. George III, for instance, could surely not have talked about Elizabeth II as she clearly can talk about him. This asymmetry, it is said, cannot just reflect the difficulty of knowing about the future. For suppose George III did by chance guess many facts about our present monarch, perhaps even her name. He would still arguably not be referring to Elizabeth; for even if she had gone the way of Edward VIII, his remarks could still have been made true by a sufficiently similar British Queen of the same name. Whereas Elizabeth, by contrast, can refer to George III in a way that attaches directly to him – so that if *he* had abdicated and not done what she said he did, her remarks would be false, even if the actual monarch (also called 'George III') had done them.

This suggests to many that George III's world contained no future Elizabeth for him to refer to, and also lacked means whereby he could refer to her as even a hypothetical future individual. But if that were so, I could hardly add tenseless facts about Elizabeth II to an eighteenth-century world that had no way of specifying the facts to be about *her*. Whereas now she does exist and can be referred to, there *are* tenseless facts specifically about her – and this constitutes a difference of actual tenseless fact between the eighteenth-century world and our own.

The short answer to this objection is as follows. First, if it assumes that George III could not talk about Elizabeth II *because* she did not then (tenselessly) exist, it begs the question. So it must be inferring her non-existence as the reason why he – obviously – could not refer to her. But once we think she *might* exist in his world's future, that inability is not really so obvious; and anyway it has other explanations. For a start, any theory of time has to say why we know so little about the future. That is, I admit, a challenge to tenseless views of time, one I shall meet later by saying why we cannot perceive events before they occur. But provided I can explain that obvious asymmetry in our knowledge of past and future, I can also use it to say why George III could not have talked about our Queen. She need not be absent from the future of his world: it suffices that he could perceive nothing of the twentieth century, and so had no way of knowing enough about it to describe her.

Much more needs to be said about all this, especially about why we cannot perceive future events. But the mere fact that we cannot is enough to generate the problems we obviously have in referring to future entities, even if they do exist. And even if future existents were denied on other grounds, these problems of reference would not prevent my adding tenseless facts about them. I can simply specify future existents hypothetically, as the things and events that *will* be at such-and-such future dates – when, being present, they will be indisputably real and capable of being referred to.

I conclude that differences of tense do after all exhaust the factual differences between eighteenth-century worlds and our own, with the proviso that tenseless facts about future (and perhaps) past things and events may have to be construed hypothetically. Subject to that proviso – to be removed in due course anyway – all tenseless facts were the same then as they are now. At all the same dates, everything was in exactly the same places, and people throughout history were seeing, thinking and doing exactly the same things. Whatever the present date may be, the world remains essentially the same in all tenseless respects.

But the world does not remain the same in tensed respects, and the tensed differences between the eighteenth and twentieth centuries are numerous and impressive. The few giant tortoises we all agree the two centuries share, old in our world, were young and relatively sprightly when late eighteenth-century dates were present. In their lumbering fashion they were still cavorting youthfully about the Galapagos, to which Darwin's celebrated visit was still future, instead of past as it is for us. Neglecting the eighteenth-century's last decade, it contained a present King of France called Louis, which our world lacks; the English Revolution was less than a century old; and the Russian one still over a century off. Even if such differences of tense between the eighteenth-century world and our own are the only factual differences, they are quite enough. They are both undeniable and undeniably objective. They are obviously no mere matters of opinion or of subjective judgment, nor is it an illusion that eighteenth-century worlds differ in these striking ways from the twentieth-century world we inhabit. These are objective differences, which must be accounted for as such. It will be no mean feat to account for them while denying that in reality things and events have tenses at all.

Tackling this problem may well seem a task both daunting and perverse. That it is not too daunting I shall show in this chapter by actually doing it, i.e. by giving a totally tenseless account of these seemingly tensed differences. But that in itself is not enough to acquit me of perversity. The question 'Why climb Everest?' is perhaps well answered 'Because it's there', but that answer hardly justifies accepting a tenseless account of these tensed facts. The account's mere existence does not prove its truth; and the existence of tenses is not disproved by showing how to save the phenomena of tense without them. To take a familiar analogy, the natural idea of the sun going round the earth is not disproved merely because the phenomena of sunrise and sunset can also be saved by the bizarre hypothesis of the earth going round the sun. That heliocentric explanation still has to be shown to be the right one. And so it is with the tenseless explanation of the phenomena of tense. I shall still have to show that the tenseless explanation is right. But I cannot well do that until I have said what it is.

Tensed facts and tensed truths

The first step in explaining away tensed facts is to trade them in for tensed truths. The objective truth or falsity of our judgments of the tenses of events and things is what we really have to explain. Whenever I say or think that some event is present, or is to some extent past or future, I will generally be objectively right or wrong, depending on when the event actually occurred. Consider the example of chapter 1, the Queen being fifty-eight in May 1984. Her birth seems then to have the tense *fifty-eight years past*. But all this means is that, made in May 1984, this judgment about the Queen's age would be objectively true. A year later, of course, it would be objectively false – i.e. the Queen would then not be fifty-eight.

Expressing tense's objectivity in the idiom of tensed judgments being true or false does not beg the question against tensed facts. They might still be what make tensed judgments true or false; and if so, these two ways of putting it are equivalent. The tensed fact that the Queen is fifty-eight in May 1984 will by definition be what makes the corresponding judgment true at that date. But I will argue that actually quite a different fact makes this judgment true, and that tensed facts are a myth, a fallacious reification of the truth of tensed judgments. Since that is my view, I have to use the idiom of tensed judgments, to prevent the question being begged against me from the start. Of course, I still have to supply my tenseless alternative, to say what makes tensed judgments true if tensed facts do not; and that is what I shall now set out to do.

The facts I am looking for must be undeniable facts, objective and tenseless, that will make tensed judgments true when they are true, and false when they are false. These facts, if I can find them, will be my tenseless surrogate for the apparent facts of tense. To get at them, however, I must first make and extend a familiar philosophical distinction: the distinction between *types* of words and sentences and *tokens* of them, a distinction which I shall need to apply also to judgments.

A token of a word or sentence is a particular specimen of it, in the sense in which a particular horse is a specimen of that species (or type) of animal. The particular specimen of the sentence which occurs immediately before this one in this copy of this book is a token, one of many tokens of that sentence – one in each copy of this book, for a start. The sentence type, on the other hand, is what I mean by 'that sentence', in the sense of it being the *same* sentence in every copy of the book. For me, the important feature of tokens as opposed to types is that a token is a particular object, in this case an arrangement of ink on the particular piece of paper you are looking at, i.e. a thing which is in a definite place at every moment of its existence. The sentence type, by contrast, is a much more wide-spread object than any of its tokens, if indeed it is an object at all. The sentence type you are now reading a token of, for instance, is scattered across the world as widely as – I hope – copies of this book are. Sentence types are in fact not so much objects as properties of objects, namely of all the objects that are their tokens; just as the type *horse* is not so much another object, over and above particular horses, as a property that all particular horses share, i.e. the property of being a horse. But whether types are objects or properties – a controversial question – is fortunately neither here nor there; all that matters here is that tokens are objects, in particular that they have definite locations in space and time.

Now all tokens are objects in a fairly broad sense (only fairly broad, because I mean to exclude properties), but in the narrower sense distinguished in chapter 1, not all tokens are *things*. The printed tokens in this copy of this book are things, because, like the copy itself, they have no temporal parts, even though they will I trust last for some time. But other token sentences are not things in this sense: they are *events*, because they do have temporal parts. Sentences can be spoken, for example, as well as being written or printed, and someone's speaking of a sentence on a particular occasion is an event, with his successive speaking of the sentence's words as its temporal parts. But even though they are not things, such events are just as much tokens of sentence types as printed and written specimens are – in particular, they are just as capable of being true or false.

But although both thing and event tokens can be true or false, they do have to be distinguished. My interest in tokens of tensed sentence types, as opposed to the types themselves, is that, having definite dates, they should be definitely either true or false without temporal qualification. That is, their so-called "truth-value", truth or falsity, should be an unchanging property of the token itself. But with some thing tokens this is not so, and the type/token distinction on its own will not suffice. This is because a long-lasting thing token of a tensed sentence type may very well change its truth-value during its lifetime, just as it may change its shape or colour. (The 'Back in two hours' notice of chapter 1, which starts off true and ends up false, is a good example.) As we shall see in chapter 7, such changes of truth-value are not real changes as changes of colour are, because they have no effects on anything and so are not real events. But they are changes in the weaker sense that one and the same thing has incompatible properties, viz. truth and falsity, at different times. To get one definite and unchanging truth-value for a thing token of a particular tensed sentence type, we must in general specify not only the token but also a particular B series instant within its lifetime.

Event tokens do not present this problem, because they cannot change truth-value as thing tokens can. The reason, indicated in chapter 1, is that temporally extended events are never wholly present at an instant, and so never have instantaneously possessed properties capable of changing from one instant to another. The full account of this distinction between things and events, and of the account of change derived from it, will have to wait for chapter 7; for the time being, an illustration of it will have to do. Suppose I say of a very shortlived event e (e.g. a flash of lightning): 'e is past'. Then if e is over before I start to speak, this event token will be true, and if not, false – and that's that. My sentence cannot change its truth-value as I produce it, not even if e occurs as I speak; the whole sentence is never present at any instant to be either true then or false then, so it can never change in that respect (or any other) from one instant to another. Unless the sentence token is wholly true, therefore, it must be wholly false; whereas a similarly dated thing token of the same tensed type could have been first false and then true.

A thing token can also be wholly true, of course, i.e. true at every B series instant in its date, and it can also be wholly false. When that happens, it is no longer worth distinguishing from an event token of the same type and date, since both are simply true or false, and the plain type/token distinction will do. In most of what follows I simply assume that this is so, and refer therefore simply to tokens, whether they be things or events. Where it does matter, a definite truth-value can always be got for a thing token by specifying a *B* series instant within its date, i.e. its lifetime; and where it doesn't, there is no merit in drawing nice but irrelevant distinctions. And usually it doesn't matter, since we deliberately restrict either the lifetime or the type of tensed tokens in order to make them wholly true. This, for example, is one reason why longlived printed tokens are usually of past tense sentence types: a token of '*e* is past' that starts off true is always true thereafter, which tokens of '*e* is present' and '*e* is future' will not be.

For the same reason, very precise *A* series positions have to be ascribed by correspondingly shortlived tokens. The obvious examples are the tokens produced by clocks, which say to within a second or a minute what *B* series time is present. Clocks with hands do this by events, such as the second or minute hand moving across the figures on the face; digital clocks do it by means of shortlived things, namely their digital displays. Thus, when a clock's hands move to indicate '2.15', or those figures appear on a digital display, that event or thing is in effect a token of the present tense sentence 'It is now 2.15'. The clock is understood to be saying that the minute-long date 2.15 contains the present moment. But that will only be true for a minute, after which the hands must move on (or the digital display be replaced) if what the clock is saying is to remain true. On an ideal clock, therefore, the lifetime of every token it presents is neither more nor less than the very minute or second of time during which what it says is true.

So much – for the time being – for the distinction between thing tokens and event tokens. Token sentences of course include other events and things besides the impersonal pronouncements and displays of clocks. They include also live people saying things and, more importantly, thinking things. Thoughts can be tokens of sentence types just as written or spoken specimens can be – in particular, they can just as easily be true or false. I need not say 'It's raining', or write it, to generate a true or false token of that sentence type. A token of it occurs each time I think it. My making a mental judgment may not be a very audible or visible event, but it is an event nonetheless, and quite able to be a token of a sentence type. Sometimes indeed such mental events make history: wars, for example, have been started by an ultimatum's recipient reading it to himself, thereby generating in his mind a mental token of its contents, and calling out his troops as a result. Even this book, although it has no pretensions to being a *casus belli*, is meant to cause its readers to consider in their minds the sentences it contains, in the hope that they will then judge them to be true. Indeed, in the end, the whole function of written and printed tokens is to give rise in their readers to further mental tokens of the same sentence types. Books that are never read, after all, might as well never have been written.

I am not trying to sell mental tokens in competition with written or spoken ones, or those produced by clocks or other mechanical devices. I need not even defend them against the – e.g. behaviourist – arguments of those who deny their existence altogether. Mental tokens are not a necessary, nor even a helpful, ingredient in my account: on the contrary, they are part of what I feel I must account for. Only, so far as I can see, tensed mental tokens do exist, and their truth-values must therefore be accounted for in tenseless terms along with those of purely material tokens.

Actually, the chief problem mental tokens pose is that some of them, although tensed, may not be tokens of any particular sentence type. This is because we may be able to make judgments without putting them into words. On looking out of the window, for example, I suppose that, in noticing the rain and other aspects of the view, I make a multitude of judgments; but I doubt if I formulate them all in specific English sentences. That would not matter much if sentences in English or some other language accurately expressed the content of all these judgments. For then we could simply take these judgments to be tokens of those sentences, even though I did not actually use them; just as we can take a clock striking two to be a token of the English sentence type 'It is now two o'clock'. But maybe some of our judgments are not accurately expressed by any sentence type in any language. Perhaps no one could say precisely what Sir Henry Baskerville thought he saw coming at him out of the mist on the moor last night. Now even this does not matter for my purposes, provided that, as in this case, at least the tense of the judgment is clearly expressible. All I want to do, after all, is to say in tenseless terms what makes it true to ascribe the tense *last night* to that terrifying event. So long as I can do that, and say enough to identify the event, I need not care how inexpressible most of its non-temporal aspects are. But if other aspects of judgments can be inexpressible, so conceivably can their temporal aspects. Some judgments might perhaps be tokens of no specifically tensed sentence type. Yet they might still be tensed, and true or false; and if so, I must suppose there to be tenseless facts which make them so.

I confess I find it hard to think of judgments whose tense is inexpressible. Certainly, when I look out of the window, however inexpressible my judgments may be otherwise, they are nearly all obviously present tense: I think I am seeing what is happening out there *now*. So I do not really think, so far as tense goes, that I would risk missing much if I did take judgments to be tokens of sentence types. But since judgments may be inexpressible in other respects and so require the type/token distinction to be extended anyway from sentences to judgments, I might as well take advantage of the extension, just in case.

What I assume about judgments, therefore, is this. On different occasions different people (or even the same person) can make the very same judgment, whether or not it be verbalised or even verbalisable, and whether it be tensed or tenseless. What the occasions have in common is the judgment type, of which the mental events – the makings of that judgment type on these different occasions – are tokens. Token judgments are episodes in people's lives, particular events, distinguished one from another by whose judgments they are and by where – and especially by when – they occur. Particular thoughts strike particular people at particular times: the token judgments they make, therefore, like the token sentences they speak and write, all have dates of greater or less duration.

I labour this conclusion because it is crucial to my case. I need dates for all tokens of tensed judgments and sentences in order to be able to say, without appeal to tensed facts, what it is that makes them objectively true or false. And I believe in fact that all tokens do have dates, with the possible exception of judgments made by the Deity "outside time". I do not really understand what people mean who say that God is outside time, but I suppose they may mean that His actions and thoughts are not in the B series, i.e. they have no dates. If so, and if in particular He makes tensed judgments which have no dates, I confess I shall be at a loss to say in tenseless terms what makes them true. I confess also that this inability does not disturb me much; and I leave it to believers to decide how serious a deficiency it is in my account. But with this one dubious exception, I can give a uniform tenseless account of the truth and falsity of all tensed tokens, both of sentences and of judgments. In what follows I refer mostly to token sentences, since these can be taken to include all linguistically expressible judgments. But I do not mean thereby to deny (although I doubt) the possibility of judgments with definite but inexpressible temporal contents; if there are any such, what I say will apply to them also.

Tenseless truth conditions

Suppose someone says or thinks sometime in May 1984 that the Queen is fifty-eight, and suppose he absent-mindedly makes the same judgment again a year later. That is, he produces two tokens of the sentence type 'The Queen is fifty-eight', each with an objective truth-value. But not the same truth-value. The first token is true, because – to put the matter for the time being in tensed terms – in May 1984 the Queen *is* fifty-eight. The second token is false, because the inexorable change in tense of the Queen's birth during the intervening year has by then made her fifty-nine. In other words, tokens of a single sentence type can differ, as in this case, in that some are true and others false. The truth and falsity of tensed sentences, therefore, are properties of their tokens rather than of their types. So in looking for tenseless facts to give these sentences the objective truth and falsity we know they have, we must look for facts which vary appropriately from token to token even of the same type.

The facts we need are easy enough to find, once token sentences have been distinguished from their types. Token sentences, we have remarked, are things and events with more or less definite dates, and tokens of the same sentence type rarely all have the same date. I have, for example, supposed that one among the tokens of 'The Queen is fifty-eight' occurs in May 1984 and another occurs a year later. These dates, together with the date in April 1926 when the Queen was born, are enough to make the first of these tokens true and the other false. Given these dates, it is no coincidence that these tokens have these truth-values. Any token of the sentence 'The Queen is fifty-eight' has to be true if its date is fifty-eight years later than that of the Queen's birth, and any whose date is a year later than that has to be false. The truth-values of these tokens follow directly from how their B series positions relate to that of the event they are about.

The truth-values of sentences depend of course on more than the temporal facts that concern me. Some sentences, although verbally tensed, are always true because necessarily so: e.g. 'The past is now earlier than the present' and 'Either it will rain tomorrow or it won't'. Others likewise are always false because self-contradictory or wrong in non-temporal respects: e.g. 'The Queen is now both fifty-eight and fifty-nine' and 'Napoleon won at Waterloo'. Sentences like these I shall ignore, since they state no A series facts in the first place. Tensed instances of analytic truths and self-contradictions need no temporal facts, tensed or tenseless, to account for their truth-values; nor do sentences made false by atemporal error. I shall confine myself therefore to sentences and judgments made sometimes true and sometimes false by the A series whereabouts of things and events; and henceforth I imply that restriction in calling them tensed.

My task then is to simulate tenselessly the effects that varying tenses have on the truth-values of otherwise sound tensed sentences and judgments. And once the dates of sentence and judgment tokens are added to those of other things and events, that task is easily accomplished. The truth-values of tokens of any particular tensed type are – so far as time is concerned – a definite function of how much later or earlier the tokens are than the events they are about. (What the function is depends on the particular type: for example, as we shall see, on whether the sentence is of a past or a future tense type.) Thus, generalising from our Royal exemplar, any token of a past tense sentence, to the effect that some event happened N years (days, or whatever) ago, will be true if its date is N years (days, etc.) later than the date of that event. Those are the tenseless conditions, and the only tenseless conditions, in which simple past tense sentence tokens will be true. They are what we may conveniently call the tenseless "truth conditions" of these tokens.

The truth conditions of future tense tokens are like those of past tense ones, only in order to be true these tokens have to be earlier, not later, than the events they are about. Suppose I predict that the sun will next be totally eclipsed in N days' time. What I say will be true provided I say it N days earlier than the eclipse; otherwise it will be false. And similarly for all other simple future tense sentences: the truth of their tokens is completely determined by how much their dates differ from those of the events they refer to.

The tenseless conditions in which present tense tokens come out true are somewhat different. For a present tense token to be true, the event it refers to must occur within a specified B series interval containing the token itself. Take for instance a remark to the effect that someone is getting married this week: the remark will be true provided, and only provided, it is made during the very week of the wedding. In general, any token of a sentence type which ascribes a present tense of N days' duration to an event will be true if made within N days of the event, and otherwise it will be false.

These then are the tenseless facts that fix the truth-values of tokens of simple tensed sentences and judgments. Since they include facts about the tokens themselves – their relative whereabouts in the B series – this account of what makes them true is called a "token-reflexive" account. On it, basically, past tense tokens are true, and only true, after the events they are about; future tense tokens are true and only true beforehand; present tense tokens are true and only true at the same time. That these simple types of tensed sentences have these token-reflexive truth conditions is really quite obvious, and is not seriously questioned. The serious question is whether this is all there is to the facts of tense. I believe that in the end it is and can be shown to be. But that conclusion is still a long way off. For a start, there are verbal tenses more complicated than the simple past, present and future, and it has not seemed obvious to everyone that all of them have tenseless truth conditions. That will now have to be shown before I can claim to have disposed altogether of the need to invoke tensed facts to make tensed sentences true or false.

Complex tenses

Consider the following example of the so-called future perfect tense:

'In a fortnight's time, he will have been married two weeks.'

That sentence is true now of any man who marries this week. What it says in effect is that in a fortnight's time, his wedding will have the A series position *two weeks past*. This of course differs from the A

series position, *this week*, which the wedding has now, because the tense of that event, like that of all events, is constantly changing. We use the simple verbal tenses I have so far considered to say what *A* series positions things and events have *now*: complex verbal tenses, of which the future perfect is one, are used to say what those *A* series positions will be in the future or were in the past.

But since tenses do constantly change, we must say *when*, if not now, an event has the *A* series position that a complex tense ascribes to it. That could be done by giving a date: by saying for instance that the wedding will be two weeks past on 23 August. Complex tenses actually do it, however, by means of another *A* series position, thus: the wedding will be two weeks past *in a fortnight's time*. In short, what complex tenses do is *iterate A* series positions. Unfortunately, *A* series positions can not only be iterated, they can be reiterated, and in theory there is no limit to the reiteration. For not only does the first *A* series position ascribed to an event keep changing, so do all the other ones. Not only is 'He marries this week' only true this week, so is the future perfect 'In a fortnight's time he will have been married two weeks'. A week ago, both those judgments would have been false. In other words, it would *now* be false to say 'A week ago, he would in a fortnight's time have been married two weeks'. What is now true is 'A week ago, he would in a fortnight's time have been married a week'. These last two sentence types, whose present tokens are respectively false and true, are one stage more complex even than the future perfect, since they involve three *A* series positions, not just two. And even they are not eternal truths, as a little reflection on them will reveal. In weeks other than the present, their truth-values would be different, thus giving rise to more complex tenses still. And so on, *ad infinitum*.

To study all these complex tenses systematically, tense logicians write them all in a standard way. They write down the successively ascribed *A* series positions in turn in front of a present tense "core" sentence. Thus, in our example, the core sentence

'He marries this week'

is successively elaborated into

'Two weeks ago, he marries this week',
'Two weeks hence, two weeks ago, he marries this week',
'A week ago, two weeks hence, two weeks ago, he marries this week',

and so on. And all these sentences have definite truth-values. If, for example, the core sentence 'He marries this week' is true, then the successive elaborations of it listed above will be respectively false, true and false. For all these truth-values I have to supply corresponding tenseless facts.

I should like to excuse myself this chore by observing that in real life, as opposed to tense logic, no one reiterates A series ascriptions. No one actually uses verbal tenses more complicated than the future perfect. One should be suspicious therefore of the apparently endless array of complex tensed facts that have to be conjured up to make all these tensed sentences true or false. They have a decided air of being generated by the system rather than by the world. But the suspicion, though sound, gives me no immediate respite. Even if tensed sentences of indefinitely great complexity never are produced, they could be; and if they were produced they would have definite truth-values. So whether they are produced or not, there appear to be tensed facts corresponding to those truth-values, and for these I have to find tenseless substitutes. Now since the reiteration of A series positions is unlimited, I cannot hope to find substitutes case by case. What I need is a general recipe that will, for any iteration, automatically specify the corresponding tenseless fact. And happily the recipe I need has already been worked out by tense logicians, anxious to be able to say in simple A series terms what fixes the truth-values of complex tensed sentences. They call this recipe the semantics of their subject; but it would be more accurate to call it their Trojan Horse, since once it is admitted, all the topless towers of tense logic can rapidly be toppled to tenseless ground.

I should say here that the semantics of tense logic contains more than the recipe I am about to consider. That only concerns itself, as I do, with the actual history of the world. It gives A series truth conditions for sentences about particular things and events which say how the world actually is now, was, will be, will have been, and so on to any degree of tensed complexity. Additional recipes are needed by those who think there is no future now (though there will be); to cater for what in the past were possible futures but are no longer; and so on. Speculation on these topics has been expressed in formal systems of impressive virtuosity. But they all ultimately depend on a foundation of tensed fact. Remove that and these Baroque superstructures will all go too. And all I need, to remove the foundation, is a tenseless version of the following.

First, put the tensed sentence to be assessed for truth-value into the standard form, i.e. with its complex tense expressed by a sequence of *A* series positions prefixed to a present tense core. Then take the first of these *A* series positions, and suppose the present moment shifted that amount from the date it now has. Starting again from there, repeat the exercise with each of the other *A* series positions in turn. Finally, ask if the core sentence would be true if the present moment actually did have the date arrived at for it by this process. If it would, the original sentence is true; if not, not.

Thus, in our example, start by transforming

'A week ago, he would in a fortnight's time have been married two weeks'

into its standard form

'A week ago, two weeks hence, two weeks ago, he marries this week'.

Then suppose the present moment shifted back into what is now last week, then forward two weeks to next week, and back two weeks again to last week. Finally, ask if 'He marries this week' would have been true last week. Since we are supposing it to be true this week, the answer is 'No'; so the original sentence is false. That is the tensed version of the recipe, and tense logicians have kindly checked that it does indeed work for all complex tenses stating facts about the actual history of the world.

But if this tensed recipe works, so will the tenseless version got by replacing references to the present moment with references to dates, starting with the date of the token sentence being assessed. That is, start by seeing how far the first *A* series position is from the present, and take the date which is that far from the token's date. Then starting again from there, repeat the exercise for each of the other *A* series positions in turn. Finally, ask if a token of the core sentence would have been true on the date arrived at by this process. If it would, the original sentence token is true; if not, not.

Thus suppose in our example that the token sentence was produced on 8 August, the day before the wedding. Taking the *A* series positions in the standard form of the sentence in turn, we first go back a week to 1 August, then forward two weeks to 15 August, and back two weeks again to 1 August. Would a token of 'He marries this week' have been true on 1 August? Since the wedding is in fact on 9 August, which is more than a week from 1 August, the answer is 'No'; so the original sentence is false. The tenseless recipe gives the same answer as the tensed one; and it is easy to see that it would do so whatever the token's date, just so long as it would be true on that date to say 'He marries this week'.

So the tenseless token-reflexive recipe works in this case. Of course one success does not guarantee success every time. But for once a general proof of it would be superfluous. I have remarked already that no one uses these complex tenses in real life. We have no independent awareness of their truth-values with which to judge the deliverances of our token-reflexive recipe. When presented with sentences as artificially complicated as my example, we have to work out whether they are true – and we do it by means of the recipe I have just given. It has to give the right answer, because it is what we use to decide what the right answer is.

However complex the verbal tense of a sentence, therefore, nothing but tenseless facts are needed to settle the truth of its tokens. The objective truth-values of tensed sentences and judg-ments give no reason to suppose that there are tensed facts, i.e. that things and events really do have *A* series positions. But of course they *may* do, and there may be other reasons for believing that they do. In particular, the apparently inescapable presence of experience itself seems to imply real differences between the past, the present and the future. That it is now the twentieth and not the eighteenth century still seems to be a fact of experience, over and above all tenseless facts about dates. That is the next, and the crucial, fact I must now explain away.

3   The presence of experience

The problem I now face is nicely illustrated in a puzzle posed by Lewis Carroll in 1849 (Fisher, 1973, p. 25). He invites us to choose between two clocks, one being right twice a day, the other right only once a year. Naturally we choose the clock that is more often right – and get a clock that doesn't go at all, instead of one that merely runs a little slow! Yet we get the clock we asked for: the stopped clock is indeed right twice a day, whereas a slightly slow clock is almost never right. Moreover, as Carroll says, we know *when* the stopped clock is right, namely at the very time shown on its face, say two o'clock.

Even so, a stopped clock is not quite what we had in mind. But why not? Carroll has given tenseless truth conditions for the unchanging tokens of 'It is now two o'clock' which the stopped clock is in effect emitting all the time. We can see what the clock says, and we know when it is true. What more could we want to know?

What more we want to know, of course, is whether it is two o'clock *now*. Is two o'clock the date of our present *experience* of looking at the clock to see what the time is? We need not look to see that 'It is now two o'clock' is true at two o'clock – *that* is true all day. Token-reflexive truth conditions never change. In particular, therefore, they do not convey the changing facts of tense that a stopped clock fails to tell us. And once we see that, we can see that they also do not convey what an accurate clock does tell us. It does indeed say '2.15' at 2.15, '3.30' at 3.30, and so on, and that is indeed what makes everything the clock says true. But it is true all day long that the clock says '2.15' at 2.15, '3.30' at 3.30, etc. So far as satisfying their truth conditions goes, there is never anything to choose between any of these tokens; so citing them does not tell us what the clock tells us, namely which of all these times is the *present* time. That is what we look at a clock to find out. And a slightly slow clock will nearly always tell us that more accurately than one which has stopped altogether. Assuming – what the absurdity of Carroll's tale anyway needs – that the slow clock is set right periodically, its dating of the present moment will only be a few minutes out, whereas the stopped clock will mostly be hours out. So we should, as we do, prefer the clock that goes slow.

That is the obvious, tensed, solution to Lewis Carroll's puzzle. A stopped clock is no good because it is mostly very bad at telling us *A* series facts. But what is wrong with it if, as I maintain, there are no *A* series facts? In order to answer that question, however, I must first tackle another puzzle, set explicitly by A. N. Prior (1959) as a problem for the tenseless view of time.

Suppose you have just had a painful experience, e.g. a headache. Now it is over, you say with relief 'Thank goodness that's over'. What are you thanking goodness for? On the face of it, the fact that the headache is no longer a present experience, i.e. is now past. So what you are thanking goodness for appears to be an essentially tensed fact, that the headache is past. That is presumably why you make your remark after the pain, and not during or before it. Can this fact still be explained when tensed facts have been traded in, as in chapter 2, for tensed tokens with tenseless truth conditions?

Prior says not. In this case the true or false token is your saying 'That's over', referring to the headache, and the tenseless fact which makes it true is that it occurs later than your headache. All this is obvious and not in dispute; but is it enough to explain your thanking goodness? After all, this tenseless fact was a fact before and during the headache as well as after it. It always was a fact that this particular token of 'That's over' occurs later than the headache it refers to. What is more, the fact could have been recognised as such in advance: you could have decided in advance to say 'That's over' after the headache, and known of the fact then in that way. So if you were thanking goodness for that fact, you could just as well have thanked goodness for it before or during the headache – which of course is nonsense. So you must be thanking goodness for some *other* fact, something that was not a fact at all until the headache ceased. The tensed conclusion seems irresistible: the headache's pastness, for which you are thanking goodness, must be something over and above the tenseless fact that makes 'That's over' true. If your headache had not really had the *A* series property of presence, and had not now lost it, there would have been nothing to thank goodness for at all.

Yet again, as with Lewis Carroll's clocks, our tenseless token-reflexive truth conditions seem to miss the tensed character of experience. Nor is this a feature only of these somewhat contrived examples. Temporal presence seems to be an essential aspect of all experience. By 'essential' I mean essential to its being experience. If I only gave the dates of my experiences, without saying which was happening to me *now*, I should on the face of it leave out precisely what makes them experiences. The headache which has just stopped, for example, is really no longer a headache at all, because it is no longer painful. Something can only be a headache, or an experience of any other kind, when it is present. The past event is only a headache in the dispositional sense in which an object in a dark room, though invisible, is yellow. If the object *were* lit, it would be yellow; if the event *were* present, it would be a pain in the head. But so far as actual pain goes, the event is merely a retired or Emeritus headache, not something still in business as the genuine experiential article. And that is why I thank goodness for its pastness: by ceasing to be present it has ceased to be the unpleasant experience it was. Having a headache, in short, inevitably includes knowing – if one thinks about it – that it is present; and similarly for all other experiences.

On the other hand, experiences are also events in tenseless time. They have dates, as other events do. My headache, for example, may have started just as the clock struck six, and that fixes the first *B* series moment of its date.

So some events with dates, namely our experiences, we know are present events, and hence located firmly in both the *A* and the *B* series. But once some events are located in both series, all events are. The tenses of all other things and events follow from how much earlier or later they are than these present events; and hence arise all the tensed facts that distinguish worlds differing in the date of their present moment.

Our knowledge of tenses comes entirely from the presence of experience. Experiences tell us directly of their presence, and the rest of the *A* series we fill in from there. We know for example how long light takes to reach us from a celestial event we are now seeing, and that tells us how past it is, namely as far past as it is earlier than our experience of seeing it. Ultimately, therefore, it is the directly perceived presence of experience which tells us what the tensed facts of our world are, i.e. that it really is the twentieth century we are living in and not the eighteenth.

The presence of experience is the crux of the matter. Without a tenseless account of it, tenseless truth conditions on their own will never dispose of tensed facts. That account I will now set out to supply. First, let us look again at Prior's puzzle, this time put slightly differently.

Before, I acquiesced in the idiom of thanking goodness for facts, but in this case that idiom is tendentious. What a token of 'Thank goodness' really does is express a feeling of relief: not necessarily relief from or about anything, just relief. So when is it natural to have a feeling of relief in relation to a painful experience? The tensed answer is: when the experience is past. The tenseless answer can only be: *after* a painful experience, i.e. at a later date, rather than during or before it. Now this answer may well seem weak. Why should relief be natural after pain if not because the pain is then past and *therefore* (as we have seen) no longer pain? To this further question I confess I see no answer. But I also see no answer to the question: why feel relief only when pain has the *A* series position *past*? The answer is not, as one might suppose, that relief *cannot* be felt while pain is present and thus still pain. It is no *a priori* truth that relief is never felt, in relation to a pain, while the pain is present. Indeed it is no truth at all. Masochists, for a start, presumably feel relief when a future pain they have been longing for at last becomes present – 'Thank goodness it's started' is what they would naturally say! And masochism, however deplorable, is certainly possible. There is no *a priori* magic in temporal presence therefore to prevent relief being felt while pain is present. So saying that relief normally occurs only when pain is past is no more of an explanation than saying that normally it only occurs after the pain.

The tenseless description of the phenomenon of relief – that usually it follows pain rather than preceding or accompanying it – is all right on its own. The tensed description makes the phenomenon no less mysterious, so there is no good reason to insist on it. Nothing about the relation between pain and relief requires us to credit pains with tenses as well as with being earlier and later than other events.

And the tenseless description, of relief coming usually after pain, gives me a tenseless solution to Prior's puzzle. We need not claim to be thanking goodness for the fact that 'That's over' is true only after the pain. There is a much more credible tenseless story than that. The fact is that 'Thank goodness that's over' is not really a single statement at all: it is a conjunction, of 'That's over' and 'Thank goodness'. This can be seen in the fact that the conjuncts are just as naturally joined the other way round: 'That's over; thank goodness'. Now the first conjunct, 'That's over', has obvious token-reflexive truth conditions; and I have just given the tenseless conditions in which the relief the second expresses is normally felt. The two things are usually said together partly because these two conditions usually coincide: the relief 'Thank goodness' expresses is usually felt only when 'That's over', said of a pain, is true, namely just after the pain. However, there is a little more to it than that. The coincidence of these tenseless conditions is not just a coincidence. The ending of the pain is also, we believe, the cause of our relief; and saying 'Thank goodness' in conjunction with 'That's over' expresses *inter alia* our recognition of this further tenseless fact.

This seems to me to explain perfectly well why most of us, wishing to tell the truth and not being masochists, will say 'Thank goodness that's over' only when our pain has stopped. Here I believe is an entirely adequate tenseless account of Prior's case. It does not after all compel us to admit tensed facts as well as tenseless ones. Pains only need to be causes of later feelings of relief; they do not also need to be in reality at first present and then past.

I have drawn out the tenseless treatment of Prior's case at some length in order to extract from it the ingredient I need to dispose in general of the presence of experience. That ingredient is a kind of self-awareness. The salient feature of Prior's case is that we not only have painful experiences, we also remember them. However relieved I feel, I shall not thank goodness for the ending of a pain I have forgotten. The recollection of past pain is what prompts the remark, rather than the pain itself. Now this recollection, which is what 'That's over' expresses, is in part a token of a past tense judgment, the judgment that I was in pain in the recent past. But it is also in part a present tense judgment, the judgment that I am not in pain – or not in so much pain – now. I shall not say 'That's over', let alone 'Thank goodness', while I still feel the same pain. A present tense awareness of being relatively free of pain is an essential ingredient in Prior's case; and this is the ingredient I need.

An awareness of being free of pain is, I contend, a token of a present tense type of judgment about my own experiences, namely that the experiences I am having now are painless. This token judgment is itself an experience, an event occurring in my conscious mind, but an event quite distinct from the rest of the experience it is about. I emphasise this distinction, because there is a temptation to identify our experiences with our present tense judgments about them, a temptation which it is essential to my argument to resist. The source of the temptation is that we distinguish experiences from other events, virtually by definition, as those events we are directly conscious of. We may easily seem bound, therefore, both to be aware of our experiences, and to be right in our conscious present tense judgments about what they are. While I might, for instance, overlook or mistake the colour of my pen, I can hardly miss or mistake the actual experience of (say) seeing it to be red. My judgment about the experience itself is so closely tied to it that there is a serious risk of confounding the one with the other. Nonetheless the risk must be avoided, not just for my argument's sake, but for a number of familiar and independent philosophical reasons which I need not digress here to rehearse. But one at least is apparent enough in this example, namely that I need not be making judgments all the time about every aspect of my experience. In particular, although I can hardly be *in* pain without noticing it, I can quite easily be free of pain without noticing it. Being free of pain does not force me to make the conscious judgment 'I am free of pain', even if I am – perhaps – bound to be right if I do so. So if I do make the judgment, that is an extra fact about me, over and above my lack of pain.

In short, to be aware that my present experiences are painless is to have a further experience, namely that of judging them to be painless. Since this judgment is about the experiences I am having now, it will have the token-reflexive truth conditions characteristic of the present tense. That is, the judgment will be true provided I am having only painless experiences at the very B series time I make it. And as for judgments of painlessness, so for judgments about all aspects of experience. If I judge myself to be seeing a red pen, for example, my judgment about that will likewise be true just in case I actually am seeing a red pen at the time I make the judgment.

Grant all this: now suppose I start making judgments, not about my present freedom from pain or about colours I am now seeing, but about temporal aspects of my experience. Specifically, suppose I judge that the experiences I am now having possess the *A* series property of being present. Notice that this restriction in the subject matter of my judgment, to the experiences I am *now* having, does not make the supposition a tautology, at least not in terms of tense. Tenses, after all, must always be ascribed to events at a particular time, because the tense of events is always changing; and the events which happen now to be our experiences are no exception to the rule. Our question therefore has to be: what tense do these events *now* have. And it is by no means tautological that they will now all have the same tense as each other, let alone that they will all be in the present. On the face of it we could now have as experiences events anywhere in the *A* series, past, present or future. Far from being a tautology, it seems in tensed terms to be a striking and impressive fact that events can only be experiences while they are present. It is indeed, as we have seen, the basis for all our knowledge of other tenses. It is what lets us infer from an event's now being an experience that it is now a present event, a conclusion that becomes in turn the premise from which the tenses of all other events and things are indirectly inferred.

However, no one actually infers the presence of experience. Rather, presence is itself an aspect of experience, i.e. something we are directly conscious of. (How else, after all, would we know that all experience *is* present?) So my judging my experience to be present is much like my judging it to be painless. On the one hand, the judgment is not one I have to make: I can perfectly well have experience without being conscious of its temporal aspects. But on the other hand, if I do make it, I am bound to be right, just as when I judge my experience to be painless. The presence of experience, like some at least of its other attributes, is something of which one's awareness is infallible.

The real, relevant – and suspicious – difference between judgments of presence and painlessness is that whereas only some experience is painless, all of it is present. No matter who I am, or whenever I judge my experience to be present, that judgment will be true. This is the inescapable, experientially given presence of experience which I now have to explain away. And once experience has been distinguished from the tensed judgments we make about it, that is not hard to do.

We are concerned with token judgments to the effect that experiences we are now having possess the A series property of being present. Now any token which says that an event is present will be true if and only if the event occurs at the same B series time as the token does. Those are the undisputed token-reflexive truth conditions of all such judgments. But in this case the events to which presence is attributed are themselves picked out by the use of the present tense. Not all our experiences, past, present and to come, are alleged to have this A series property, only the experiences we are having now. But these, by the same token-reflexive definition of the present tense, are among the events which *do* have the property now ascribed to them: i.e. events occurring just when the judgment itself is made. So of course these judgments are always true. Their token-reflexive truth conditions are such that they cannot be anything else. In tenseless terms they are tautologies after all.

That is the tenseless explanation of the presence of experience. And for once it is not merely an alternative to a tensed explanation of the same thing. There is no tensed explanation of this phenomenon. If events can in reality have a range of tenses, I see no good reason for experience to be confined as it is to present events. In tensed terms, that is just an unexplained brute fact about experience. The nearest thing to a tensed explanation of the fact is given by the extreme view discussed in chapter 2, that in reality only what is present exists at all. And of course, if only present events exist, then in particular experiences will all have to be present. To that extent the phenomenon is explained by this tensed view, albeit in an implausibly Procrustean way. What it does not explain, however, is how experience differs in this respect from other events. Other events and things at least seem to be spread out throughout the whole of A series time: the events we see (especially celestial events) all over the past; the events we predict, or plan to prevent or to bring about, all over the future. Only our experiences, including our judgments (i.e. our thoughts), and our intentions, decisions and actions appear to be restricted to the present. Of that contrast, the token-reflexive account I have just given alone provides a serious explanation.

The tenseless fact is that experiences themselves, like all other events and things, are neither past, present nor future. But we can make past, present and future tense judgments about them, just as we can about other matters. We have indeed, as we shall see in chapter 5, compelling reason to do so. In particular, we have compelling reason to make present tense judgments about our thoughts, actions and experiences as they occur. Without making such judgments we should be unable to communicate with each other – and there is nothing tautological about our ability to do that. Nor are most of these judgments tautologies. There is no tautology in my being aware of having a headache. It may be a necessary truth of some kind that I have a headache when I think I have one; but even that is not a trivial truth. The only trivial truth is that the experiences I am having now possess the *A* series property of being present. That is not, after all, a profound experiential restriction on our temporal awareness of the realm of tense. It is nothing more than the fact that experiences which occur when we judge them to be occurring now are bound, by the token-reflexive definition of the present tense, to make that judgment true.

What then of Lewis Carroll's clocks? Consider first the clock that goes dead right. It is true that nothing tenseless about the clock itself picks out the present position of the hands; but something tenseless does, namely the time the clock is looked at, say 2.15. If the clock is going right, it will then be emitting what is in effect a token of the sentence 'It is now 2.15'. Assuming I believe the clock, that token will generate in me another, mental token of the same tensed type. Neglecting the time this message takes to get through to my brain, this means the clock will make me think 'It is now 2.15' *at* 2.15, so my thought will be true. That, in token-reflexive terms, is the virtue of an accurate clock: it generates, in those who look at and believe it, true tensed judgments about what time it is – which is what, after all, clocks are for.

   A slightly slow clock generates, in those who believe it, tensed judgments which are not far out. That is, although they are actually false, most of their tensed consequences will be true. If I never need to know the time to more than a minute, a clock which is ten seconds slow will never deceive me in anything that matters. But a stopped clock can deceive people in matters of great moment, for mostly it is hours out. At most times of day, someone who looks at and believes it will make wildly inaccurate judgments about the time, judgments whose inaccuracy could cause him to be hours late for very important occasions. That is really what is wrong with a stopped clock. So even in token-reflexive terms, a slightly slow clock is much to be preferred. Lewis Carroll's puzzle does, after all, have a tenseless solution.

Finally, what of the difference between our twentieth-century world and a world with its present moment shifted back two hundred years? Actually, this is just the clock writ large, for we might as well ask how a good clock at 2.15 differs from the same clock an hour later. In tenseless terms, the answer is that the clock itself does not differ. Similarly, there is no tenseless difference between the two worlds. Indeed, there are not two worlds, any more than there are two clocks. There is only one world, with things and events scattered throughout *B* series time as they are throughout space, including both the eighteenth and the twentieth centuries.

But among these things and events are token judgments people make from time to time, the token sentences thought, spoken and written, including tokens of tensed sentence types. And since as a matter of tenseless fact, we are located within the twentieth century, so are all the token sentences we produce. Their tenseless truth conditions therefore differ by two centuries from eighteenth-century tokens of the same types and many of them will therefore differ also in truth-value. Many eighteenth-century tokens of 'The present King of France is Louis XV' are true therefore, because they occurred during the reign of that French monarch; whereas, as is well known, all twentieth-century tokens of that particular type are false. There is the real objective difference between the eighteenth and twentieth centuries: not a difference of tensed fact, but a difference in truth-value of tensed tokens of the same type located in the two centuries.

Some, I fear, will not be satisfied by this token-reflexive account. If I gave tenseless truth conditions for every token sentence and judgment in the history of the world, they would still ask: but which of all these token judgments is being made *now*? To them I can only say that their question is itself a token, with a date that determines of what type an answer must be in order to be true. The judgments that are being made on the date of the question are those the true answer must give. So that answer too is made true by purely tenseless facts.

Of course the question can be asked again of any token answer: is it being given now? An endless regress is possible of such questions and their answers. But the regress is not actual, nor is it vicious. Every question in it has an answer made true by tenseless facts, because every question has a date. Those of us who eschew tensed facts are sometimes accused of trying to take an impossible eternal view of the world, neglecting our own immersion in the stream of time. But the accusation might more justly go the other way. It is those who cling to tense who fail to take seriously that all things are in time – and so are all our judgments about them. Things, events and judgments alike all have dates, dates that suffice to settle, without tensed fact, the truth or falsity of every tensed judgment there ever was or ever will be.

4 Tenseless time and tenseless space

I have not yet tried to prove that there is in reality no difference between past, present and future, i.e. that there are no tensed facts. So far I have shown only that all tensed sentences have tenseless token-reflexive truth conditions. My tenseless explanation of the apparent presence of experience depended on that thesis, and so will my subsequent disproof of the reality of tense. The thesis, though insufficient for the tenseless view, is nonetheless essential to it, and it must be rightly understood. Yet although it is simple enough, and by no means new, it is still quite often misconstrued. In particular, its significance is apt to be exaggerated. Three things especially have been wrongly inferred from it; and since all three are clearly false, the inferences only discredit it. Before going any further, therefore, I will now discredit them, so that readers may not be misled by them to reject the thesis.

The inferences are these. First, if tensed sentences have tenseless truth conditions, they must mean the same as the tenseless sentences which state those truth conditions; so we could translate all our tensed sentences, and express all our tensed judgments, in tenseless terms. Secondly, whether or not tensed sentences have tenseless translations, tenseless facts are all the facts there are; so we could in principle give up tensed discourse altogether, and talk and think about the world in purely tenseless terms. Thirdly, the spatial analogue of the token-reflexive thesis about time is clearly true; the thesis therefore explains – and is perhaps implied by – the essential unity of space and time, a unity which has moreover been demonstrated by the success of the special and general theories of relativity.

Each of these inferences is false. Tensed sentences are not translatable by tenseless ones; tensed judgments are not dispensable; and time is not like space (and relativity does not show that it is). My task in this chapter and the next will be to scotch the canard that the tenseless view says otherwise, and I will show first that tenseless time need not be spacelike. I have to draw the spatial analogy anyway in order to show its limitations, and the analogy will then help in chapter 5 to make the other two points – since everyone takes a tenseless view of space, despite spatial tenses being as clearly untranslatable and indispensable as temporal tenses are.

Spatial dates and spatial tenses

Since space has three dimensions to time's one, the arrangement of things and events in space is more complicated than it is in time. But this does not prevent the *A* and *B* series, and in particular the relation between them, having spatial analogues. It just makes the spatial analogue of the temporal relation *earlier* (or *later*), common to the two series, more complicated. And since the extra complication is irrelevant, I will reduce it by developing the analogy only for a two-dimensional array of spatial positions on the surface of the earth.

The analogues of dates are the spatial positions of things and events depicted on terrestrial maps. These spatial "dates" can be specified by latitude and longitude or, within the UK for instance, by National Grid references. That corresponds to giving temporal dates in the system of years BC and AD. As in that system, latitude and longitude locate things and events by how far they are, and in what direction, from some more or less arbitrarily chosen thing or event. Thus the Equator and Greenwich correspond in space to Christ's birth in time, degrees of latitude and longitude correspond to years, and the directions North-South and East-West correspond to earlier-later.

Spatial dates need not of course be stated in a comprehensive system, any more than temporal dates do. *Ten miles North of Cambridge* is a perfectly good spatial date, just as *ten years after the Russian revolution* is a perfectly good temporal one. The point in each case is that dates, as opposed to tenses, are given by fixed spatial or temporal relations which things and events have to one another.

In saying that spatial dates are fixed, I am not overlooking the obvious fact that people and things can move. That indeed marks a major difference between space and time, relating to time's role as the dimension of change, including change of spatial position. But I am not yet ready to deal with change. That comes later, and has to do with how the temporal relation *earlier* differs from its spatial counterparts. Here I want only to draw an analogy between spatial and temporal positions. And to this analogy the fact that things can move is irrelevant, for the following reason.

In giving the temporal date of something spatial, I am not saying that it fills the whole of space throughout that time, only that it has *some* spatial position, not necessarily the same from moment to moment. In giving Mozart's date (1756–1791), for example, I am saying at most that he is somewhere on the earth throughout this interval of *B* series time. Analogously, in giving the spatial date of something temporal, I am not saying that it occupies that whole region for all eternity. It merely has to be everywhere within the region at some time or other. Whether it stays still, and is every-where within its spatial date all at once, or whether it moves about from one part to another, is immaterial.

Because space has more than one dimension, the spatial dates of things are apt to be more convoluted than their temporal dates. Mozart's spatial date, for example, is a rather web-like region of the earth's surface encompassing all the ground he ever stood, sat or lay on (or was ever over or under) during his lifetime. It is not a feature of his – or anyone's – life that we normally think of, because it tells us very little about him. If you want to meet a traveller, it is no use knowing where he will be at some time or other, which is all his spatial date tells you. You need to know *when* he will be at various more specific places within his spatial date. In short, you need to know his so-called "world-line", which is a plot of his spatial position against *B* series time. From someone's world-line you can read off that he is, say, in Vienna on 26 August 1788, in Salzburg on 19 November 1790, and so on. His spatial date suppresses all this useful temporal information by projecting his whole world-line, regardless of time, onto the surface of the earth – just as his temporal date projects it, regardless of his spatial location, onto the dimension of time.

Usually, therefore, it is only worth giving the spatial date of something whose world-line is closely parallel to the time axis, so that its projection onto the earth's surface is not much larger than the thing itself. In other words, only to things which do not move much, like mountains, rivers and towns, do we normally bother to ascribe spatial dates. They are the only kind of things worth depict-ing on maps, because only they can be relied on to be at the places indicated at any time within a period of years. People and other mobile things are not worth putting on maps, not because they have no spatial dates, but because their spatial dates are so much larger than they are.

What I mean by calling spatial dates 'fixed', therefore, has nothing to do with things being immobile. It is simply the spatial analogue of what I meant in chapter 1 when I said that temporal dates are fixed. The *B* series positions of things and events do not change with time as tenses do; and analogously, the spatial dates of things and events do not vary from place to place. Thus, just as it is always a fact that World War II ends in 1945, so it is everywhere a fact that Cambridge has latitude 52° North. Or, to put it more perspicuously in the idiom of truth, 'World War II ends in 1945' is true *whenever* it is said, and 'Cambridge is 52° North' is true *wherever* it is said. A statement of Cambridge's latitude does not have to be varied to be kept true as one moves about the globe. That is what I mean by saying that Cambridge, like all other things and events, has a fixed spatial date.

It follows that spatial dates say nothing about how near or far things and events are from *here*, the spatial analogue of the present moment *now*. For that information we need the spatial analogues of tenses. There are analogues of the tenses like *this week* which are present because they contain the present moment: *less than a mile away*, for example, is a spatially present tense, because it includes *here*. Similarly, there are analogues of non–present tenses, past and future, like *ten days hence* and *ten days ago*: e.g. *ten miles South of here* and *ten miles North of here*.

Moreover, spatial distances South and North of here are fixed by the spatially tenseless relation *North of*, just as temporal distances into the past and future are fixed by the tenseless relation *earlier*. If one event is ten days earlier than another, it will always be ten days *more past* or *less future*, whatever the date of the present may be; analogously, if one place is ten miles North of another, it will always be ten miles *more North of here* or ten miles *less South of here*, wherever *here* may happen to be. Fix the latitude of the spatial present, and the latitudes of all distances South and North of here are settled, just as the dates of all *A* series positions are settled by fixing the date of the present time. In all these crucial respects, the array of positions North and South (or West and

East) of here is exactly analogous to the array of tenses in the *A* series.

The correspondence between spatial and temporal tenses is of course not perfect. There is the greater dimensionality of space, which complicates the structure of both spatial dates and spatial tenses. And so far as positions on the earth's surface are concerned, the correspondence there is in some ways defeated by the earth's shape. Nowhere is North of here at the North pole, for example, whereas I see no reason to believe in an end to the future. Similarly, wherever here is, going West of here around the globe eventually brings us to places East of here, whereas the future will not eventually turn into the past. Also, nothing much depends on spatial distinctions between what is North and South (or West and East) of here, certainly nothing comparable to the fact that we can see and hear only what is past, not what is future. Consequently, it makes no real odds which way the analogy is drawn, i.e. whether North rather than South, or West rather than East, is taken to correspond to the future.

But these differences in no way vitiate my limited comparison. I am not trying to show time and space to be alike in all important ways. On the contrary, that is the inference I am trying to resist. But the inference, to be resisted fairly, must be given the benefit of all reasonable doubt. And there is no doubt that, at least within the confines of a country such as the UK, the array of spatial positions centred on *here* is in all relevant respects exactly analogous to the array of *A* series positions centred on *now*.

In particular, spatial tenses, like temporal ones, vary as their corresponding dates do not. Here in Cambridge, for example, the spatially tensed fact is that London is sixty miles to the South. But that is not a fact everywhere. Forty miles North of here, the fact is that London is a hundred miles to the South; and eighty miles West of here, the fact is that London is a hundred miles away, roughly to the South-east. While in London itself, i.e. sixty miles to the South, the fact is that London is here and Cambridge is sixty miles to the North. The spatial tenses of London and Cambridge – and of all other places, things and events – vary systematically with spatial position, whether that be specified tenselessly by Grid reference or by distance or direction from here, just as temporal tenses vary with temporal position. Admittedly they vary in a more complicated way than temporal tenses do, because space has more dimensions than time does, but that is irrelevant. In the relevant respects the analogy is exact – and, I take it, obvious enough not to need spelling out in more detail.

Besides fixed and spatially tenseless facts about distances and directions between places, then, there seem to be variable spatially tensed facts about how far, and in which direction, places are from here. But these apparent spatially tensed facts can be explained away, in spatially tenseless terms, along token-reflexive lines exactly analogous to the token-reflexive treatment of temporal tense in chapters 2 and 3. This explanation I also take to be obvious and, in the spatial case, not seriously disputed. So I need not develop or defend it in great detail. I will merely sketch it briefly, leaving interested – or sceptical – readers to verify the details for themselves.

The first step, as with time, is to exchange tensed facts for tensed truths. All we really have to account for is the objective truth of 'London is sixty miles South' said in Cambridge, and its objective falsity said in London. We start as before by distinguishing types of spatially tensed sentences and judgments from tokens of those types. A signpost in Cambridge pointing South and reading 'London 60' is in effect a token of the sentence type 'London is sixty miles South'; and someone in London mistakenly saying or thinking that he is sixty miles to the North of it thereby generates another token of the same sentence type. The first token is true, the second false – because the first is sixty miles North of London and the second is not. The spatial dates of these tokens fix their truth-values. Any token of the type will be true if it is sixty miles North of London; tokens elsewhere will all be false. Those are the obvious and indubitable token-reflexive truth conditions of that particular sentence type. And the spatially tenseless token-reflexive truth conditions of all other simple spatially tensed sentence types are just as obvious and indubitable. Spatially tensed facts are redundant – they are not needed to account for the objective truth and falsity of simple spatially tensed sentences and judgments.

There are spatial analogues of complex tenses too, in which simple spatial tenses are iterated and reiterated. I have given examples already: e.g. 'Eighty miles West, London is a hundred miles away South-east'. Since space has three dimensions to time's one, reiterating simple spatial tenses into complex ones makes for a spatial tense logic even more rebarbative than the temporal variety.

Yet despite its formidable formal potential, it has never been developed, nor do I think it ever will be, because no one seriously believes in the spatially tensed facts it purports to present. No one believes there are really spatially tensed facts such as London being sixty miles away from here. Everyone knows that nothing but latitude and longitude is available to make statements, however complex, about what is here and what is elsewhere, true or false.

Nor is anyone impressed by the evident fact that all our experience appears to happen to us *here*, wherever here may be. This is the spatial analogue of the temporal presence of experience and, like it, the basis of our knowledge of other tensed truths. It is only because I know my experience is both *here* and *in Cambridge*, that I know Cambridge is here, that London, sixty miles from Cambridge, is sixty miles away from here, and so on. The spatial presence of experience should be as striking and central a phenomenon as its temporal presence is. But of course it isn't. We all know that the spatial presence of experience is a token-reflexive tautology: my experiences are wherever I am, so the token-reflexive definition of the spatial present tense makes me bound to be right if I judge them to be happening here.

In short, despite there being spatial analogues of all the phenomena that have led many philosophers to believe in real temporal tenses, nobody believes in real spatial tenses. No one thinks that as well as being at latitude 52° North and longitude 0° East, sixty miles North of London, etc., Cambridge also has such spatially variable properties as being *here*. Whatever their views on time, all parties agree that, so far as space is concerned, things and events are – literally – neither here nor there.

In chapters 2 and 3, I gave the temporal analogue of this universally accepted account of spatial tense; and I shall later use it positively to disprove the reality of the *A* series. Just as things and events are really neither here nor there, so I will show they are really neither now nor then, neither past, present nor to come. In this respect, space and time will be treated in exactly the same way, and the treatment will be supported with exactly analogous arguments: i.e. arguments which, if they work in either case, will work in both. These arguments, moreover, provide in my view the only means of disproving the reality of tenses, whether spatial or temporal. No one who rejects them in order to save the temporal *A* series can consistently explain why, as everyone admits, there really are no spatial tenses. Space and time can only be distinguished in this respect by maintaining that the difference is too fundamental to admit of explanation. And that is generally what upholders of real tense do maintain. For them, the existence of real differences between past, present and future is what distinguishes time from the dimensions of space; above all, it is what explains the peculiarly temporal character of change. Without it, they think, temporal change cannot be sufficiently distinguished from its spatial counterparts.

This is simply not true. Even if there are no tenses, the tenseless relation *earlier* still differs from all spatial relations. Often the difference is a plain matter of observation. Towards the end of chapter 1 I cited seeing the second hand of a clock moving clockwise as opposed to anti-clockwise. This simple observation involves both seeing and distinguishing a spatial and a temporal relation between two events: seeing, for example, that the hand passing the figure '1' is both *earlier* and *to the left of* its passing the figure '2'. Seeing this, moreover, as I remarked in chapter 1, in no way depends on seeing the tense of these events. Normally indeed I will suppose the clock to be nearby, and the events therefore to be going on more or less here and now. But I could equally well be looking through a telescope at events long past and far away, or even precognising events still in the future. The events would *look* the same in any case. In other words, their tenses are not observed but inferred, via the tenseless physics and metaphysics of the observation, from what in chapter 3 we saw was the tautologically present tense experience of seeing them. What tells me how long ago they occurred is how long I know it takes light to get from them to my eyes; and I only know the events are not future because I know light does not go backward in time. All I learn about the events' tenses from the observation itself therefore is what follows from its tenseless content: since the hand visibly passes the figure '1' before it passes the figure '2', that must be the more past or the less future of the two events.

The crucial point, however, is not what and how I might learn about tenses in making such observations. The point is that I need learn nothing about tenses at all. We can quite well see one event precede another without seeing the tense of either; and we can simultaneously see (and distinguish) the fact of its being to the left of that other event. So I can perfectly well deny both spatial and temporal tenses without denying our obvious ability to perceive temporal relations, and in particular to distinguish them from spatial ones.

Nor need I deny change and its peculiar association with time. The second hand moving is a case of change, and I see it as such. Because I can see the difference between temporal and spatial relations, I can clearly distinguish temporal change in the hand's spatial position from, say, spatial variation in its width from one end to the other. I must still of course explain why variation in time should count as change when variation in space does not; but it does not take real temporal tenses to do that. The peculiar association of change with time can quite well be explained tenselessly, on the basis of a causal account of what happens when someone sees one event precede another. Developing and defending that account is matter for later chapters, on which for the present I can only issue a promissory note. But all I need here, pending the delivery and defence of a tenseless account of change, is the admission that treating both space and time tenselessly need not involve denying this and other important differences between them. The tenseless view of time should not lead anyone to think of it as spacelike, nor to deny the reality of temporal change; those who rightly steer clear of such paradoxical opinions need not part company with me on that account.

Relativity

Nor need they part company with Einstein's theories of relativity. Contrary to some early misconceptions, the special and general theories do not obliterate the distinction between space and time. They do indeed combine space and time into a unified spacetime, with a four-dimensional geometry quite different from that of classical Newtonian spacetime. Moreover, they make it arbitrary to some extent how the spacetime separation of remote events is to be divided up into spatial and temporal distances, and this is what leads to the suspicion that they confound time with space. The suspicion is less widespread than it was, but is still perhaps persistent enough to warrant another attempt to dispel it. And since the suspicious feature shows up just as well in the simpler special theory, it will be enough to show its innocence there. The gravitational complications of the general theory will not make time any more like space than the special theory does.

Consider then, in the special theory, a star which is about a thousand light years away, i.e. such that no signal sent off to it from earth in AD 1000 could return again until AD 3000. Now think of an event occurring on the star when the signal reaches it, and ask what terrestrial date that event should have. The natural answer is of course AD 2000, and if the earth were more or less at rest in the universe (neglecting its rotation round the sun), that would be right. But the special theory provides no way of distinguishing being at rest from moving with a constant velocity, any more than Newton's theory does; and moreover – unlike Newton's theory – it makes different assumptions about the earth's motion generate different terrestrial dates for this celestial event: dates ranging from just after AD 1000 to just before AD 3000. To these different dates, however, there correspond different spatial distances between us and the star in question, so as to preserve, under all assumptions about the earth's motion, an invariant spacetime separation between events there and events here.

The theory says, therefore, that the spacetime separation of things and events is what is physically fixed. How it divides up into spatial and temporal components is – within limits – a matter not of fact but of an arbitrary choice of a so-called "reference frame", i.e. in effect of an assumption about what is at rest in the universe. What follows from this about the distinction between space and time, and about the relative prospects for tensed and tenseless views of time?

To take the second question first, I must say that I think relativity on its own makes a tensed view of time very hard to maintain. It prevents distinctions between past, present and future bearing the factual loads that provide the main motive for drawing them in the first place. Take the view discussed in chapter 2 that only the present exists. On that view the only celestial events that now exist are those with the terrestrial date at which you are now reading these very words. But according to relativity, which celestial events have this present date is decided by an arbitrary choice of reference frame, which in the above example could put the event in question anywhere in an *A* series from centuries past to a millennium into the future. Events we can now see will admittedly be past in all local reference frames, so they at least will definitely *not* exist now; and the same goes for events which we could still affect, since they will be future in all local reference frames. But in between, only things and events that span the gap separating definite past from definite future – a gap, on our star, of 2000 years – will come out present in all such frames, and therefore definitely exist as a matter of physical fact. And since this gap increases with distance from here, the more shortlived a thing or event is, the closer to here it must be for it ever, as a matter of fact, to exist at all.

Combining relativity with the view that only the present exists, therefore, restricts existence more or less to what is here as well as now. And that is a much less attractive proposition. For objective existence (or possibility or necessity) to depend credibly on presence, the present really needs to extend as a matter of fact across the whole spatial universe; and relativity essentially denies that it does any such thing. Whereas to a tenseless view, on which distinctions between past, present and future are not factual anyway, it makes no odds that they can be drawn in many different ways, all equally true to what physical facts there are. Alternative *B* series, in short, matter much less than alternative *A* series – provided relativity sets *some* limits to the range of alternatives, as we shall see shortly that it does.

So relativity poses a serious problem for tensed views of time. It is not, however, a problem I shall press, for two reasons. One is that a sufficiently determined upholder of tense might just as well use it to attack relativity. That might be rash, but it would be a perfectly healthy reaction: philosophers of late years have been altogether too deferential to the metaphysical speculations of physicists, especially about time. But my real reason for not pressing the problem is that I do not need to. The tenseless view of time does not need relativity to support it, as chapter 6 will show. That it readily accommodates the special and general theories is just as well for them, but it is not a *sine qua non* of the view itself.

The important question about relativity is the first one: does it deny the distinction between space and time? If so, it would perhaps support a tenseless view of time as being at least consistent with that denial, which the tensed view of time is not. I confess, however, that I should not welcome such support. If relativity did confound time with space, I should join upholders of tense in rejecting relativity, since our common experience distinguishes time from space far too certainly for physical theory to deny the distinction. We need no theoretical authority for it, any more than we need such authority to distinguish colours. I have remarked already how readily we can see one event following another in many cases and can distinguish that sight from seeing how the events are related in space. We see such things, and make this distinction, every time we see something move; and the perception of movement is as undeniable by theory as the perception of colour is. No theory can tell us there is really no difference between different colours, for we can see there is. Likewise, no theory can tell us there is no difference between space and time: we can see there is.

But relativity of course tells us no such thing. It does indeed allow a rather striking latitude in the terrestrial dating of celestial events, with a compensating latitude in their spatial distance from the earth. But this does not make time in the theories at all like space. Temporal distance figures in them quite differently from spatial distance. In special relativity, for example, the fixed spacetime separation s of two events is related to their variable spatial and temporal distances x and t in any reference frame as follows:

$$s^2 = x^2 - c^2 t^2;$$

where c is the speed of light (the same in all reference frames) and x is related to coordinate distances x_1, x_2 and x_3 along any three spatial directions at right angles to each other by the Pythagorean formula

$$x^2 = x_1^2 + x_2^2 + x_3^2.$$

The temporal distance t is thus clearly distinguished by its sign from any Cartesian coordinate of the spatial distance between the events. Moreover, t and x are of course measured respectively by clocks and by metre rules (or other stock ways of measuring spatial distance), the results being values of t and x for frames in which these measuring devices are at rest. The theory therefore presupposes, rather than denies, a distinction between the spatial and temporal components of spacetime.

The theory, moreover, draws a clear and absolute distinction between so-called "timelike" and "spacelike" separations. For any two events, if s^2 is negative, the events have a timelike separation; if positive, a spacelike separation. The point of these labels is that s^2 can only be positive if the events are spatially separated in all reference frames, although some frame will make them simultaneous. For if there were a frame in which they coincided spatially, i.e. in which $x = 0$, we should in that frame have $s^2 = -c^2 t^2$; which, since c^2t^2 cannot be negative, means that s^2 would not be positive after all. Similarly, s^2 can only be negative if t is never zero, so that in no reference frame are the events involved simultaneous, although some frame will put them in the same place. When s^2 is negative, therefore, the separation of the two events always has a temporal component. They are separated in time absolutely, as a matter of physical fact independent of choice of reference frame, and that is why their spacetime separation is called timelike.

If $s = 0$, then $x = ct$ in all reference frames: i.e. the two events lie along the spacetime path – the world-line – of something travelling at the speed of light, which according to relativity is as fast as anything can travel. Such a world-line, therefore, the world-line of a photon, marks a boundary between spacelike and timelike separations of events. More importantly, it also gives a clue to what is taken in relativity to distinguish these two kinds of spacetime separation.

I gave another clue to this earlier, in remarking that any event we can now see will come out past in every reference frame, and any event we can still affect will come out future. This means that my seeing of an event – which is itself another event – always has a timelike separation from the event I thereby see; and likewise any event I affect has a timelike separation from the action by which I affect it. The timelike separation follows from the two events in each case having a definite temporal order, the same in every reference frame. That is, not only are they never simultaneous, the one is always later, not earlier, than the other. In each case, therefore, the one is *absolutely later*, and the other *absolutely earlier*, as a matter of physical fact. And the basis of this fact in relativity is that the one event is directly or indirectly affected by the other. In the case of action this is obvious. For me to kill someone by shooting him, for example, my moving my finger to pull the trigger must be what indirectly causes his death, by causing the explosion which causes the bullet to reach him at high speed, thereby causing damage to his tissues, etc. And though it may be less obvious, a similar chain of causes and effects must also occur when we see things or events, or perceive them by any of our other senses. When I perceive an event, such as a light being turned on, the event must cause me to perceive it, directly or indirectly: by causing light to be emitted or reflected into my eyes, for example, or by causing sound waves to reach my ears.

Causation, in short, is how relativity distinguishes time from space. Events cannot have a spacelike separation if they are related directly or indirectly as cause to effect; and most events so related have a clearly timelike separation. The only exception is for $s = 0$, where events are linked causally by light or other radiation that transmits causal influence as fast as it can go. The separation of these events, although not spacelike, is also officially not timelike because there is (in a degenerate sense) a reference frame in which they are simultaneous, namely that in which even light would be at rest. However, this is a "frame" quite inaccessible to anything travelling more slowly, since nothing in relativity can be accelerated to that speed. In particular, no clock can be; and at all the speeds clocks can reach they will give these events the same temporal order. So we do no violence to any relativistic measurement of time in insisting on the obvious fact that even light sets out before it arrives. Here too causes come absolutely earlier than their effects.

Relativity gives causes and effects an absolute temporal order: different reference frames can only reverse or annul the temporal order of causally unrelated events. Thus it distinguishes absolutely between space and time, provided some events cause others, as they must for perception and action to occur – and even, as we shall see, for there to be any things or processes in the world. In no such world will any relativistic *B* series, i.e. a temporal ordering of all things and events in some reference frame, ever also be a one-dimensional spatial ordering of them in some other reference frame. There is an absolute causal limit to the range of alternative *B* series, which effectively distinguishes all of them from any dimension of space.

Not everyone agrees that all causes precede their effects. No one, of course, denies that most of them do. But it remains to be seen why, and whether the general rule admits exceptions. This too is matter for a later chapter, where I show why the causal test of temporal order is right, and conclusive. But right or not, its use suffices to acquit relativity of treating time like space. Indeed, there has never really been a charge to answer. Relativity uses only standard methods for measuring spatial and temporal distances, and they are clearly distinct: clocks are not metre rules, and metre rules do not tell the time. Relativity then treats these different kinds of measurement quite differently in its equations. And finally, as we

5   *The need for tense*

So much for the canard that tenseless time is spacelike time. I shall have more to say in later chapters about how time differs from space, especially in relation to change and causation. But at least I trust I may now take some difference for granted, and that in particular I will not be charged with spatialising time when in what follows I draw on spatial analogies. I use spatial analogies, to help to sell the ensuing argument, because they make it more obvious that something must be wrong with the inferences I mean to discredit, namely that tenseless sentences could translate, or at least supplant, tensed ones. Not that the falsity of these inferences is more obvious in the spatial case: it is equally obvious that neither 'Cambridge is here' nor 'It is now 1980' can be either translated or replaced by spatially and temporally tenseless sentences. The point is rather that this does not make anyone adopt a tensed view of space, whereas it does seem to encourage tensed views of time. The spatial inferences must therefore to start with be more obviously discreditable. Yet the temporal inferences are only valid if the spatial ones are. So to encourage a proper scepticism about them, I shall start by treating the two cases together.

The untranslatability of tense

Why should tenseless space or time be thought to imply tenseless translations for spatially or temporally tensed sentences? The reasoning seems to be as follows. Tenseless facts provide the truth conditions for all tokens of tensed sentences and judgments: tokens of 'Cambridge is here' are true if and only if they are in Cambridge, tokens of 'It is now 1980' are true if and only if they occur in 1980, and so on. For many, stating a sentence's truth conditions gives its meaning; and if it does, a sentence which states another sentence's truth conditions surely has the same meaning. For example, any English sentence of the form 'X is half empty' is true if and only if X

is half full; so '. . . is half full' means the same in English as '. . . is half empty'.

Now apply this train of thought to the tenseless truth conditions of tensed sentences, allowing for the fact that the truth conditions of tokens of 'Cambridge is here' and 'It is now 1980' vary respectively from place to place and time to time. Nonetheless, although these truth conditions vary, they do so in peculiar and characteristic ways; and a statement of how they vary does seem to give the meanings of those sentence types. Anyone who knows that for any place X tokens of 'X is here' are true if and only if they are at X, and that for any date T tokens of 'It is now T' are true if and only if they occur at T, surely knows what '. . . is here' and 'It is now . . .' mean in English. So the tenseless sentences I have just used to give those meanings should themselves mean the same thing, and hence provide tenseless translations of these tensed sentences.

But they don't. Let X = Cambridge and T = 1980, and let R be any token of 'Cambridge is here' and S be any token of 'It is now 1980'. ('R' and 'S' must of course not themselves be token–reflexive names or descriptions.) Then R is true if and only if it occurs in Cambridge, and S is true if and only if it occurs in 1980. If a sentence giving another's truth conditions means what it does, R should mean the same as 'R occurs in Cambridge' and S should mean the same as 'S occurs in 1980'. But these sentences have different truth conditions. In particular, if true at all, they are true everywhere and at all times. If R does occur in Cambridge, that is a fact all over the world, and if S occurs in 1980, that is a fact at all times. You need not be in Cambridge in 1980 to meet true tokens of 'R occurs in Cambridge' and 'S occurs in 1980'. But you do need to be in Cambridge in 1980 to meet the true tokens, R and S: for only there and then can R and S themselves be true. At all other places and times those tensed sentences would have been false, whereas their alleged translations are true everywhere and always.

Now it may be contentious whether meanings are in general given by truth conditions, and whether sameness of truth conditions guarantees sameness of meaning. But few will deny that same meaning means same truth conditions. Two sentences can hardly mean the same if, as here, they are true in quite different circumstances. And for all those reluctant to relate meaning to truth conditions at all, there is the following consideration. Because these tenseless sentences, if true at all, are nowhere and never false, the truth of any token of them says nothing about where or when it occurs. To be told, of some token *R*, '*R* occurs in Cambridge', is to be told nothing at all about where you are; and '*S* occurs in 1980' is similarly unenlightening about what time it is. Tokens of these tenseless sentences are quite useless for telling people where they are or what the time is. But those are the chief uses of the tensed sentences they purport to translate. Now, however meaning may relate in general to truth conditions, it is an undisputed canon of modern philosophy to relate it to usage. And however loosely that canon is applied, no sentence could possibly mean the same as another when, as here, it cannot be used at all as the other one standardly is. No theory of meaning, therefore, could make *R* mean '*R* occurs in Cambridge' or *S* mean '*S* occurs in 1980'.

Obviously, nothing tenseless will translate tokens *R* and *S* if '*R* occurs in Cambridge' and '*S* occurs in 1980' do not. And if simple tensed sentences such as these have no tenseless translation, then no tensed sentence does. The fact, I think, needs arguing no further, least of all to opponents of tenseless time. The only question is what it implies for tenseless time. It is tempting to infer from it that tensed sentences mean more than their token–reflexive truth conditions reveal; and that tensed facts may after all be needed to say what. How is the temptation to be resisted?

First, by resisting a bad analogy. Sometimes indeed there must be more to meaning than truth conditions: in mathematics, for example. If mathematical truths are all necessarily true, then each is true in the same conditions, namely in all conditions. Thus '2 + 2 = 4' is true if and only if there is no greatest prime number. But '2 + 2 = 4' does not mean that there is no greatest prime number. Someone who already understands '2 + 2 = 4' will not learn what 'There is no greatest prime number' means by learning that they have the same truth conditions.

But the contingent tensed sentences we are concerned with are not like that. They may not *have* the same meaning as the tenseless sentences that give their truth conditions, but those truth conditions surely *give* their meaning. As I have already remarked, anyone who knows that, for all dates *T*, 'It is now *T*' is true during and only during *T* knows what 'It is now . . .' means. Given just this knowledge, he can use and understand tokens of any such present tense sentence, and distinguish it from all past and future tense sentences of which he also knows the token-reflexive truth conditions. (Granted, he also has to recognise what in chapter 3 I called the "presence of experience", in order to tell that he is *now* hearing someone say 'It is now *T*'; but I have already given a tenseless account of that phenomenon.) Here, unlike mathematics, correct usage *is* explained by people knowing how the truth of what they say depends on when and where they say it; in particular, the *different* meanings of different sentences are differentiated, as they are not in mathematics, by their different truth conditions. 'Cambridge is here' and 'Cambridge is ten miles away' are used differently because they are known to be true in different places; and similarly in time for 'It is now 1980' and '1980 is two years ago'.

Truth conditions give meanings less problematically here than in mathematics and elsewhere for another reason too. For a sentence's truth conditions to give its meaning, its being true in them must be more than a coincidence. Otherwise, so far as truth conditions go, the English sentence 'Snow is white' could just as well mean that grass is green, since 'Snow is white' *is* true and grass *is* green. 'Snow is white' is indeed true if and only if grass is green. But that, of course, is just a coincidence. Even if grass were not green, 'Snow is white' would still be true – provided snow was still white. 'Snow is white' is not only true in the real world, it would also be true in any other world in which snow was white, and false in any world in which it wasn't. That is really why the sentence means in English what it does, rather than meaning that grass is green. To give meanings, therefore, truth conditions generally have to include imaginary conditions as well as real ones. But it is a very moot point how enlightening about meanings reference to truth in imaginary conditions is. I could not, for example, teach anyone that 'Snow is white' doesn't mean that grass is green by taking him to a world in which it isn't, and showing him there that the English still take 'Snow is white' to be true, because there is in reality no such world. On the contrary, we only know that 'Snow is white' would be true in some such imaginary world because we already know what it means, and assume for that very reason that snow could be white even if grass were not green.

This is a serious objection to using truth conditions to give meanings, but it does not apply when the conditions are token-reflexive. I *can* teach someone what 'Cambridge is here' means by showing him, or describing to him in tenseless terms, the real places where it is true, and thus distinguishing them from the real places where it is false. And likewise for 'It is now 1980'. When truth conditions are being given for token sentences, they need not include imaginary conditions in any problematic way. They must admittedly apply to imaginary as well as to real tokens. All the tokens of 'Cambridge is here' in Cambridge could by chance have occurred in King's College, making tokens of that sentence true as a matter of fact if and only if they occur in King's. But that again would only be a coincidence, and would not give the real meaning of 'Cambridge is here'. So we must consider all the actual places where tokens of this English sentence *would* be true, even if none are actually there. But although we have therefore to consider imaginary tokens, we have only to consider them in actual places.

To give the (spatial or temporal) meanings of essentially tensed contingent sentences, we need only say when and where in the real world they would actually be true. In this case truth conditions seem to me both innocuous and effective: I find it hard to see what aspect of tensed meaning they fail to accommodate. And certainly they fail to do nothing that tensed facts could do better. For the only aspect of a sentence's meaning which tensed facts could supply is its truth conditions. That is after all what they are defined to do. That Cambridge is here and that it is now 1980 make 'Cambridge is here' and 'It is now 1980' objectively true if they do anything at all. They do nothing to make these sentences important, or memorable, or short, or poetic: merely true. But that job has already been done by the tenseless facts adduced in chapter 2. If doing that job does not suffice to give the meaning of tensed sentences, the lacuna will not be filled by tensed facts.

But if their tenseless truth conditions give the meaning of tensed sentences, why have they no tenseless translation? Actually, the reason is quite simple. To translate a sentence is to find another sentence with the same meaning: in particular, therefore, one with the same truth conditions. Now the truth conditions of tokens of spatially tensed sentence types vary, as we have seen, with their spatial position, and those of temporally tensed types vary with their temporal position. So therefore must the truth conditions of tokens of their translations. But what makes sentence types tenseless, as we saw in chapters 1 and 2, is that the truth conditions of their tokens do *not* vary in this way. Spatially tenseless tokens' truth conditions are the same at all places, and temporally tenseless ones' are the same at all times. So far as space and time are concerned, the truth conditions of tenseless sentences are not token-reflexive. No tenseless sentence, therefore, can have tokens whose truth conditions are everywhere and always the same as those of a tensed sentence, because by definition the latter vary from place to place or time to time and the former do not. That is why no tenseless sentence can mean the same as a tensed one does: tenseless token-reflexive and non-token-reflexive truth conditions are bound to differ. Far from the tenseless translatability of tensed sentences following from the tenseless view of space and time, it follows that they are not thus translatable. So that obvious fact is no objection to a tenseless view of either space or time. On the contrary, only the tenseless view explains it. For if tensed sentence types had tensed and non-token-reflexive truth conditions, i.e. stated (if true) tensed facts which did not vary from token to token, it would so far as I can see just be an unexplained axiom of tense that no such fact is ever identical with what any tenseless sentence states.

The indispensability of tense

But if tensed sentences are not translatable, why are they indispensable? If there are no tensed facts, why must we think and speak as if there were? Here, after all, we are only concerned with sentences expressing judgments, i.e. stating what people take to be facts; not with expressing emotions, giving commands, etc. Someone saying 'Cambridge is here' or 'It is now 1980' is stating what he takes to be a fact. But if all facts are tenseless, why not state them tenselessly? Why on the tenseless view must we make tensed judgments at all?

Yet it is as evident that we must as it is that tenseless sentences will not express them. We must obviously know more than the dates and grid references of things and events. To govern our interactions with them, and with other people, we must also know which we are faced with at any time, i.e. which are spatially and temporally present. But does this not mean that tenseless fact, like patriotism, is not enough, that we need tensed sentences because they state other, tensed, facts that we also need to know?

Not at all. We do need to make and express tensed judgments, but not because we need to know and state tensed facts. The fact is that we need to make and express judgments whose truth conditions are token-reflexive. That is the real reason tensed judgments are indispensable to our thought and speech, despite there being no tensed facts. But why do we need to make token-reflexive judgments? To answer that question I must first say more clearly what judgments are.

I have so far left the idea of judgment deliberately inexplicit. I introduced it in chapter 2 by remarking that we can think things past, present or future without saying or writing anything, i.e. there can be mental as well as physical tokens of tensed sentences. I said no more about them then, except that they have dates, because that was all I needed to give them tenseless token-reflexive truth conditions. What else judgments are like was immaterial. But now that I have to explain why we need to make judgments with these truth conditions, I shall have to go into more detail.

Basically, to judge that something is so is to believe it. So far I have given only cases of conscious belief, and only then, I dare say, do we talk of "making a judgment". But belief, including tensed belief, can exist without being conscious. I keep left while driving in Britain, for example, because I believe that is still the rule, but I do not have the rule consciously in mind all the time I am following it. Again, I suppose a dog can believe it will soon be fed, without it being capable of making conscious judgments at all. Of course not everyone accepts animal or other unconscious beliefs, but since it costs me nothing to admit them, I might as well sidestep that controversy by doing so. So from now on I shall talk of tensed beliefs rather than tensed judgments.

The idiom of belief also helps me to apply to mental tokens an important distinction drawn in chapter 2. I have so far called judgments events, namely event tokens of whatever types of sentence would express them. Having a belief, however, is not an event. Acquiring or losing one is, since it is a real change (see chapter 8) in a believer's state of mind; and so is making a judgment, because it involves the conscious acquisition or reinforcement of a belief. But once acquired, beliefs persist to guide action even when the believer's conscious attention has turned elsewhere (as my beliefs do about which side of the road to drive).

A person with a belief is what in chapter 2 I called a "thing token", not an event token, of a sentence type that would express the belief. That is, a believer is like a printed sentence rather than a spoken one.

The difference, the reader may recall, is that, unlike event tokens, thing tokens have a truth-value at each *B* series instant, and can therefore change in truth-value from one instant to another. And the truth-values of tensed beliefs do change from time to time as the things and events they are about change their *A* series positions. So to keep them true, one must every so often change their tenses, from tokens of future, to tokens of present, to tokens of past tense types. These changes are the psychological reality behind the myth of passing time, as will emerge in more detail at the end of chapter 7. Here their importance is that we need them to undertake timely action. That is why beliefs themselves need to be changeable properties of believers, rather than events.

This way of distinguishing judgments from beliefs is unusual, but it suits my purposes, and will not, I trust, be as contentious as the role of consciousness in judgment is. Consciousness is of course not the only contentious aspect of belief, but fortunately I can afford to be agnostic about most of the others as well. All I shall need to assume about belief is that it is a state of mind aimed exclusively at truth, is what perception produces, and combines with desire to generate action. Whether belief needs language, whether it is a relation believers have to propositions, whether it comes by degrees, how it manages to be about particular people and things, how it is embodied in the brain – all these hard and important questions I can evade, because different answers to them make no odds to the ensuing argument.

I should however enlarge somewhat on what I am assuming. It is nothing very contentious, and needs, I think, no more explanation and defence than plausible illustration can provide. But that much it does need, since there is more to it than the last paragraph might suggest.

To start with, belief's peculiarly intimate connection with truth is not easy to pin down. It is not just that believing a sentence or proposition *p* is believing it to be true. Hoping that *p* is likewise hoping that *p* is true, and similarly for intending, regretting and all the other so-called "propositional attitudes". What for my purposes is special about belief can best be illustrated by the paradox pointed out by G. E. Moore (1942, p. 543). It would, he said, be absurd for anyone to say '*p* is true but I don't believe it'; whereas there is generally nothing absurd in saying '*p* is true but I don't regret it', '*p* is true but I don't intend it', etc. Now this is not because '*p* is true but I don't believe it' could not be true: there are many truths we don't believe. But even if (e.g.) the post has come without my realising it, 'It is true that the post has come but I don't believe it' would still, though true, be a most paradoxical thing for me to say. The reason is that I cannot say such a thing sincerely without turning it into a falsehood, because I cannot think something to be true without consciously believing it. Other propositional attitudes produce no such paradoxes, because settling for oneself a proposition's truth-value does not automatically settle one's other attitudes towards it. But it does settle whether one believes it. For me to believe something just *is* for me to have settled (for myself and for the time being) that it is true. This is what I mean by saying that belief is a state of mind aimed exclusively at truth in a way that other propositional attitudes are not.

This means in particular that, in order to dispose of tensed facts, we need only account tenselessly for the truth of tensed beliefs. Whenever other attitudes seem to imply tensed facts, they do so only by implying either a correspondingly tensed belief or the truth of such a belief. Regretting that something happened in the past, for example, implies believing that it did; and all there is to the *temporal* rightness of that regret is the truth of the tensed belief it incorporates. (Whether the happening was regrettable in other respects is not my business.) Similarly for other propositional attitudes; even knowledge, which differs from the others in implying truth and not merely belief. Some philosophers admittedly deny that knowledge implies belief; but even they will admit that I can only know something if, had I believed it instead, that belief would have been true. So in this case too, accounting tenselessly for the objective truth or falsehood of a tensed belief will also account, so far as tense goes, for the objective rightness or wrongness of the other tensed attitude to the same proposition. In short, if tensed facts are not needed to make tensed beliefs true or false, they will not be needed at all. In discussing what the indispensability of tensed attitudes implies for tenseless time, therefore, we need not run the whole gamut of propositional attitudes. We need only consider tensed belief.

What makes tense indispensable, therefore, is that we cannot help having tensed beliefs. Partly we cannot help it because belief, including tensed belief, is what perceptions give us. To see or hear something is in the first place always to acquire or reinforce a belief about it: perception is nothing if not the acquisition or reinforcement of belief. Whatever has perceptions therefore must also have beliefs.

And whatever *acts* on its perceptions must have tensed beliefs. Action is what really makes tensed belief indispensable. That action is, as I have said, generated by combinations of belief and desire is obvious and not seriously disputed. But that – and why – actions need *tensed* beliefs is less obvious. The fact that they do, however, and especially the token-reflexive reason for the fact, is both the crux of my case and the reason for the persistent and fatal attraction of the idea that tenses are real. The fact therefore, and the reason for it, need developing in some detail, largely as before by illustration.

Suppose I push a switch to turn on the radio. To motivate this action I need some beliefs and desires: a desire to hear something on the radio, presumably, and a belief that pushing the switch will turn it on. But whatever the desire and the belief, desire and belief are both needed, since neither attitude engenders action on its own. I will not act unless I desire some outcome of my action; but nor will desiring an outcome make me act unless I believe it is an outcome. It is not enough for the switch actually to turn the radio on: I will still not push it unless I believe that it does.

(One must allow in general for comparative degrees of belief and desire, since people sometimes act to avoid a relative evil rather than to get anything they positively want, and sometimes they gamble on what they believe are very unlikely outcomes. But the greater complexity of other cases is not really germane. Any action needs some degree of belief in its efficacy as a means to some end, and it also needs some degree of tensed belief. The need for tense does not depend on the degree of belief involved; so we may as well stick to a simple case. The ensuing discussion will I think make it evident enough that tense, if needed there, will be needed everywhere.)

Now suppose more specifically that I want to hear the one o'clock news; so I push the switch at one o'clock. Why did I do that at one o'clock, and not some minutes or hours earlier or later? Well, obviously, because I wanted to hear the one o'clock news. But that on its own is not enough, even given that I know that pushing the switch turns the radio on. I could have been wanting to hear the one o'clock news for hours; and I could have mastered the radio years ago. Something more than these two steady states of desire and belief is needed actually to propel my finger to the switch at a specific time. Obviously, what I also need to believe is that it is *now* one o'clock. Until I acquire that present tense belief I shall do nothing, however much I want to hear the news, and however strong my tenseless belief in the efficacy of the switch.

What action needs, in short, is the belief, not the fact. Even if there were tensed facts such as one o'clock being now, they would not make me turn the radio on, or do anything else. I turn the radio on when I *believe* it is now one o'clock, whether it actually is or not. My beliefs are what make me act, not the facts that make them true or false. But of course, when I act on false beliefs, tensed or tenseless, my actions are apt to fail, i.e. not to get me what I want. If it is not in fact one o'clock when I push the switch, or if the switch does not in fact turn on the radio, I am likely to miss the news I want to hear. So although the truth-value of my beliefs is irrelevant to explaining my actions, it is by no means irrelevant to explaining their success or failure. And since actions are meant to be successful, the truth conditions of beliefs are highly relevant to determining how actions depend on them. Truth being the sole aim of belief, it is all belief can contribute to successful action. Action therefore in general so depends upon the truth conditions of the agent's beliefs that their being satisfied will suffice for its success. (Waiving again the extra complexities of action based merely on degrees of belief.)

In particular, action will be timely if it satisfies the token-reflexive truth conditions of the tensed beliefs it depends on. To hear the one o'clock news, I need to turn the radio on at one o'clock. I turn it on when I believe it is *now* one o'clock because the truth conditions of that belief are satisfied, and only satisfied, at one o'clock. It is a belief such that, if I act on it when it is true, my action will succeed. And to have that desirable property, it must be a tensed belief, because only tensed beliefs have truth conditions that include the time at which the belief is held. Tenseless beliefs, if true, are always true; so acting when they are true does nothing to secure the success of an action which needs to be done at a particular time.

This dependence of timely action on the token-reflexive truth conditions of tensed beliefs is no coincidence. Nor is it merely the result of acting on a prudential maxim ('If you want to succeed in life, act when your beliefs are true') which feckless people might ignore. That might be so if believing something were a state of mind independent of how one acts as a result of being in it – but it isn't. Suppose it was: suppose for example people's beliefs were what they consciously thought them to be, so that self-deception about belief was not merely rare but impossible. Now imagine a husband who is always finding implausible pretexts to return home unexpectedly, i.e. is acting in a way that only makes sense as being designed to succeed in showing his wife to be unfaithful if the belief that she is is true. Yet the husband is quite sincere in the flimsy pretexts he gives: he is consciously quite unaware of believing his wife to be unfaithful. We should have to say then that he did not really believe it after all, because he did not think he did, even though he acts in a way that then makes no sense. But we should say no such thing. He really is jealous, as his actions show, only he is at the same time deceiving himself into thinking that he isn't.

If a man wants above all else to do something at a particular time, knows how to do it and is able to, it makes no sense to suppose he believes that time to be present, but still does nothing because he is too feckless to act on his belief. If in those circumstances he does not act on that present tense belief, he does not have it. To have it just *is* to be disposed to act in ways that will succeed if it and the other relevant beliefs are true. Explaining people's actions by their beliefs and desires means crediting them willy-nilly with beliefs whose truth would ensure the actions' success. And in particular, explaining the timeliness of people's actions means crediting them willy-nilly with temporally token-reflexive and therefore tensed beliefs.

It follows from all this that a tensed belief, conscious or unconscious, must be a real psychological property of whoever has it. By this I mean that a change in the belief has to be a real event in a believer's mental life, i.e. an event which has effects. This must be so because that is how tensed beliefs explain actions, viz. causally. If I already want to hear the one o'clock news and know how to work the radio, a change from future to present in the tense of my belief about one o'clock is what *causes* me to turn the radio on. Unless my states of tensed belief were real properties of mine, changes in them could not be, as usually they are, the immediate causes of my actions.

A proper discussion of change and of the distinction between real and other properties of people and things must wait for chapter 8. For the time being, an illustration will have to serve to indicate the significance of the distinction. Fame, for example, is not a real property of a famous man, since it resides in the acclaim of others, not in him. That is, although his hearing of his fame can immediately affect him, his merely becoming or ceasing to be famous cannot. Fluctuations in his fame occur at a distance from him, and causes do not produce their immediate effects at a distance. Conversely, what does affect him immediately, e.g. by being an immediate cause of his actions, is not remote from him. That is the crucial difference between his beliefs and his fame, the difference that puts them among his real psychological properties – i.e. among those which materialists will have to suppose to be embodied somehow in definite and distinct states of his brain.

Changes in tensed beliefs, being real events, will normally have causes as well as effects. The change from my thinking one o'clock future to thinking it present does not occur automatically at one o'clock; it takes a cause to set it off. The cause could come from the "internal clock" that any agent, human or animal, needs to have to change its tensed beliefs from time to time to try and keep them true. Or it could be external, for example my seeing a real clock change its display from '12.59' to '1.00'. This perception of course needs tenseless beliefs as well to make it work – for example, that the clock is accurate, and that my perceptions of its changes occur virtually as soon as they do. But given that I have those beliefs, the change in the clock will at once cause me to believe that it is now one o'clock and hence to turn on the radio to hear the news.

As this example illustrates, tensed beliefs about *B* series times like one o'clock are really only intermediaries between perceiving some events and acting to affect others. The primary subjects of our tensed beliefs are events, not dates. We only have beliefs about dates because, being fixed attributes of many events, they conveniently sum up what we need to know about them. To know that one o'clock is present is to know that any event is present which has that date. But ultimately, coming to act on what we see and hear is a process of acquiring past or present tense beliefs about what we perceive, inferring present or future tense beliefs about events we wish to effect or affect, and then acting on those.

These inferences, from what we have perceived to what we wish to affect, need mediating of course by tenseless beliefs, e.g. that the radio news starts as the clock strikes one, or that a ball I am trying to catch will reach me a second or so after I see it. But mediation is no use without something to mediate; the timing of our action depends in the first place on the tense of beliefs our senses give us, about clocks striking, things to be caught or avoided, etc.

This, more precisely, is what I meant earlier by action based on perception needing tensed belief. The main function of perception indeed is to give us the tensed beliefs we need to act on at the right time. That needs to be done for all action whose desired outcome needs to occur at a particular time – or at the same time as a particular event – and that means almost all action. My radio example is no isolated case. To catch a train or a bus, as well as a ball, I must be in the right place at the right time; even to talk to someone, I must get him and the soundwaves I emit somewhere simultaneously. There may be actions to whose success timing is completely immaterial, but not many. And for the rest, we need perceptions to give us tensed beliefs, because we need to derive from them beliefs with the right token-reflexive truth conditions to make us act in time.

Conversation is an important special case of an activity that calls for tensed belief, which it does for two main reasons. First, conversation conveys information whose value, we have seen, often depends upon its being tensed. People can say what time it is, for example, as well as clocks can, and they use explicitly tensed forms of words, e.g. 'It is now one o'clock', to do so. These spoken tokens are meant to do what a clock does, namely give their hearer corresponding mental tokens just when they are true, i.e. in time to be acted on successfully. They may not do that in fact, because people can lie or be mistaken just as clocks can go wrong, but that is their function; and knowing that is all it takes to use – or misuse – these tensed expressions. Similarly of course for tensed information about particular events: 'The bus is due in half an hour' tells you how soon and how fast to set off to meet it at the bus stop. Here again the importance of tense lies in the way the sentence only being true at certain times makes for the success of actions caused by coming to believe it at those times.

But even if I know all this, and want to tell the truth, I produce tensed sentences when I believe them to be true, not necessarily when they actually are true. There is no more magic in its now being one o'clock to make me say 'It is now one o'clock' than there was to make me turn the radio on. It is the beliefs tensed sentences express, not the tensed facts that allegedly make them true, which cause us to use them when we do. Now many philosophers take the content of a belief to be whatever we need to know to use and understand sentences expressing it; and although the moral to be drawn from that claim is in general debatable, it seems to me plain enough here. We have seen that using tensed sentences demands nothing more than knowledge of when they are true and when false, i.e. of their tenseless token-reflexive truth conditions; so that, I suggest, is all there is to the tensed beliefs they express. The idea that tensed sentences also express non-token-reflexive beliefs in tensed facts, while not yet positively disproved, is a gratuitous and idle supposition. It adds nothing to the token-reflexive explanation of why and how uses of these sentences, and reactions to them, depend on how action needs to be timely in order to be successful.

The token-reflexive truth conditions of tensed sentences incidentally explain not only how we usually use them, but also how our usage varies when their tokens take time to arrive. So far I have taken it that you hear what I say almost as I say it, so that what you hear will be true if what I say is. When that is so, as it usually is, all I need do, to try and tell the truth, is to say what I believe. But when it takes a substantial or unpredictable time for my message to reach you, this may not work for tensed sentences. I cannot, for instance, expect to tell you the time by writing 'It is now one o'clock' in a letter, since I have no idea at what o'clock you will read it. That being understood, the rule is that if I do write such a thing, you should ignore its truth-value when read, and infer instead that it was true when I wrote it, i.e. that I wrote it at one o'clock. On the other hand, if I do want to tell or celebrate a time or an event in a tensed way at a temporal distance, I am allowed by convention to do so by despatching a message that is false when I send it, so long as I intend it to be true when it arrives. That, for example, is why signing and sending birthday and Christmas greetings in advance, when what they say is still false, is not a case of lying.

These variant uses of tensed sentences are commoner still in the case of spatial tenses, since we more often communicate at significant spatial distances. In reading my letters, no one dismisses my tales of life "here" just because they are not true there. The reader infers instead that 'here' refers to wherever I wrote the letter. And it is of course mainly to facilitate such inferences, both spatial and temporal, that correspondence customarily includes the date and place of its composition. Where that information is wanting, the tensed contents of correspondence become correspondingly unintelligible. 'I wish you were here now' says a postcard, undated, unstamped, unsigned and unaddressed. What, in tensed terms, could be more explicit? Yet the postcard clearly tells us almost nothing: not who, not where, not when. The token–reflexive account tells us why not.

The second reason conversation needs tensed beliefs stems from its being a means of communication. Even if I am telling you something tenseless, I still need tensed beliefs in order to tell you it. The reason lies in a psychological mechanism of communication described by H. P. Grice (1957) as part of a theory of linguistic meaning. Whether or not the whole theory is right, the part that demands tensed beliefs is undeniable, and runs roughly as follows. When I tell you something, I may or may not persuade you that it is so. But I should at least persuade you that I believe it, so that insofar as you accept my authority you will incline for that reason to believe it too. This at any rate is the normal situation, on which the exceptions are parasitic. In lying, for instance, I try to exploit the normal assumption, that people believe what they say, to mislead you about my beliefs and thereby about the facts. Either way therefore I mean you to form a belief about my beliefs, correct if I am speaking sincerely, incorrect if I am lying. And either way, the beliefs I intend to make you believe something about are the beliefs I have as I am speaking. But I cannot intend something without knowing what it is, which in this case means having a belief (as I speak) about what my own beliefs (as I speak) are, so that I know what I am trying to get you to believe I believe. Which means having a belief about what other beliefs I have at the same time, i.e. a belief with the token–reflexive truth conditions of the present tense. So even if the belief I am trying to communicate is wholly tenseless, I still need a present tense belief about what it is in order to communicate it.

In short, tensed beliefs are indispensable, not only for timely action in general and timely conversation in particular, but also for the conscious communication, sincere or insincere, of anything at all, tensed or tenseless. And the reason in both cases is that no agent, and above all no user of language, can do without token–reflexive beliefs. So far from the tenseless view of time, with its token–reflexive analysis of tensed belief, implying that tensed beliefs are dispensable, it alone explains exactly why they are not.

6   *The unreality of tense*

The last two chapters have discredited three discreditable inferences drawn from the tenseless view of time. I set out now to discredit its rival, which I do by discrediting the tensed idea of change. Change is clearly of time's essence, and many have thought it the downfall of tenseless time – that only a tensed view of time can account for it. In fact the opposite is true. The *A* series is disproved by a contradiction inherent in the idea that tenses change.

Change, obviously (if vaguely), is having a property at one time and not at another. More specifically, it is something having incompatible properties at different dates, such as being at different temperatures or in different places. Cooling is a change of temperature, being first hot and then cold; movement is a change of place, being first somewhere and then somewhere else. Similarly, there are changing sizes, shapes, colours and other properties of things. In each case something has one of several mutually incompatible properties at one *B* series time, and another one later.

This tenseless idea of change is basically right as well as being obvious. But there are objections to it, of which two especially have long preserved a tensed alternative. The first is that it does not really distinguish change through time from change across space. Properties can after all vary from place to place as well as from time to time. A poker, for example, may be at once hot at one end and cold at the other: why is that not change, as much as the whole poker being hot one day and cold the next? We could of course define change to be variation in time as opposed to variation in space – but only given some other way of distinguishing time from space. If time is marked off only as the dimension of change, we should be arguing in an indecently small circle. But it is not obvious how else to distinguish it from spatial dimensions.

Consider again a clock's second hand passing successively the figures '1' and '2'. The latter event is both later than the former and to the right of it. We see this as change (namely movement), which is how we distinguish the temporal and spatial relations of the two events. Specifically, it is how we tell a thin hand moving across the clock face from a fat one spread statically across it in two spatial dimensions. In short, we perceive the temporal relation in this case by perceiving change. Similarly for changes of place, temperature, colour and everything else. To see that one event is later than another is to see something change. How else could time be perceived or understood, except as the dimension of change? But change cannot then be defined as variation in time. And the objection to tenseless time is that it has no other way of defining change; and so in particular no way of distinguishing change from spatial variation.

This objection is reinforced by the other one, namely that the tenseless view reduces change to changeless facts. If a poker is hot one day and cold the next, then those always were and always will be its temperatures on those two days. *B* series facts of this kind do not change with time: that, we saw in chapter 1, is the mark of the *B* as opposed to the *A* series. And as for time, so for space. There is no spatial change in a poker being at once hot at one end and cold at the other. The hot and cold ends of a poker are not a case of change, because they coexist: the spatially tenseless world contains them both, only located in different parts of tenseless space. Likewise, the hot poker and the cold coexist in a temporally tenseless world. It contains them both, only located in different parts of *B* series time. And if, as everyone agrees, coexistence prevents change in the spatial case, how can it be compatible with change in time?

The *A* series provides a ready answer to all these questions. Change is the changing tense of things and events moving from future to past. It is peculiar to time because the *A* series has no real spatial analogue. The token-reflexive facts of spatial tense given in chapter 4 are all there is to it; but on the tensed view they are not all there is to temporal tense. In the temporal case, over and above those tenseless facts, there is a present moment which is forever changing its date. The reality of the clock hand's movement consists ultimately in the events of its passing the figures '1' and '2' becoming successively present and then past; and similarly for all other changes.

On the tensed view, change is first of all the successive presence of earlier and later things and events. This defines the temporal relations *earlier* and *later*: one event is tenselessly earlier than another if and only if its ever-changing tenses bring it to the present first. Since there are no real spatial tenses, this definition has no spatial analogue. The tenseless spatial relations of events and things are *sui generis*, and that is the difference between space and time. In time, but not in space, the tenseless *B* series is supposed to be derived from the *A* series, and thence the idea of tenseless change I started with. Change is still defined as variation through time; but by defining time first as the dimension of changing tense, the tensed view prevents this definition of change begging the question against its spatial analogues.

This tensed view of change may be supported by further doctrines about what else turns on the difference between present and future. We have already noticed the view that existence turns on it, i.e. that coming to be present is coming to exist. This provides a still more profound basis for distinguishing time from space, as the dimension in which things come successively into existence. However, it makes no odds what else turns on tense unless the idea of changing tenses actually does account for change; and, appearances to the contrary notwithstanding, the fact is that it doesn't.

To start with, one might accuse the tensed view itself of begging the question against spatial change, in denying the reality of spatial tenses. They after all vary across space just as temporal tenses vary through time. If change is different events becoming temporally present from time to time, why is it not different things becoming spatially present – here – from place to place? To such accusations upholders of tense reply that we have a direct intuition of temporal presence which is lacking in the spatial case. We see things laid out tenselessly in space, whereas we do not see things laid out tenselessly in time. But we have in fact, in chapters 1 and 3, already disposed of this supposed intuition of temporal tense. We have seen how observing tenseless temporal relations is independent of observing tenses, and how the apparent temporal presence of our experiences can be tenselessly accounted for.

Although the tensed view of change could easily be convicted of distinguishing time from space no better than the tenseless view, I will not press the charge. To prefer debatable and relatively trifling charges is pointless when a capital offence can be proved against the same party. The capital offence is self-contradiction, of which tensed views of both time and space are guilty. But as the tensed view of space has been put away already, I only need to prosecute the temporal case.

The proof of contradiction in the tensed account of change is not new. It was given by J. E. McTaggart in 1908 and has been much debated since. To me it seems beyond all reasonable doubt, but since it is still disputed, I fear I must prosecute it yet again. Two factors however encourage me to hope for more success than McTaggart had. One is that he prosecuted time itself. He thought that time needs change and change needs changing tense, and so thought to convict time along with tense. However, the obvious unimpeachability of time defeated him, and unfortunately drew suspicion on his whole case. Tense in fact has been wrongly acquitted to save the innocent time. But we need not acquit the guilty in this case in order to save the innocent. What is wrong with McTaggart's prosecution of time is not his prosecution of tense but his contention that disposing of tense disposes of change. We shall see in chapter 7 that change can be explained and distinguished from spatial variation without any appeal to tense. And given that, the reality of changing tense can safely be denied without imperilling the reality of change and hence of time itself. Once that is realised, McTaggart's proof will, I hope, meet much less resistance.

The other factor encouraging me is the token-reflexive treatment of tense outlined in chapters 2 to 5. Although this factor is not new, it was not there in McTaggart's time, and it should make his proof more persuasive. On the one hand it should make its validity more obvious and, on the other, its conclusions more palatable. Tense, it will turn out, is not being banished altogether, merely replaced where it belongs – in our heads.

McTaggart's proof

McTaggart's proof (1908; 1927, ch. 33) is very simple. Many *A* series positions are incompatible with each other. An event which is *yesterday*, for example, cannot also be *tomorrow*. Past, present and future tenses, as was remarked in chapter 1, are mutually incompatible properties of things and events. But because they are forever changing, everything has to have them all. Everything occupies every *A* series position, from the remotest future, through the present, to the remotest past. But nothing can really have incompatible properties, so nothing in reality has tenses. The *A* series is a myth.

The defence has an immediate and obvious riposte to this attack, and its rebuttal is unfortunately much less obvious; which is why McTaggart's proof has rarely carried the conviction it deserves. The riposte is that nothing has incompatible tenses at the same time. Nothing is present *when* it is past, or future when it is present. Things and events only have these properties successively: first they are future, then present, then past. And nothing prevents things having incompatible properties at different times. On the contrary, that is how change is defined: the successive possession of incompatible properties. All McTaggart has shown is that changing tense fits that definition, as it should.

To rebut this riposte, McTaggart asks when, in tensed terms, things and events have their various tenses; and here it will help to use some symbols. Let P, N and F be respectively the properties of being past, present (i.e. now) and future, and let *e* be any event. Then *e* being past, present and future I write respectively as 'P*e*', 'N*e*' and 'F*e*'. Complex tenses I represent by repeated ascription of P, N and F: thus 'PF*e*' means *e was* future, 'FPN*e*' means *e will have been* present, and so on. '~', '&' and '⊦' as usual mean respectively 'not', 'and' and 'entails'.

Then McTaggart's basic argument is that, on the one hand, the three properties P, N and F are mutually incompatible, so that for any event *e*

$$P e \vdash \sim\! Ne; \quad Ne \vdash \sim\! Fe; \quad Fe \vdash \sim\! Pe; \quad \text{etc.} \tag{1}$$

On the other hand, the inexorable change of tense means that every event has all three *A* series positions, i.e.

$$Pe \ \& \ Ne \ \& \ Fe. \tag{2}$$

But (1) and (2) cannot both be true; since if (1) is true, two of the statements in (2) must be false, so (2) as a whole must be false. But our concept of tense commits us to both (1) and (2); so it leads us inevitably into contradiction and thus cannot apply to reality. Reality therefore must be tenseless: there are no tensed facts.

To this the riposte is that *e* has no more than one of these incompatible properties at once, so there is no contradiction after all. Suppose for example that *e* is actually present, i.e. N*e*. Then *e* is neither past nor future, i.e. both 'P*e*' and 'F*e*' are false, as (1) requires. The truth rather is that *e will be* past and *was* future, i.e. not (2) but

$$FPe \ \& \ Ne \ \& \ PFe, \tag{3}$$

which is quite compatible with (1).

So it is. But, as McTaggart remarks, there are more complex tenses than those in (3), and not all combinations of them are so innocuous. Specifically, there are also PP and PN, FF and FN, and NP, NN and NF. And just as every event has all *A* series positions if it has any of them, so it also has all these other complex tenses. For example, whatever has any simple tense obviously also has it *now*, i.e.

$$Pe \vdash NPe; \ Ne \vdash NNe; \ Fe \vdash NFe.$$

Obviously also, whatever is past *was* present and *was* future, and whatever is future *will be* present and *will be* past, so that

$$Pe \vdash PNe; \ Pe \vdash PFe; \ Fe \vdash FNe; \ Fe \vdash FPe.$$

Moreover, whatever is sufficiently past also *was* past, e.g. what happened two days ago was already past yesterday; and sufficiently future events likewise also *will be* future: which gives us PP and FF as well as P and F.

In place then of the original three simple tenses, we have the nine compound tenses PP, PN, PF; NP, NN, NF; FP, FN, FF. But McTaggart's argument applies just as well to them. Because of the way tense incessantly changes, every event that has any of these nine tenses has to have them all; but they are not all mutually compatible. For example, FF and PP are incompatible, since what will be future cannot also have been past. And NP, NN and NF are even more clearly incompatible, because they are equivalent to the simple P, N and F.

The riposte will again be made, that events do not have these incompatible tenses all at once. But again, saying in tensed terms just when they do have them only generates another set of properties, including mutually incompatible ones like PPP, NNN and FFF, all of which every event has to have. There is, in other words, an endless regress of ripostes and rebuttals, a regress that is vicious because at no stage in it can all the supposed tensed facts be consistently stated.

The defence of McTaggart

That, basically, is how McTaggart put his case. His critics have reacted by denying the viciousness of his regress. At every stage, they say, the appearance of contradiction is removed by distinguishing the different times at which events have different tenses. They ignore the fact that the tensed means they use to distinguish these times are also subject to the contradiction they are trying to remove. However, the debate by now is too well worn to be settled by mere repetition of McTaggart's proof, sound though it is. To change the metaphor, too many people have managed to inoculate themselves against it. If it is to wipe out belief in real tenses, as it should, a more immediately virulent strain of it is needed, a strain that I believe is best nurtured on the token-reflexive facts that make tensed sentences true or false.

Before developing the new strain, however, it is worth neutralising some antidotes that have been proposed to McTaggart's original proof. First, I should perhaps remark that although I have dealt only with the unqualified past, present and future, the proof applies also to more precise *A* series positions. *Yesterday* and *three days ago*, for example, are likewise incompatible properties of things and events of less than a day's duration, both of which they must all nevertheless possess. But there is no point in complicating the discussion by bringing all these other tenses into it explicitly. If the argument works for P, N and F, it will work for all tenses; and if not, for none.

Secondly, I have followed McTaggart in ascribing these problematic *A* series properties to events. Tense logicians mostly prefer to treat 'P', 'N' and 'F' as "operators" (analogous to 'It is not the case that' or 'It may be the case that') prefixed to present tense core sentences or propositions. This is tantamount to regarding P, N and F as properties, not of events, but of tensed facts. Where, for example, McTaggart and I start with a thunderstorm, tense logic starts with the sentence or proposition saying that a thunderstorm is happening now. Where we say the thunderstorm is two days past, they say the fact of its happening now is two days past, i.e. the present tense sentence or proposition saying that it is happening now was true two days ago. In the symbolism above, this amounts to replacing '*e*' throughout by 'N*e*'. But it makes no odds to the argument, as readers may verify for themselves: facts are no better at being at once both and not both past and present, present and future, etc. than events are.

Nor does it help to distinguish the "object language", in which events are said to be past, present or future, from a "meta-language" in which object language sentences are said to be true or false. At least, it helps only if the meta-language sentences are the tenseless ones used to give the token-reflexive truth conditions laid out in chapter 2. When the meta-language sentences are themselves tensed, the problem simply reappears in a new guise. Truth and falsity are now the incompatible properties of the object language sentence types (since tensed truth conditions are supposed not to be token-reflexive: if they were, as we shall see later, they would not be tensed). But to say that a particular sentence type is true – i.e. that any token of it would be true – is to say that it is not false, and *vice versa*. Yet any true contingent tensed sentence type must also be (sometime) false – otherwise it would not be tensed. This now is McTaggart's basic contradiction, and the riposte to it is the same: no tensed sentence type is both true and false at the same time. Meta-language sentences then say when these object language sentences are true and when false. But if the meta-language sentences are themselves tensed, they too will be both true and false. The contradiction simply recurs in the meta-language. Removing it from there by using a tensed meta-meta-language to say when meta-language sentences are true and when false only leads to McTaggart's regress. Iterating tensed meta-languages no more refutes McTaggart than iterating tensed properties of events or facts does, or than iterating tensed operators on propositions or sentences within a single language.

The plain fact is that nothing can have mutually incompatible properties, whether they be tenses or truth-values: neither events, things, facts, propositions, sentences, nor anything else. I prefer therefore to stick to events and things, as being the natural inhabitants of *A* series positions. I will eschew translations of the problem into other and more fashionable idioms, since it only panders to the erroneous conviction that McTaggart is thus easily answered.

Thirdly, however, I must deal with the complaint that in symbolising McTaggart's argument I have myself begged the question against tenses. Specifically, in using 'P*e*' to say that *e* is past, I have left out the verb 'is'. By so doing I have tacitly treated the 'is' in '*e* is past' as a tenseless copula, which is why *e*'s being past, present and future appear to be contradictory. For in fact the verb 'is' in '*e* is past' is tensed, i.e. it really means that *e* is *now* past. And given that, the contradiction vanishes, since if *e* is now past, it is not also now present or now future. Of course, it *was* future and it *was* present, but that is quite compatible with *e* being now past. In short, the supposed contradiction has been artificially generated by suppressing the essentially tensed verbs used in ascribing to *e* the properties P, N and F.

This complaint misses the point of tense completely. The *A* series is supposed to be a feature of the world, not of verbs. We saw in chapter 1 that adverbs and phrases like 'yesterday', 'this week' and 'next year' make verbal tenses redundant, and so do 'in the past', 'now' and 'in the future', i.e. 'P', 'N' and 'F'. That is their function: to take over the roles respectively of the past, present and future verbal tenses to which by definition they are equivalent. Given these expressions, verbs might as well be tenseless, i.e. take the same form regardless of the *A* series position of the events they refer to. Suppose for example that 'happens' is made such a tenseless form. Then 'It happened' means 'It happens in the past'. If the past tense form of the verb in 'It happened in the past' were not redundant, it would have to mean PP rather than P, which it clearly doesn't. It simply means 'It happened'. Just as 'in the past' is superfluous given the past verbal tense, so the verbal tense is superfluous given 'in the past'.

As for the past, so for the present. Adding 'now' to 'It happens' or 'It is happening' makes the present tense connotations of the verb superfluous. Given the 'now', 'happens' is as tenseless in 'It happens now' as in 'It happens in the past' and 'It happens in the future'. And as for 'happens', so for 'is'. The temporal meanings of '*e* is past', '*e* is present' and '*e* is future' are supplied entirely by the words 'past', 'present' and 'future'. The 'is' *is* a mere tenseless copula, present only because English grammar gives sentences verbs even when, as here, they contribute nothing to the content. Nothing therefore is left out by abbreviating these sentences to 'P*e*', 'N*e*' and 'F*e*'. So the abbreviation can generate no contradiction that was not already there.

Anyone who still says the 'is' in '*e* is past' is present tense, so that '*e* is past' means '*e* is now past', will have to say what tense 'is' then has in '*e* is now past'. It is clearly either tenseless or present tense – and if tenseless, McTaggart's contradiction reappears at once, because '*e* is now past' is not always true. It is true only when '*e* is past' is true (which is why the two sentences mean the same). So all we have to do to regenerate McTaggart's proof, as readers may again easily verify, is replace 'P', 'N' and 'F' throughout by 'NP', 'NN' and 'NF'.

But if the 'is' in '*e* is now past' is tensed, as in '*e* is past', the same vicious regress appears in the form of the verb itself. For '*e* is past', meaning '*e* is now past', must now also mean '*e* is now now past', in which again the 'is' must either be tenseless or present tense. If tenseless, we again get McTaggart's argument, starting this time with 'NNP', 'NNN' and 'NNF'; and if present tense, the regress continues with '*e* is now now now past', '*e* is now now now now past', and so on *ad infinitum*. And for no sentence type in this endless sequence can we consistently give tensed truth conditions. It is no use saying, at any stage in the sequence, that the last sentence type in it is true *now*, because whether that is so depends on when *now* is. Saying that merely generates the next type in the sequence, concerning which the same question arises. To stop and give a definite answer at any stage only produces a contradiction, because if the sentence is true (at some present time) it is also false (at some other). The only way to avoid contradiction is never to stop at all, which is tantamount to admitting that the original sentence type has *no* tensed truth conditions, i.e. cannot be made true or false by any tensed fact such as that *e* is past, *e* is now past, *e* is now now past, etc. In short, supposing that there are such facts is either self-contradictory or useless for saying what makes tensed sentences true or false.

McTaggart and token-reflexives

So much by way of reinforcing McTaggart's own proof. But in case it still does not convince, I will now put it explicitly in terms of token-reflexive truth conditions. First, recall that tensed facts are supposed to provide *non*-token-reflexive truth conditions for tensed sentences and judgments. Just as all tokens of 'Snow is white', whenever and wherever they occur, are made true by the single fact that snow is white, so all true tokens of '*e* is past', whenever they occur, are supposed to be made true by the single fact that *e* is past or, if for some reason that won't work, by the fact that *e* is now past, or that *e* is now now past, etc. All tokens of the same tensed sentence type are supposed to have the same tensed truth conditions, however much their tenseless truth conditions may vary from token to token.

Now chapter 5 showed that tensed sentences have no tenseless translations, because tokens of the translation would all have the same tenseless truth conditions, whereas those of tensed sentence tokens vary from time to time. That is, no one tenseless fact can make true all true tokens of a given tensed type regardless of when they occur. However, *e* being past, or being now past, etc., should be able to do this because, unlike tenseless facts, they are not facts at all dates. They should be able to make tokens of '*e* is past' true just when it is a fact that *e* is past, is now past, or whatever.

Now we know when it is a fact (if it is) that *e* is past, is now past, etc.: namely at all and only dates later than *e* itself. Tokens of '*e* is past', '*e* is now past', etc. are all alike true if and only if they occur later than *e*. In tenseless terms, all these sentences are merely different ways of saying '*e* is past'. But in tensed terms, all this means is that true tokens of '*e* is past' could be made true, consistently with their agreed tenseless truth conditions, by any one of these facts, that *e* is past, *e* is now past, etc. And in tensed terms these are, arguably at least, different facts. For although *e* is admittedly not just, i.e. not always, past, it is supposed to be *now* past; and if not always now past, at least now now past; and so on. Adding 'now' to any of these claims is supposed to help to make it – now – true. So the additions presumably somehow affect the claims' tensed truth conditions, which is to say that *e*'s being past, being now past, etc. are somehow different facts.

Yet in *B* series terms none of them will do the job. None gives '*e* is past' non-token-reflexive truth conditions, because even when they *are* facts, its tokens' truth-values still depend on their own dates. Thus at any date *t* later than *e*, the facts are that *e* is past, now past, now now past, etc. But none of these facts makes tokens of '*e* is past' which occurred before *e* true at *t*. They are false then, just as they always were and always will be. The whole point of the type/token distinction, it will be recalled from chapter 2, is that tensed tokens, as opposed to types, have definite and temporally unqualified truth values. True, long-lasting thing tokens can vary in truth-value during their lifetimes – e.g. a token of '*e* is past' printed before *e* will start off false and end up true. But that does not change its truth-value at the earlier dates, any more than my slimming in 1984 will require me to rewrite, Newspeak-fashion, the record of what I weighed in 1983. A saying or writing of '*e* is past' which occurs before *e* always was and always will be just plain false.

But can the tensed facts we are considering give '*e* is past' non-token-reflexive truth conditions when times are specified in *A* series terms? Unfortunately for them, no. Even when it is *now* a fact that *e* is past, *e* is now past, etc., tokens of '*e* is past' are not all true now regardless of their *A* series position. Tokens that are now more past than *e* itself will be false now, as they always were and always will be. Even in *A* series terms the truth conditions of '*e* is past' are token-reflexive: they depend on the *A* series position of the token itself.

And as for '*e* is past', so for all tensed sentences. We saw in chapter 2 that all tensed sentences have tenseless token-reflexive truth conditions. That is, some tokens of the same tensed type will differ in truth-value depending on their date. But we also saw in chapter 1 that whatever has a date has at every moment a corresponding tense. In particular, tensed tokens with diverse dates will always have correspondingly diverse *A* series positions, with which their diverse truth-values will therefore also vary. So if the tenseless truth conditions of tensed sentences are token-reflexive, so are their tensed truth conditions.

So giving any tensed sentence non-token-reflexive truth conditions, tensed or tenseless, always leads to contradiction. That, for tenseless truth conditions, is how I proved that tensed sentences have no tenseless translations; the translation would give all tokens of the type the same truth-value regardless of their date, thus inevitably contradicting the truth-value of some tokens of the tensed sentence, which differ from date to date. And the same goes for tensed truth conditions. Since the truth-value of tensed tokens is never independent of their *A* series position, giving them now all the same truth-value will inevitably make some past or future tokens both true and false.

This, in token-reflexive terms, is McTaggart's contradiction. That it is so is most easily seen in the meta-language version of his argument (p. 96). Because the tensed truth conditions of '*e* is past' are token-reflexive, any attempt to state in a tensed meta-language the one tensed fact that makes all its true tokens true is bound to fail. The alleged fact would by definition have to make all tokens of the type true, regardless of their *A* series position, whereas in fact some are always true and others always false. Hence the contradiction. And it is, I hope, easier to see in this version of the argument that complex tenses are no better off, i.e. that the regress of meta-languages McTaggart's critics invoke is indeed vicious. For the above argument applies to tenses of any complexity. Provided, as was shown in chapter 2, they have tenseless token-reflexive truth conditions, their tensed truth conditions will also be token-reflexive. And whatever doubts there may be about the token-reflexivity of some complex tenses, there can be none about those McTaggart's critics resort to. Unless '*e* is now past', '*e* is now now past', etc., had the same token-reflexive truth conditions as '*e* is past', they could not be substituted for it. And if they do have those truth conditions, McTaggart's argument disposes of the tensed facts they allegedly state, just as it disposes of the alleged fact that *e* is past.

Finally, I suppose defenders of tense might ask why tensed truth conditions cannot be token-reflexive, if tenseless ones are. The answer is that they then cease to be tensed. Suppose for example it is now N years after e: e is now past, but that fact alone does not suffice to make all tokens of '*e* is past' now true. However, consider a token that is only M years past, where M is less than N. The token is true, because it is less past than e itself. Those are the ostensibly tensed truth conditions of any token of the type: it is true if and only if when it is present e is past, i.e. N-M is positive. But if N-M is ever positive, it is always positive, because the temporal distance be-tween A series positions never changes. The values of N and M continually increase, therefore, but always at the same rate, so the value of their difference does not. The fact is simply that the token is – tenselessly – N-M years later than e. The variably tensed elements N and M in the supposedly tensed token-reflexive truth conditions cancel out, leaving the already familiar tenseless truth conditions: true if later than e, false otherwise.

Similarly for all other tensed sentence types. Their tensed truth conditions are either self-contradictory or token-reflexive; and if token-reflexive, they reduce to tenseless truth conditions. As McTaggart saw, the truth conditions of tensed sentences are either tenseless or self-contradictory.

My version of McTaggart's proof started from the fact, shown in chapter 2, that all tensed sentences and judgments have tenseless token-reflexive truth conditions. In that chapter it was left open whether tensed sentences also state tensed facts, but we see now that this is not a real option after all. And while those immunised against McTaggart may need something like the above argument to convert them, there is a simpler argument which should serve to sway more open minds.

The sole function of tensed facts is to make tensed sentences and judgments true or false. But that job is already done by the tenseless facts that fix the truth-values of all tensed sentence and judgment tokens. Provided a token of '*e* is past' is later than *e*, it is true. Nothing else about *e* and it matters a jot: in particular no tensed fact about them matters. It is immaterial, for a start, where *e* and the token are in the *A* series; and if that is not material, no more *recherché* tensed fact can be. Similarly for tokens of all other tensed types. Their tenseless truth conditions leave tensed facts no scope for determining their truth-values. But these facts by definition determine their truth-values. So in reality there are no such facts.

7   *Change*

We saw in chapter 6 that tenses cannot change, as they must to be tenses, and therefore cannot exist. Nothing real therefore can depend on differences between them. What exists cannot be restricted to what is present, or present or past, because the restriction has no basis in reality. The world can neither grow by the accretion of things, events or facts as they become present, nor can increasing pastness remove them. Put another way, token sentences, whether tensed or tenseless, can neither first acquire nor then lose truth-value by their subject matter becoming first present to our senses (and so verifiable) and then becoming veiled from us by the mists of antiquity. Nor can facts become fixed or necessary by becoming present, in contrast to as yet unfixed, contingent or merely possible facts about future things and events. Differences of necessity and possibility can no more depend on non-existent differences of tense than existence and truth-value can.

McTaggart's proof thus disposes of much more than tense. Distinctions of existence, truth and modality which have been drawn between past, present and future all have to go, and high time too. But other things can and must be saved from the wreck of the *A* series. We must for example say in tenseless terms why we can only perceive the past and affect the future. But first we must revive the tenseless account of change, and overcome the objections to it cited at the start of chapter 6.

Change, I said there, is a thing having incompatible properties at different dates, and the objection to this was twofold. First, it lacks means of distinguishing change from spatial variation; second, it reduces change to changeless facts. The reply, briefly, is that the first objection is false, and the second not an objection. For a change to be a fact, the fact need not change as well. If the facts, for example, are that a poker is hot one day and cold the next, why is that not change, just because those always were and always will be the facts? Why should things be unable to change unless facts do?

The first objection is false because change need not in fact be appealed to to distinguish tenseless time from space. We saw in chapter 4 what will do the job: causation is the rule that even in relativity distinguishes succession in time from spatial separation. We still have to say why it is the rule, and whether it admits exceptions, i.e. whether some causes can be later than their effects. That is matter for chapters 9 and 10, where time's dependence on causation will be explained and backward causation shown to be impossible. Here a promissory note will have to do: causation does distinguish time from space, and we can appeal to it to distinguish change from its spatial counterparts.

But these are not the only obstacles to defining change as things having incompatible properties at different times. The definition will not do unless limits are set both to properties and to things, and that too must be done without question-begging appeal to change. Doing this is the business of the next two sections.

Things and events

I said in chapter 1 that things are not events. The difference is that things have no temporal parts, even when their dates span extended intervals of *B* series time. In other words, things are wholly present throughout their lifetimes, and events are not. (Here of course things include both animals and people, who are also wholly present throughout their lives, as well as social entities like nations, churches, firms and trade unions.) This is why things can change and events cannot, which is the immediate point of the distinction. Apparent changes in events are no more than differences between their temporal parts, analogous exactly to differences between spatial parts of things. Whereas things, lacking temporal parts, undergo change in their entirety.

This distinction between things and events is crucial to my account of change. Being contentious, it will have to be defended therefore, principally in the next chapter, against those who, zealous for conceptual economy, would reduce things to events or *vice versa*. Some such distinction of course is clearly drawn both in everyday life and in the sciences, both natural and social. But I still have to defend what I claim the basis of it is; since being wholly present at an instant may not be an immediately evident mark of what I am calling things. Now part of my defence will be the plausibility of my account of change. That in itself, especially failing credible alternatives, will give content to the idea of things lacking temporal parts, and some reason to believe it. But to meet accusations of *adhoc*ery, the idea really needs to be defensible on other ground as well, which I shall therefore now briefly show it to be.

First, the idea fits the distinction as drawn in ordinary and scientific usage. Philosophers who have persuaded themselves that things are really just events admittedly write professionally as if people, animals and such other things as electrons, tables and committees had temporal parts. But no one else would say that only temporal parts of Hilary and Tenzing climbed only a temporal part of Everest in 1953. The rest of us think the two whole men climbed the one whole mountain, and that all three parties were wholly present throughout every temporal part of that historic event. Likewise, when Churchill published an account of his early life, that is what he called it: *My Early Life*. He did not call it 'Early Me', and the silliness of such a title is no mere triviality. Similarly with other things in the natural and social sciences. No one thinks a committee has temporal parts, even though its meetings do, nor that a hailstone has just because its falling is a temporal as well as a spatial part of a hailstorm. Nor do physicists suppose only temporal parts of an electron and a positron are annihilated when the two collide: the whole particles are what collide and thereupon disappear.

Contrariwise, everyone talks of the temporal parts of events. The rapidly successive stages of explosions, for example, are distinguished and described in theories of the subject, just as geologists detect epochs in the evolution of the earth. On an intermediate domestic scale, meals have temporal parts (the eating of each course, for example) even though dishes demolished during them do not. And in larger social and historical contexts, the temporal parts of World War II adverted to in chapter 1 are no isolated case. Historians are always picking out significant stages in the unfolding of historical events; though never, be it noted, in peoples or countries. The French Revolution has temporal parts, but France herself and the French people do not.

I need not multiply examples: the distinction, thus drawn, is so ubiquitous and familiar that it really only needs pointing out. But to remove any lingering suspicion that nothing but my account of change turns on it, I will now show briefly how it accounts also for something quite different, namely the limited application of ideas of moral and legal responsibility.

I have already mentioned some social things, or "groups" as they may conveniently be called, and the reader will readily think of others. Nations, churches, firms, unions, committees, political parties, shops, orchestras, families – the list may be extended *ad lib*. To all such groups the concept of moral or legal responsibility applies, much as it does to people. That is, they are all agents, and for their acts they may later be called legally or morally to account. But now consider the following psychological and social events: speeches, illnesses, engagements, company mergers, elections, parliamentary sessions, riots, concerts – again the list may be extended *ad lib*. Yet however long the list, nothing in it can be legally or morally responsible for anything, even though everything in it is causally responsible for multitudes of other events. But why not? The only reason I can see is that events such as engagements and mergers have temporal parts, and people and companies do not.

Recall that the first prerequisite for moral and legal responsibility is identity through time. Nothing and no one can be held responsible for an earlier action unless he, she or it is identical with whoever or whatever did that earlier action. That is the point of an alibi, to show the defendant to be not the same individual or collective entity as the earlier doer of the deed complained of. Now whatever identity through time may call for elsewhere, here it evidently requires the self-same entity to be wholly present both when the deed was done and later when being held accountable for it – a condition satisfiable by things, but not by events. Because they have temporal parts, extended events like long engagements or protracted mergers are never wholly present. In particular, whatever temporal parts of them caused the deed in question will never be the same as the parts which might be later brought to court for it. In short, social and psychological events can never be held morally or legally responsible for anything because they always have temporal alibis.

There is of course much more to be said about moral and legal responsibility; but nothing I can think of, besides my idea of what things are, explains why the concept does not apply also to events like those I have listed. So quite apart from its use in accounting for change, the idea supplies a strong concept of identity through time, which things have and events lack, that is needed to make sense of a concept central both to law and to morality. That I think suffices to acquit it of being tailored merely to the tenseless account of change that follows.

Changes and properties of things

So much *prima facie* for the distinction between things and events. Of course it (and the concepts of responsibility and change which depend on it) might still not apply to reality. But at least the burden of proof is on sceptics either to admit it or actually to reduce things to events or events to things, explaining change and responsibility away as they go. In chapter 8 I shall deal with several such reductive arguments; meanwhile I feel free to get on with showing how to use the distinction to account for change.

Having limited the range of things to exclude events, it remains to limit the range of their properties. Not every alteration in *prima facie* properties of things can count as change. Take the property of being an only child. I cease to be an only child when my parents have another offspring, but that event is not itself a change in me. Any relational property of things can similarly cease or come to apply to one thing because of a change in something else, without the thing itself changing. Change in one thing does not automatically change everything related to it. When I leave my house, for example, every thing in it increases its distance from me, but that is not a real change in those things. Likewise with fame, the example of chapter 5. I can come or cease to be famous unawares; that is a change in the attitudes of other people, but not a change in me.

What is wrong with all these cases is that the apparent change involved has no immediate contiguous effects. Naturally there are effects: my sibling's birth has effects, as do my walking from my house and other people's changing attitudes toward the more or less famous. But the immediate effects of these events are nowhere near the things in which they are alleged to be changes, and this is why we deny them that location. The far off birth of an offspring to my parents is not a change in me, because it produces no immediate effects on me or in my vicinity. The immediate effects of changes in my fame which I know nothing of are on the people in whose changing views of me my fame consists, so that is where these changes also must reside. And I cannot immediately affect the contents of my home merely by walking away from it, which is why their changing distances from me are no real changes in them.

Real changes in short must have effects, and their immediate effects must be next to them in space and time. Why this is we can postpone saying until chapter 8 explains the relation between change and events; for the time being, I simply take this causal test of change for granted, and use it to fend off some well known counter-examples to the tenseless account of change.

This test of change also provides a test for real properties of things, namely properties whose alteration is a real, i.e. a contiguously effective, change. Being famous, therefore, and being an only child are not in this sense the properties respectively of famous and siblingless people. Ascriptions of fame and siblings are of course objectively true or false, but what makes them so is not the person concerned having or lacking some property. What makes people famous is the attitude of other people; what makes someone an only child is that his parents have no other children. Or to put it another way, you cannot tell whether someone is famous or an only child by inspecting him, not because these properties are hard to observe, but because you are looking for them in the wrong place – as properties, they do not inhere in him at all.

Among other bogus properties this causal test excludes are the factitious properties made infamous in philosophy by Goodman (1965, ch. 3), "grue" and "bleen" and their numerous ill-gotten progeny. Roughly, being grue is, up to some specified time t, being green, and thereafter it is being blue; while 'bleen' is defined the other way round. What makes these properties phoney is that, at t, a thing changing from grue to bleen (or *vice versa*) is no real change – because there are none of the effects of a change of colour. Whereas staying grue or bleen at t does have the effects of a colour change, namely those of a change from green to blue or *vice versa*, and so really is a change of colour after all.

More does need saying about 'grue' and 'bleen' and others of their ilk, but it has more to do with the notorious problem of induction than with anything that matters here. For example, to see before t that anything is green is also by definition to see that it is grue; so the question arises why, if the observation could be put either way, it supports the prediction that things will stay green rather than grue. This is no place to add to all the literature on that question, except for one remark. Because it would have the effects of a colour change, staying grue at *t* would *be* a colour change, and it is not in general rational to predict change without specific cause. (Why not is a question we shall return to in chapter 8.)

Another apparent property our test disposes of is that of being a certain age. The age of a thing is the past tense of its first *B* series moment, and as that tense keeps changing, so does the thing's age. Every thing therefore ages inexorably throughout its lifetime: from birth to death we all get one year older every twelve months. Now we saw in chapter 6 that this cannot be because past events really change their tenses. But nor is it because things have a real and ever-changing property, namely their age. Age is not a real property, because its incessant changes are not real. They have no effects, mediate or immediate, contiguous or otherwise: nothing ever was or ever will be caused merely by the passage of time.

Real ageing is something quite different. When we say a man has grown old before his time, we mean for example that sixty years after his birth, he is in a state of physiological decay which most healthy, happy and uninjured people take eighty years to reach. The changes that take us from our prime into such states as these are quite real. They have real tenseless causes, and they have real and often disagreeable effects on whoever they are changes in. We may, as with the advancing years themselves, be unable to prevent or reverse them, but at least that is a serious and contingent fact of physiology, not a trivial necessary truth about time.

Real ageing is thus, paradoxically enough, not an effect of a process of getting older, because there is in reality no such process. Getting older is not what takes the Queen from being fifty-eight in 1984 to being fifty-nine a year later. What does that, as I remarked in chapter 1, is simply that she was born in 1926, i.e. fifty-eight years earlier than 1984 and fifty-nine years earlier than 1985. Facts about chronological ageing are just tenseless facts about temporal distances between the first and later *B* series moments of things, not about changeable properties of the things themselves.

This causal test makes identifying properties of things a matter of saying what apparent changes have real and contiguous effects. And so far as I can see, that is how disputes about the identity of properties are settled. Take the classic case of inertial mass. A thing's mass is any force applied to it divided by the resultant acceleration. Now the result of this division does not have to be the same for all forces: doubling the force on a thing might, although it doesn't, triple or quadruple its acceleration instead of doubling it. So we might distinguish two or more inertial masses: e.g. m_1 displayed in accelerations under forces less than the earthly weight of 1 kilogramme, and m_2 displayed in other accelerations. That m_1 always equals m_2 is a natural law, not a necessary truth. Why then are m_1 and m_2 not separate properties of things but merely diverse manifestations of a single inertial mass? Obviously because changes in m_1 and m_2 are not independently effective. If they were, they would be real enough by our tests, since a change in either m_1 or m_2 would *inter alia* immediately cause a change in the other. But no one thinks a change in something's inertial resistance to small forces is an effect of changing its resistance to large ones, or *vice versa*. A change in a thing's inertial mass is a single event, demanding a single cause (like knocking a lump off the thing or accelerating it close to the speed of light), and being itself the single cause of other effects, such as changes in the thing's gravitational field. That is why inertial mass is a real and single property of things – or at least was thought to be, until the same test showed it to be itself merely one manifestation of a still deeper property, namely a combined gravitational and inertial mass.

Change

A change, then, is a thing having incompatible real properties at different times. But events, as well as things, can have incompatible properties at different times. Why is that not change? Well, suppose some thing or event a has a pair, G and $G^\star$, of such properties (e.g. two different temperatures) at two different times t and $t^\star$. That is,

$$a \text{ is } G \text{ at } t \tag{1}$$

and

$$a \text{ is } G^\star \text{ at } t^\star. \tag{2}$$

Now if a is an event, it will have different temporal parts containing t and $t^\star$. Call the relevant parts respectively p_a and $p_a^\star$. Then the apparent change in a really consists in the fact that

$$p_a \text{ is } G \tag{3}$$

and

$$p_a^\star \text{ is } G^\star. \tag{4}$$

In other words, the properties G and G★ are really properties of two different entities p_a and $p_a^\star$. But different entities differing in their properties do not amount to change even when, as here, one is later than the other and both are parts of something else. (3) and (4) no more constitute change than would *a*'s spatial parts differing in their properties – e.g. a poker being hot at one end and cold at the other. Change requires one and the same changing thing to have both the incompatible properties concerned, and this is not so either in the spatial or in this temporal case. The whole poker is neither hot nor cold – only its ends are – and *a fortiori* does not change from being hot to being cold. The event *a* likewise is neither G nor G★ – only its parts p_a and $p_a^\star$ are – so it too does not change from the one state to the other.

But if *a* is a thing, it has no temporal parts to take over properties G and G★. They are properties of *a* itself, albeit at different times. They are in short relations *a* has to the times at which it has them. That is, adopting the usual symbolism for relations, (1) and (2) should be read in this case not as (3) and (4) but as

$$G(a, t) \tag{5}$$

and

$$G\star(a, t\star). \tag{6}$$

(5) and (6), unlike (3) and (4), make *a* itself own the incompatible properties G and G★, incompatible in that no one thing could have both relations G and G★ to the same time. So the prime requirement of change is met: a single changing thing. Moreover, (5) and (6) are peculiar to time, as change is. Unlike (3) and (4), they have no spatial analogue. No thing or event is at once wholly present at two places in which it has different and incompatible properties. The poker at once hot at one end and cold at the other is not wholly present at each end as a poker first hot and then cold is wholly present at both times. Provided then chapter 9 vindicates relativity's causal test, for timelike as opposed to spacelike separation, without itself invoking change, we can now distinguish tenseless change from spatial variation.

Pending that vindication, one objection to (5) and (6) must be disposed of straightaway. This is that temperatures, colours, shapes etc. are not relations between things and times because they are not relations at all. They are non-relational properties, with no more temporal than spatial connotations. So the account of change (5) and (6) deliver is false. The facts given in (1) and (2) should be represented by temporal "operators" like those mentioned earlier, i.e. in this case

at t, Ga (7)

and

at $t^\star$, $G^\star a$, (8)

where the core sentences 'Ga' and '$G^\star a$' are supposed to have truth-values on their own. (That is the point in calling G and G* non-relational properties: they can be truly or falsely ascribed to things without reference to anything else, and specifically without reference to times.)

But if 'Ga' and '$G^\star a$' are tenseless sentences, they will only have definite truth-values if a is either always G, always G* or always neither. If a is sometimes G or G* and sometimes not, no one truth-value can be consistently assigned to either 'Ga' or '$G^\star a$'; and since G and G* are by definition changeable this is always liable to happen. So, the objectors conclude, these sentences cannot be tenseless; in which case, obviously, they are present tense. To say that a is G is to say that a is *now* G.

Now 'a is now G' is indeed not a relational sentence, i.e. it cannot be translated by a tensed but non-token-reflexive sentence saying that G relates a to the present. (The proof is an obvious application of the arguments of chapter 6, which I leave the reader to make.) But 'a is now G' *is* temporally token-reflexive, and that is just as bad. We have seen that what makes it true cannot be any single non-relational tensed fact like a being now G, now now G, etc. The fact can only be that a is G at the very B series time at which the token ascription is made. So although changeable properties are usually ascribed in the present tense, and these ascriptions are not relational, the facts which make them true or false are nonetheless tenseless, and the right representation of those facts is (5) and (6).

The crux of the matter, however, is tense, not whether (5) and (6) or (7) and (8) are the right way to represent the facts of (1) and (2). Nothing prevents believers in tense using (5) and (6): t and $t^\star$, in (5) and (6), could just as well be A series instants like *exactly twenty minutes ago* or *10.3000 . . . seconds hence*. That is perfectly compatible with (7) and (8). Indeed the standard "semantics" of tense logic would take (7) and (8) to be made true by the relational facts stated in the tensed versions of (5) and (6). Tense therefore affords no reason for rejecting (5) and (6), only for using A series rather than B series times in them. But since in reality there are no A series times, t and $t^\star$ must in fact be B series times, so that is what I shall henceforth take them to be.

Some however may still jib at thinking of temperatures and the like as relations, whether to A series or B series times; so I should emphasise how little this entails. It really only entails three things. First, when such properties are ascribed to things, a time must generally be either specified or understood for the ascription to be definitely either true or false. That is undeniable.

Secondly, the truth of such an ascription does not depend on how the thing or the time is specified. Suppose that a is the heaviest and the ugliest thing in the room, and that t is 8.15 p.m. and sunset. Then all the following must be true if a is G at t:

'The heaviest thing in the room is G at t',
'The ugliest thing in the room is G at t',
'a is G at 8.15',
'a is G at sunset',

etc. In other words, both the contexts

'. . . is G at t'

and

'a is G at . . .'

are what is called "referentially transparent".

Thirdly, for 'a is G at t' and its variants to be true, a and t must exist. This implication of 'a is G at t' may be less obvious than its transparency, but it is no less undeniable once a couple of side-issues are disposed of. The first concerns fictional characters. In some sense Hamlet was a Dane despite his not existing, and in that sense 'Hamlet is a Dane' is true without implying his existence. This is no place to start analysing fictional discourse, so all I will say here is that at least 'Hamlet is a Dane' was never true in any sense that impugns Danish census returns that left him out – and no other sense matters here. The other side-issue is whether times exist independently of events, or regardless of relativistic complications. In implying t's existence, 'a is G at t' implies neither that times could exist without events nor that spacetime divides uniquely into time and space. A particular time like the end of 1984 may well depend on there being events that much later than Christ's birth; and temporal positions on *a*'s world-line, which is all *t* and *t*★ need to be, need not correspond uniquely to positions on the world-lines of other things far off in space.

Once all this is realised, the existence of *a* and *t* is as undeniable an implication of '*a* is *G* at *t*' as its referential transparency. And these are all the implications of calling *G* a relation between *a* and *t*. (5) and (6) really assert nothing about properties that anyone could seriously deny. So I shall take it henceforth without more ado that (5) and (6) do together state the general form of tenseless change. In short: things, being devoid of temporal parts, change when they have incompatible properties at different *B* series times, provided that the difference of properties has contiguous effects.

Changes of belief and the flow of time

People are among the things capable of tenseless change, and among the changes people undergo are changes of belief. I remarked in chapter 5 that beliefs are instantaneously possessed properties of believers, capable of having a truth-value at a *B* series instant, a value which in the case of tensed beliefs is apt to vary from one instant to another. Thus my premature belief that it is now one o'clock will suddenly change from being false to being true as the clock strikes one. Now because such variations of truth-value are not real changes (since they have no effects), the truth-values of their beliefs are no more real properties of believers than their ages are. Indeed ages are merely a special case of tensed beliefs having truth-values: I am forty, for example, when the belief that my birth is forty years past is true. And just as chronological ageing is not in reality a sequence of events, so changes in the truth-values of tensed beliefs are by our causal test likewise not events.

But changes from beliefs of one tensed type to beliefs (about the same thing) of another tensed type *are* events. Suppose *G* is the property of believing it is not yet one o'clock, *G*★ is the property of believing it is, and that *a* is a believer who is first *G* and then *G*★. Assume moreover that these properties are incompatible, i.e. that whenever people come to believe it is now one o'clock they stop believing one o'clock is yet to come. (This may be obvious, but it needs saying: people can to some extent harbour inconsistent beliefs.) So a is not $G^\star$ at t, nor is he G at $t^\star$. And these incompatible properties, G and $G^\star$, are also real, since a's changing from one to the other between t and $t^\star$ has immediate and contiguous effects. In chapter 5 this change was the immediate cause of a's turning on the radio to hear the one o'clock news. And of course this really is a case of change in a, not of difference between temporal parts of him. It is a himself, the whole man, who believes first that one o'clock is future and then that it is present.

So changes of tensed belief are real events, even though changes in its truth-value are not. Nevertheless we only keep changing our tensed beliefs because they are constantly changing their truth-values. Our object of course is to keep our beliefs true, truth being as we saw in chapter 5 the sole object of belief. So naturally we try to acquire tensed beliefs when they are true and get rid of them when they become false. But this we also saw needs causation: either by our internal clocks or by our perceiving external clocks or other events temporally related to those the beliefs are about. And our perceptions are as fallible in temporal as in other matters. Neither internal nor external clocks always change our tensed beliefs at the right B series time.

When clocks do go right, however, their changes, and those they induce in us, correspond to what believers in tense have mistaken for the reality of change, namely change of A series position. If I keep my belief in the A series whereabouts of one o'clock true at all times by appropriate changes in the tense of my belief about it, then I will in particular change its tense from future to present just when one o'clock actually becomes present – i.e. at one o'clock. And similarly for all other changes in the A series position of that B series instant. So although things, events and dates themselves are in reality neither past, present nor future, and so are not capable of change in that respect, the idea that they are is not a complete illusion. Real changes do correspond to the apparent movement of things, events and dates from future to past via the present, viz. the changes of temporally token-reflexive truth conditions that tensed beliefs about these items, and the tensed deliverances of timepieces, must continually undergo in order to stay true.

This tenseless surrogate for A series change is both real and objective. It is real, because the changes of tensed belief and the tensed output of clocks it appeals to are real events with real effects. It is objective, because it appeals not just to any old change in tensed beliefs, clock displays, etc.; only to changes that keep them true, and thus correspond to real temporal relations between the changes and whatever they are about. Nevertheless, real and objective though it is, the surrogate will hardly satisfy adherents of the *A* series. For the changes it offers are not changes in the things and events themselves, only in clocks and in states of mind of people and animals. And what makes these changing clocks and tensed thoughts true are purely tenseless relations they have to whatever they are about, not real and changeable *A* series facts.

But like it or lump it, the tenseless surrogate is all there is. In the form of tensed belief, it is the psychological reality behind the myth of tense, the myth of the flow of time. The reality is the changing truth conditions of true token-reflexive beliefs; the myth results from mistaking these beliefs to have non-token-reflexive contents, and so to correspond to real movement along the *A* series, when in reality they do no such thing.

Space and the flow of time

Why have we no spatial myth corresponding to the myth of the flow of time? Spatially tensed beliefs have to vary from place to place to stay true, just as temporally tensed beliefs have to vary from time to time. Yet no one mistakes them to have non-token-reflexive content. Why not?

The reason lies in the lack of spatial analogues for (5) and (6). My spatially tensed beliefs can of course change, i.e. they can be different at different times; and if they are also temporally tensed, they will have to change as I move about in order to stay true. As I travel from Cambridge to London, for example, my present tense belief that Cambridge is here has to change into the belief that London is.

But this is still only temporal change. A spatial analogue of the flow of time needs something else entirely, namely one person wholly present in two non-overlapping places u and $u^\star$ at the same time, at u believing truly that u is here, and at $u^\star$ believing truly that $u^\star$ is. Then the spatial change would consist in one and the same believer's having incompatible beliefs in different places at the same time, the truth of the two beliefs in this case corresponding to the spatial analogue of positions in the *A* series.

What prevents this of course is that nothing with incompatible properties in different places at the same time is wholly present at both places. I remarked earlier that a poker hot at one end and cold at the other is not wholly present at either end, and the same goes for people. No one thinks people are wholly present both in their bald feet and hairy pates. Parts of them are bald and other parts are hairy; that is all there is to it.

If spatial change in people's physical properties makes little sense, spatial change in their mental properties makes less. But the effort to make sense of it is quite instructive. First, assume that the beliefs, in u and u^* being here, are incompatible as well as inconsistent, i.e. no one can have both beliefs at once in the same place. Then the closest I can get to spatial change is this: a schizophrenic with the two beliefs embodied in different halves of his brain located respectively at u and u^*! But even then we should ascribe the two beliefs to two different personalities, not to a single believer wholly present at both u and u^* and changing spatially from the one belief state to the other. And anyway the two beliefs could not of course be so precisely located. What matters to the location of beliefs is not just where bits of the brain are, but where the bodily actions are of which changes of belief are supposed to be the immediate cause. In fact this case only really presents three possibilities, none of which amounts to spatial change. First, someone's behaviour might be so confused as not to display either belief properly but rather to suggest in him some mixture of the two. In that case he simply does not know where he is, and there is no change in that. Secondly, he might systematically display the two inconsistent beliefs in different (non-spatial) circumstances and therefore at different times. Then he has the two beliefs successively, which is temporal, not spatial, change. Or thirdly, systematic inconsistencies in his behaviour might show that he really does have both beliefs at once. But then, despite their being inconsistent in content, the beliefs are not incompatible properties of people, so there is no change at all, either temporal or spatial.

In short, the spatial analogue of temporally changing tensed beliefs will always fail in one of three ways. Either the beliefs, although inconsistent, will be compatible, or they will not be possessed simultaneously, or they will be properties of different believers, and so no more a case of change than is a poker hot at one end and cold at the other. The fact is that spatial variation of spatially tensed belief, like all other spatial variation, is always to be construed analogously to (3) and (4), never like (5) and (6) which give the form of real change.

Although we do have spatially tensed beliefs, therefore, just as we have temporally tensed ones, there is no spatial analogue of temporal change in them, because we lack temporal parts but do have spatial ones. But the temporal changes in our temporally tensed beliefs were the source of the myth of the flow of time. So we have no analogous spatial myth, because it has no analogous source.

8   *Events, causes, things and parts*

Changes and events

I have said what change is, and said also that changes are events, i.e. that they are or have temporal parts and so cannot themselves change. Now this does not follow from anything I have so far assumed, but it is obviously true, and needs explaining. Perhaps the explanation is that events just *are* changes, and can be so defined.

The idea is attractive, but for two reasons will not do. First, I have defined change as things having different properties at different times, and need events to supply the times. This is so despite general relativity's showing spacetime to be an entity distinct from the things and events it contains, with a structure that affects and is affected by them (see p. 130 below). Events are still needed to identify regions and points in spacetime: general relativity gives no sense to the idea of the same distribution of matter occurring elsewhere in spacetime. So particular times cannot without vicious circularity be used to define all changes and hence all events. Anyway, trading in events, via changes, for times is no great conceptual economy. It is also risky, since there is still much less evidence for general relativity – which is what tells us spacetime exists – than there is for the existence of events.

Secondly, even if all changes are events, not all events are changes. The beginning or ending of a thing, for a start, is unlikely to be a change. It is obviously not a change in that thing, and often not a change in anything else. The creation of a positron and an electron, for instance, with the annihilation of a corresponding amount of gamma radiation, is a notable event with significant effects; yet with no previously existing thing for it to be a change in. Similarly, the endings of macroscopic things are not always changes. Sometimes they are: an animal's death, for example, is usually just a change in its body. But not if it is killed by being vaporised; and likewise when any thing is ended by the scattering of its spatial parts. Once erstwhile parts no longer interact, they cease to be the parts of a whole, for reasons that will emerge later in this chapter. So even when a thing's parts survive it, they will not in general constitute anything else in which its demise could be a change.

Moreover, some events are not even beginnings or endings of things, let alone changes in them; some are no part of the history of any thing. Of what thing's history is a flash of lightning a part? Of course things can be concocted *ad hoc* for events to be changes in – the universe itself, as a last resort. But that is a poor way of making events changes, and no way at all of defining them. And anyway, it would not work for the beginning and end of the universe itself – a fact which only a rasher metaphysician than myself would take to disprove the Big Bang theory *a priori*.

Events and causes

So there are more events than changes in the world: if anything, change must be defined as some kind of event, not the other way round. The need for events to supply the times things change at itself suggests such a definition, as does the need for real changes to have contiguous effects, since causes and effects seem in general to be events.

This is, I believe, the way to go: I will follow Davidson (e.g. 1970a, b) and others in individuating events by their causes and effects. That is, if the event fitting one description has the same causes and effects as the event fitting another description, then it is the same event. (Suppose the loudest piece in a concert has all the same causes and effects as the longest piece: then it *is* the longest piece.) However, this beguiling little principle will obviously not individuate all events, since the causes and effects of events are themselves events, so somewhere we must start without it. Some events will just have to be recognised as such. Thereafter, the principle may identify their causes and effects, the other causes and effects of those events, and so on.

With what events can this process start, and how is it carried on, i.e. how are causes and effects discovered? These sizeable questions are fortunately larger than I need cope with. To answer the first one, I need only produce some credible events for the process to start with: events which clearly have or are temporal parts and which need not be defined as changes in things. That much, albeit sketchily, I can do.

My paradigm events are on the one hand our own actions, and on the other our own experiences, especially our perceptions of other things and events. Experiences are obviously events, because they obviously both have temporal parts (not necessarily experiences), and are temporal parts of other experiences. This is especially obvious of experiences like listening to music, watching plays or films or reading books, but it is clearly true of experience generally. We never have just one persisting experience, wholly present all the time, only changing in its experiential properties. Rather, we have first one experience and then another. The succession of our experiences, indeed, has long been recognised as the epitome of temporal succession.

So experiences are events. And although they are changes, namely in whoever or whatever has them, they need not be defined that way. In fact, the great virtue of experience here is that it need not be defined at all, merely pointed to. Even if experience will not define everything else, as empiricists have hoped, at least it needs no defining, least of all in terms of change.

Similarly for actions. They too have temporal parts and are themselves parts of longer actions. When I leave a room by walking to the door, opening it and passing through, those are all temporal parts of my leaving, just as each step is a part of my walking to the door. And – also like experiences – although actions are changes, namely changes in agents, that is not how they are defined. What makes an event an action is indeed that it is caused (as was illustrated at length in chapter 5) by changes of desire and belief, including tensed belief; but that defines it as the effect of a change, apt to have other intended effects, not as being a change itself.

Actions and experiences should therefore be acceptable paradigm events for causation to apply to. They should also be sufficient, since interest in events and in causation stems entirely from wanting to affect the world and to find out what goes on in it. We intentionally affect the world by acting in it: causation is both the mechanism of action and the means by which our actions get us what we want. To walk is to cause one's legs to move, and walking causes us to get where we want to be; to speak to people is to cause them to hear what we are saying, which in turn, we hope, will cause them to act or react as we wish. Whatever else causation is, it is how we act in and on the world. To discover new effects, therefore, is *ipso facto* to extend the range of possible action to them from their causes – which is why science, whose business it is *inter alia* to seek out causes and effects, is a natural basis for technology.

Causation is likewise how our senses work. Whenever we see or hear, touch or taste something, what we perceive is directly or indirectly a cause of our perception. The lightning I see causes me to see it (by causing photons to travel to my eyes) and similarly for the seeing of other events, and for perceiving them by our other senses. Causation is the mechanism of all our perceptual experience.

Action and perceptual experience are respectively the beginning and end of chains of cause and effect by which we – and all agents – affect the world and learn about it. And however far the chains stretch from action and perception, they must still in the end remain linked to them. However large, small or otherwise remote the events which our science studies become, it must always relate them causally to what we can see and hear. If science did not say how the events it hypothesises can affect our senses, we should have no means of testing its hypotheses by observation; nor, until we know how to affect them, can we actively set up experiments to that end. Science may indeed greatly alter our conception of the world, including our conception of our own experiences and behaviour; but it must still always be able to tell us in its own terms what we can see and do.

Actions and experiences therefore are both acceptable and adequate starting points for a recursive causal definition of events. Nothing agents can observe or affect can be unconnected to them by some more or less lengthy chain of causes and effects; so the definition will at least cover all events that agents, including people, can know of or take any practical interest in.

It remains to say something of how science discovers causes and effects, thus extending the range of knowable events from actions and experiences to other kinds of happening. That this is part of science no one will deny. Astrophysics studies the causes and effects of celestial events, from sunspots to the origin of the universe, as microphysics likewise does for events of the smallest kinds. In between are myriad special sciences and technologies based on them that look for the causes and effects of all sorts of other events. And, in finding them, they uncover yet more sorts of events, whose other causes and effects then come themselves to be sought out by the same or other sciences.

It is obvious that science discovers causes and effects, but less obvious how. The methodology of science is still controversial, partly because the nature of causation is; and unfortunately I cannot evade this controversy completely. In particular, I shall have to assume something about causation to be able to say in chapter 9 why causes precede their effects. But I need not assume much, and that not much disputed. I shall assume, for example, as I have just been arguing, that causation is *inter alia* how we perceive the world and act in and on it, and no one seriously disputes that. Also, few would deprive events of effects next to them in space and time, which will explain why, as we saw in chapter 7, changes in particular have immediate contiguous effects.

The only other thing I need assume about causation is this: causes make their effects more likely than, in the circumstances, they would otherwise have been. Smoking causing me to get cancer, for example, means at least that my getting cancer would in the circumstances have been less likely had I not smoked. As in action, so in perception: when I see a lightning flash, that visual experience would in the circumstances have been less likely had the flash not taken place. And similarly in inanimate causation. If being hit by a brick causes a window to break, the window must have been less likely to break just then had the brick not hit it.

In order to discover causes and effects, therefore, science must at least establish statistical correlations between kinds of events which it claims to be causally related. The correlations must moreover be more than mere coincidence, i.e. they must have the force of statistical laws, however limited in scope. Otherwise nothing follows about how likely an event of the effect kind is to follow an event of the kind supposed to cause it. If hitting a window causes it to break, it must be more than a coincidence that windows of that sort more often break when hit like that than when not so hit.

What this statistical requirement amounts to is still much debated, and so is the conception of probability needed to make sense of it. All I need say here is that the probabilities involved must be both objective and not merely inductive. When I say smoking makes cancer more likely, I do not just mean that I have a greater degree of belief in smokers than in non-smokers getting cancer. I mean the greater incidence of cancer among smokers can be explained only by something that makes this difference in the degrees of my belief objectively right. And I also mean that provided I want very much to avoid cancer, I should give up smoking even though I would prefer to smoke whether I have cancer or not. If the probabilities were merely inductive, that would not be so. If for example the causal connection were the other way round, so that incipient cancer made people *inter alia* more likely to smoke, the statistics would show smoking to be a more or less reliable symptom of cancer, i.e. it would give cancer a correspondingly increased inductive probability. But that would be no reason to give up smoking if I preferred to smoke in any case, however afraid I was of getting the disease. What I mean by 'likely', 'probable' and cognate terms in this connection is that they *do* have these implications for sensible decision-making.

What else causation needs, besides this causal sort of probability and the correlation that reveals it, is also debatable, although it clearly needs something. But besides the assumptions I have already made, I can and will keep out of the debate; all I need is the statistical requirement itself. Even that has been disputed, but in causation it seems to me quite certain. Indeed it follows in my view from causation's connection with action and perception, and so is not really a separate assumption at all. For whatever others may mean by causation, I mean whatever *inter alia* makes our actions more or less effective and our perceptions more or less reliable. These, as I have indicated, are the original and indispensable functions of causation, and accounts of the concept must make sense of them. But that means accepting the statistical requirement. Without it, doing an action to bring about an effect of it would make no sense, because it would not in the circumstances make the effect more likely to occur. Nor likewise would causation serve as it must to make perceptual experience evidence for the occurrence of the event supposedly perceived. Unless in the circumstances the event made the perceptual experience more likely, the experience would be no good evidence that it had happened, and would be no sort of perception at all.

Events and things

I have used causation to say recursively what events are without defining them in terms of things, either as changes in them or in any other way. So a change in a thing may now be defined as the thing having different properties at different times, provided the difference constitutes an event. This explains how, as we saw in chapter 7 in the case of mass, properties of things are individuated by individuating their changes, namely by using causation to settle what prospective changes count as single events. It explains why changes have to have contiguous immediate effects, a requirement we found necessary to rule out sundry pseudo-changes in relational and other apparent properties of things. Changes have contiguous effects because events have them and changes are events. The principal function of the maxim 'No action at a distance', in fact, is to use their effects to identify, and to locate in spacetime, events in general and changes in particular.

But if events will serve to define changes in things, perhaps they will serve to define things altogether? True, we seem to need the concept of a thing to distinguish events which are changes from events which are not. But perhaps in reality every thing is itself just a sequence of events to whose properties and relations its own – including its changes – are all somehow reducible. In fact this is not so; but there are some temptations to think it, to which I should encourage resistance.

To bring out the first temptation, I must amplify the remark made in chapter 7 apropos of "grue" and induction, namely that we should not expect change without cause. The remark needs qualifying in two immediately relevant respects. First, the persistence of some real properties, not just "grue" and "bleen", entails change in other respects. A steadily turning wheel, for instance, has an angular momentum, a real property in which changes have real and contiguous effects. Without external causes of change in it (friction, air resistance, etc.), a wheel will go on turning indefinitely. But by so doing its eccentric parts are constantly accelerated towards its axis, a continuous change in their velocity that requires continuous causation (by centripetal forces produced by compressing the wheel's outer layers). Here, persisting angular momentum in the whole wheel entails continuous change in its parts, which may therefore reasonably be predicted on that basis alone, without any other cause of change.

Secondly, the remark was not meant to imply that all changes have causes. The spontaneous decay of an atom of radium-226, which changes it into an atom of radon-222, has no cause. But radioactive decay is nonetheless governed by statistical laws, which attribute to each radioactive atom a definite propensity to decay shown in the chance of it decaying spontaneously in any given stretch of time. For short stretches, the chance of spontaneous decay is roughly proportional to the length of time, and in general the propensity can be specified by the so-called "half-life", i.e. the time in which the chance of spontaneous decay is 1/2. Again, the half-life of an atom is a real property of it, changes in which have real – sometimes, *en masse*, explosive – effects, and which themselves require to be caused by changes in the atom's nuclear structure. Until these occur, whether by external bombardment of the nucleus or by the very spontaneous decay whose chances display this propensity, the half-life of a radioactive atom will persist unchanged.

In both cases, therefore, a prediction of change, either definite or statistical, is entailed by some other property persisting. And in general, properties should be expected to persist unless some cause of change in them occurs, except where the change is thus entailed or given a definite causal probability by some other property persisting which, being a case of persistence, is itself therefore to be expected.

A weak corollary of this is that, subject to the above qualifications, an unchanging thing having a property at one time is more likely to have that property thereafter than it would otherwise have been. Thus a thermally insulated thing is more likely to be at a given temperature at any given time if it has been in thermal equilibrium at that temperature just before than it would be had it then been in equilibrium at some other temperature. A thing moving at a given velocity under no net force is more likely to have that velocity an instant later than such things moving at other velocities are. And what makes this so, as with the analogous probabilifying of events discussed in the last section, is causation. A thing's having a property at any time is causally explained by its having had it earlier, given that the thing was not then in another state entailing or probabilifying change in this respect, and that no cause of change in it has occurred meanwhile.

So, for example, one way of causing a thing to have a property at some future time is to cause it to acquire the property now, and then to protect it hereafter from further causes of change in that respect. This is the rationale for deep-freezing cooked meals, for shielding paint from light, beer from air, etc., until they are wanted. These things are by these means protected from thermal, radiative and chemical causes of change in the properties we wish preserved; and that, we conclude, is a good causal basis for predicting their preservation.

But if the successive temporal "stages" of a thing are thus causally related, are they not events, of which therefore every thing embodies a causal sequence? Well, this certainly does not follow from my recursive causal definition of events, and there is good reason to deny it. It does not follow, because I have used causation to define events, not the other way about. All events have causes or effects, but causes or effects need not all be events. Admittedly 'event' has by now become rather a term of art, and I cannot prevent people stipulating that all causes and effects are to be called events. But the stipulation would be very foolish, since it would preclude the most natural way of drawing a distinction which has to be drawn somehow between "thing-stages" and (other) events.

The point is that whereas events proper have all sorts of causes and effects, an unchanging thing's stages only explain its own lack of change. The only cause of a stage of an unchanging thing is an immediately preceding and otherwise identical stage of the same thing, whose only effect is its similarly undistinguished successor. Unlike real events, thing-stages lack a heterogeneous range of independently discoverable and describable causes and effects by which they can be characterised. A stage can be identified only as a certain thing having a certain property at a certain time. So whether or not stages are by stipulation called events, things cannot without vicious circularity be defined by them as changes can by what I call events. Therefore, because calling thing-stages events would only foster the illusion that things can be so defined, I will not do it. I will simply say instead that causation relates a thing's unchanging properties from time to time, as well as relating its changes to other events.

Things and events in physics

A thing's world-line may in fact be occupied by sequences of real events, with independently characterised causes and effects; and some properties of things do reduce to properties of such processes. The turning wheel is one example, its angular momentum being largely due to the centripetal acceleration of its eccentric parts. Temperature is another. The temperatures of macroscopic things reduce to statistical properties of a process of incessant interchange of kinetic energy among their molecular parts.

But not every property of things is thus reducible by natural laws to processes going on inside the things. The angular momentum of fundamental particles, for instance, need not be a lawlike consequence of their parts accelerating, for they may have no parts. Nor is inertial mass reducible to any sequence of events: nothing need be going on inside a thing to keep its mass constant. Even the classical kinetic theory reduces gas temperatures to changing properties, namely the energies and momenta of gas particles, which need no processes to conserve them in between the particles' collisions.

Classical kinetic theory has of course long been superseded, and the entities of modern microphysics are more problematic than their predecessors. However, the problems they present, especially those of interpreting quantum mechanics, are in no way aggravated by the concept of a thing: crediting all quantum mechanical entities with temporal parts would not make the conceptual problems of that science any easier to solve. Isolated fundamental particles, as seen wending their way through bubble chambers, no more need incessant internal processes to keep constant whatever properties they can consistently have than classical particles do.

If anything in modern physics threatens the concept of a thing, it is relativity, not quantum theory. Its unification of space and time has been thought to demand temporal as well as spatial parts of spatiotemporally extended entities, i.e. to make them all events rather than things. And this has gone significantly along with the idea that four-dimensional spacetime and its contents – the so-called "block universe" – are all changeless. In fact relativity has neither implication, but the grounds for thinking it does are numerous enough, despite being individually negligible, to seem collectively impressive; so they had better now be countered *seriatim*.

First, I admit that a universe composed of events in spacetime would not change. It and its contents could only change by changing tense, and that idea I hope is now sufficiently disposed of. But events can still *be* changes, namely changes in things which a block universe can also contain. Events need not change themselves to be changes in things.

Secondly, the canard that relativity makes time spacelike, so that if spatial variation in a thing's properties demands spatial parts, temporal variation likewise demands temporal parts, has also I hope been adequately scotched. However, there is in this connection still one argument to meet, more specific than those disposed of in chapter 4. Relativity does after all make spatial and temporal dimensions of extended things and events somewhat interchangeable from one reference frame to another; so perhaps spatially separated parts in one reference frame imply temporally separated parts in others.

In fact they do not. I remarked above that successive "stages" of even an unchanging thing are causally connected and this, it will be recalled from chapter 4, makes their spacetime separation timelike. That is, they are never simultaneous in any reference frame, and *a fortiori* never simultaneously in different spatial locations. But that is just what different spatial parts must be, in at least one reference frame, to distinguish them from one spatial part being in different places at different times. So even in relativity temporal stages cannot be spatial parts of anything. Conversely, spatial parts, whose spacetime separation really is spacelike, never lie along a world-line and so are never temporal parts of anything. By founding on causation an absolute distinction between timelike and spacelike separation, relativity distinguishes absolutely between spatial and temporal parts. Consequently, it gives no reason whatever to infer from a thing's having spatial parts that it must also have temporal ones.

Thirdly, the idea that entities extended in spacetime must have temporal parts is reinforced by the practice of drawing world-lines on spatial diagrams, using a dimension of space to represent the dimension of time. The spatial regions of the diagram of course have parts, including parts of world-lines separated in the direction used to represent time. From such spatial parts of the representation of a thing's whereabouts from time to time it is all too easy to infer corresponding temporal parts in the thing represented. But a little reflection should suffice to show how invalid the inference is. When spatial dimensions are used to represent pressures or temperatures, for example, no one infers that these quantities must have parts corresponding to the spatial parts of lines representing them; nor should we infer it with time.

The itch to spatialise, however, is peculiarly strong with time, and unfortunately encouraged by carrying into physics the mathematically harmless habit of calling a four-dimensional spacetime manifold a "four-space", as if all its dimensions were spatial. The best prophylactic for this untimely itch is to keep in mind that time need not be represented by a spatial dimension. If world-lines were represented by animated cartoons in which time itself was used to represent time, the itch would disappear. If we only depicted people's movements by moving images of them about on maps, we should never think of investing them with temporal parts.

All the above, however, are quite superficial sources of the idea that relativistic spacetime gives things temporal parts, and once exposed quite obviously fallacious. But a more sophisticated train of thought also runs to that conclusion from the "geometrical" explanation general relativity gives of gravity, and that route takes rather more blocking. The train of thought is this. According to general relativity, the non-Euclidean structure of spacetime, induced by the distribution of mass in it, restricts the world-lines of things falling freely under gravity alone to geodesics of that structure, which then entail in any reference frame the acceleration we ascribe to gravity. Because this geometrical explanation of gravity starts from world-lines, and specifically from the variable curvature of their temporal parts, the theory makes them the reality behind the apparent spatial world of gravitating things. Just as the theory explains gravitational attraction away, so it explains away the things which appear as a result of it to be accelerating through space. The theory shows that in reality there are no such things, only their trajectories, which we conceive to be things because we still apply to them the outmodedly separate classical concepts of space and time.

This train of thought, however tempting, is completely mistaken. To see why, compare an exactly analogous explanation in pre-relativistic optics. The path of light through a succession of differently refracting media (air, water, glass, etc., through which light travels at different speeds) follows from its always taking the quickest path between any two spatial points in the path. That is, given its speed in each medium, the spacetime path of a photon is such as to minimise the temporal separation of every pair of its intersections with spatial coordinates. Now a photon's spacetime path through refracting media is a temporal part of its world-line, so the (classical) spatiotemporal geometry of these parts is what here explains the phenomena of refraction. But no one would infer from this that photons have temporal parts because their world-lines do, still less that the explanation reduces photons to their world-lines. For one thing, photons have too many other properties, besides their velocities in refracting media, which this optical theory does not pretend to explain. So it is with gravity. Things have many properties and undergo many changes, other than gravitational acceleration, which general relativity does nothing to derive from their spatiotemporal geometry.

Neither the optical nor the relativistic explanation shows the things it applies to to be merely misleading classical appearances of their own eventlike world-lines. To see that clearly, however, one must sharply distinguish the region of spacetime a thing occupies from the property it has of being there. Whether in reality there are such regions is a moot point: it depends on whether spacetime is an entity distinct from the spatiotemporal relations of the things and events in it. If it is, then the region a thing occupies is a part of it, and itself has other such regions as temporal and spatial parts. But whether that is so or not, the property of occupying such a region has neither spatial nor temporal parts, because properties, being abstract entities, have no parts at all. Of course, if the thing itself has parts, they will by definition occupy corresponding parts of the spacetime region the whole thing occupies. But nothing compels things and events to have parts corresponding to all possible subdivisions of their world-lines; in particular, nothing compels things to have temporal parts just because their world-lines do.

All that these optical and relativistic explanations show (if true) is that world-lines are real properties of things. As a property, a world-line is indeed unusual in being unchangeable: since it already encompasses a thing's whereabouts at all times, a thing cannot have one world-line at one time and another one later. So the property's reality does not in this case consist in its changes being real events, because there are no such changes. But this does not put world-lines completely beyond the causal pale. In particular, the cause of a thing's gravitational acceleration at any time is not its whole world-line, but the local spacetime curvature to which the line is subject at that point. And *that* property of a thing is as changeable as its colour, shape or temperature. It is moreover a real property, since changes in it have real and contiguous effects – namely the changes of acceleration which Newton took to be caused by changes in the net gravitational force on the thing. Newton, it turns out, was wrong about that: Einstein has indeed disposed of gravitational forces. But not the things on which they were supposed to act, nor their gravitational accelerations. All Einstein has done is supply new causes for the same effects.

Events and parts

My distinction between things and events rests on the concept of a part. So far, in rebutting proposed reductions of things to events, I have taken that concept for granted. I have for instance assumed that it takes more to generate spatial or temporal parts of a thing or an event than merely specifying spatiotemporal boundaries for them. That much I hope is evident enough. At least, someone who wants to apply 'part' to any arbitrary spatiotemporal subdivision of a thing or event, must admit that we also have a stronger concept, which is what I mean by 'part'. Just how much stronger the concept is, however, is less clear; and while I need not try to give it a comprehensive definition, I must say enough to give definite and credible substance to my use of it.

Again I start with events. We have a causal test for events, and hence in particular for changes in things, including human actions. A sequence of causally related events may constitute another event, such as an action, which the members of the sequence are therefore parts of. In the example given earlier of my walking to the door, the action's parts are the successive steps *en route*. They are the deliberate causal mechanism of the action as a whole, i.e. each step is itself an action which is a causal precursor of the step that follows it; from which it follows even in relativity that the steps are temporal, not spatial, parts of my walking to the door. Each step in turn also has a causal mechanism, namely the succession of nervous and muscular changes by means of which I move my legs to take a step. These are not actions, in that they are not events I am able immediately to bring about; but they are still genuine events. None is defined in the trivial way I jibbed at above, by arbitrarily dividing the time it takes me to walk a step and calling whatever goes on in me during such a division an event. It takes more than mathematical surgery to uncover the physiology of locomotion.

What it takes is the finding of events – mechanical, chemical, electrical – identified by causes or effects independently of the step they are parts of, between which we can then trace causal connections that show how, as a causal sequence, they constitute such a step. Each of these events may itself have a causal mechanism, whose elements are again independently identified and linked. And so on, perhaps *ad infinitum* and perhaps not, depending however not on Zeno or the mathematics of indefinitely divisible spacetime so much as on whether the smallest scale stuff of microphysics is discrete or not.

Temporal parts must be causally identifiable independently of the wholes they are parts of – and *vice versa*. Temporal wholes must be genuine events identifiable by their own causes and effects independently of the parts that make them up. A whole event can no more be generated just by drawing a spatiotemporal boundary round an arbitrary collection of prospective parts than parts can be generated by thus subdividing an authentic whole. There are, for instance, many spacetime regions containing the fall of Troy, the French Revolution and World War II, but that does not make these three events occur together in the causal mechanism of a single long-running historical event. Nor can such an event be conjured up by thinking of the set of these three happenings. A set of events is not a whole they are parts of, if only because no set is an event. Sets are abstract objects, which events are not. At any rate, it takes more than set theory or the mathematics of spacetime to make whole events out of prospective parts.

When, therefore, events *are* parts, the event they are parts of is neither the set they are the members of nor merely the contents of some spacetime region large enough to contain them all. The part-whole relation is not a merely formal relation like set membership, nor is it just spatiotemporal inclusion (although it entails that). My walking to the door, for example, is not the set of steps by which I do it, nor does it just spatiotemporally contain those steps. There must be more than a spatiotemporal connection between my steps and the walk they are parts of, if only because that region of spacetime also contains many events – e.g. the decay of passing cosmic rays – which have nothing to do with my walk and are no part of it. Similarly, when causal sequences of molecular events constitute a change of temperature in a macroscopic thing, that constitution is plainly not just set-theoretic or spatiotemporal. It is a material and contingent law of nature that such-and-such microscopic events provide the causal mechanism of thermal phenomena in general, and changes of temperature in particular; just as it is that such-and-such physiological and anatomical changes will propel a human body across a room.

There is more to say about the identity of events and about how a number of them can combine as parts of wholes. For example, most properties of events are explained by reference to their parts rather than to wholes they are parts of. Why that should be is itself a philosophical question, but not one to be tackled here. Here I need only insist that whole events are related to their parts contingently by laws of nature, not by laws of logic or geometry, and consequently that both wholes and parts must be identifiable independently of each other by their other causes and effects. That is really why the temporal "stages" of things are not temporal parts. We have seen that a thing's stages are not identifiable independently of the thing they purport to be parts of. So while a thing's having a property at one time does generally cause it to have the same property later, its having that property at successive times gives no causal explanation of its lack of change; whereas my successive steps across the room do causally explain my progress to the door.

Things and parts

As for temporal parts so, *mutatis mutandis*, for spatial parts. So in particular for spatial parts of things, which are not generated just by marking off spatial regions within them at arbitrary times. A thing's spatial parts must also be things, and it takes more than a spatial boundary to make a thing. Parts of people, for example, are things such as their internal organs, whose parts in turn are cells, whose parts are molecules, then atoms, parts of atoms, and so on down to quarks (or whatever). Discovering a thing's parts, like discovering parts of an event, means doing serious empirical research, not just making geometrical divisions *a priori*.

Whole things also, like their parts, must be things in their own right. Whole things no more just contain their parts than whole events do, nor are they merely sets of them. This should be obvious, but since certain things are still mistaken for sets of their parts, I had better say why they are not.

The things most often confounded with sets of parts are the social groups mentioned in chapter 7 – nations, churches, firms, unions, etc. – membership of which is still quite often mistaken for set membership. Yet it is evidently not, because groups can evidently gain or lose human parts while preserving their own identities, which sets of people could not do. Different members by definition means a different set, which is almost never true of groups. All those listed in chapter 7 can survive the admission of new members or the expulsion, resignation, retirement or death of existing ones, and I think the reader will find few if any groups of which that is not true.

To take just one example, the Church militant here on earth does not change its identity with every baptism, burial and excommunication it performs. In the long run, indeed, continual replacement of its members will lead to its sharing no human parts at all with those it had some time before. The Church militant today has none of the terrestrial members it had two centuries ago, yet it is still the same earthly institution.

As for social wholes, so for organic ones. People, animals and plants can clearly survive the growth of new cells and the sloughing off of dead ones. I do not become a different person with every morsel of food I ingest or excrete. And if people do not actually suffer a complete turnover of cells during their lifetime, as the Church does of its human parts, that is just a curious fact about biology, not a consequence of people having cells for parts.

People, then, are no more sets of cells than groups are sets of people. But although people, groups and other things can replace their parts one by one, they cannot replace them all at once. Some continuity of parts is needed to sustain a thing's identity through time, and this should give us a clue to what the part-whole relation between things is. Suppose I meet a person or a group at noon which shares no parts at all with a person or group I met an hour earlier. It surely follows that I have met two individuals (human or social), not one individual twice: no one individual person or group could have replaced *all* its parts so quickly. Why not?

The continuity of parts a thing needs is best seen to start with in groups with definite objectives, where there is a need for continuity of function. The function of members of the Hallé orchestra, for example, is to play particular instruments needed for the performances that are its *raison d'être*; and what the Hallé needs, to continue in existence, is sufficient continuity in the people fulfilling these functions. It can afford to gain, replace or lose a violinist because (a) it will still have enough of a string section and (b) its identity is secured through this change of personnel by the rest of the orchestra remaining. And once a new Hallé violinist has (so to speak) played himself in, his own continued membership will itself help to sustain the Hallé's identity as other players come and go. So in the end all the players could be replaced one by one in this way and we should still have the self-same Hallé orchestra. What the orchestra could not survive is (a) losing all its players – or, say, the whole string section – so that there ceased to be an orchestra at all, or (b) every section splitting to form two new bands, with no way of saying which was the same as the old Hallé.

Similarly for people and other organisms. People can survive the growth, replacement or loss of cells, even of major organs, so long as (a) there are enough such parts after the change to constitute a whole person, and (b) enough of them were there before the change to constitute the same person. But here the question is more pressing: what makes a cell or organ part of a person in the first place? People do not have as obvious a *raison d'être* for their parts to subserve as orchestras do; yet the existence and identity through time of people and their parts is quite as definite as that of orchestras.

We do of course attribute functions to parts of organisms, which reduce in the end to helping the organism – or species, or gene – to survive. But even this attenuated sense of function is lacking for the parts of inanimate things. Artefacts aside, inanimate things have no *raison d'être*. But they too have definite identities and definite part–whole relations to other kinds of things.

Still, perhaps survival is the point, even in inanimate cases. Continuity requirements apply to stones and atoms as to people and orchestras. Maybe all things need parts to secure their identity through time in the way its players secure an orchestra's identity. Perhaps, in short, the continued existence of a thing supplies its own *raison d'être* and hence functions for its parts to fulfil.

This suggestion is temptingly simple, but it will not do. It makes the identity of things depend on that of their parts, at least in the short run: what keeps the Hallé the same orchestra from one moment to the next is that most of its members are the same people. Similarly, the identity of the people from moment to moment depends on that of most of their cells; and so on. So either there is no end to the smaller parts of things, or we come in the end to things whose persisting identity does not depend on that of their parts, for they have none. And I see no *a priori* reason to deny the existence of fundamental particles with no parts of their own.

Things then cannot in general need parts just to keep them in existence. Parts must play a role at once less rudimentary and more active, even if not always as consciously active as players in an orchestra. The fact of the matter, I believe, is this. What makes one thing part of another is that some of its changes are spatial or temporal parts of the other's changes. Thus the musical activities of its players are the causal mechanism, the parts, spatial and temporal, of the orchestral events which constitute a Hallé concert. That is what makes those people parts of the Hallé at that time. The players' activities in turn likewise have causal mechanisms – the movements of their limbs, and changes in their nerves and muscles, which is what in turn makes those limbs, nerves and muscles parts of those people.

Similarly for inanimate things. The mechanism of a macroscopic thing heating up is the increase in kinetic energy of the molecules inside it, which is why they are among its parts and passing cosmic rays are not. Similarly for molecular and atomic changes, which may themselves be parts of macroscopic chemical reactions: their parts in turn are changes in energy in the sub-atomic particles of which atoms and molecules are (consequently) composed. And so on. Fundamental particles, if any, that have no parts are those whose changes, while being the causal mechanism of other changes, either have no such mechanism themselves or consist solely of events other than changes in things.

Parts of things have therefore to be characterised in terms of parts of events that are changes in those things; but this does not mean that things can after all be reduced to events. We still have to distinguish events that are changes from events that are not, which requires independent concepts of things of various kinds. And besides that, one thing's being part of another goes beyond the happening of actual events. Things need not be forever changing in order to exist and to have other things as parts. The Hallé, for example, continues to exist between concerts, and continues then to have its players for its parts. It does so, of course, because if those people *were* to play together, whether they actually do or not, that *would be* a Hallé concert. This is what it is for the Hallé, as an orchestra, to exist at any time, and for certain people to be at that time parts of it.

As for the Hallé, so for other things. For them to exist is for them to have properties, typical of the kinds of things they are, changes in which would take the form of (5) and (6) above (p. 111), not (3) and (4). A thing having such properties is in general not a matter of events occurring, but of what events would occur if others did. In short, properties of things are dispositions: dispositions to produce changes in other properties of the thing, or events which are otherwise parts of or contiguous to its history. To be brittle, for example, is to be disposed to come to an end by breaking if e.g. suitably dropped. To have a certain inertial mass is to be disposed to change one's velocity at such-and-such rates if acted on by specified forces. To believe that the one o'clock news is now on is to be disposed *inter alia* to turn on the radio if one acquires a strong enough desire to hear it. And so on.

In other words, what things with properties embody is not events but restricted cases of causal laws relating events of different kinds. Newton's laws of motion, for example, are embodied in any thing with an inertial mass. The embodiment is a singular fact about the thing, but a quite general and lawlike fact about the events that would display it. It is true of the thing, not merely that it accelerates appropriately when subjected to a specific force, but also that it *would* do so, whether or not the occasion actually arises. Only the restriction of this generalisation about the effects of forces to the world-line of a single thing distinguishes it from the full blown law of motion; but that is just what enables it to be embodied in particular facts about particular things. And as for mass and Newton's laws, so for colour and laws of reflection, brittleness and laws of solid fracture, temperature and laws of radiative absorption and emission, etc.

For a thing to have parts, therefore, is for a causal law embodied in the thing itself to depend on more detailed laws relating intermediate events, laws which the thing's parts embody. And this is why the identity through time of things with parts requires continuity of them. For changes in one part would only produce change in the whole thing if the other parts are there to change as well. One violin playing on its own would not be part of an orchestral concert, any more than one molecule moving on its own is part of a thing with a temperature corresponding to its mean kinetic energy. For the whole thing to be present in these cases, all the parts needed, to provide the mechanism of whatever changes would display the thing's properties, must be present as well – and be so related, spatially in particular, that their changes would interact causally to produce the requisite change in the whole they are parts of. Of course this need not be true of all a thing's properties all the time. A thing can survive the loss of some properties, so long as it does not lose too many all at once. So a thing can indeed survive the loss, and *a fortiori* the subsequent replacement, of some of its parts from time to time. But only if enough remain at any time to preserve some sufficient number of the whole thing's changeable properties.

The above is just a sketch of what needs saying about the identity of things through time, about their parts, about how properties of things relate to their potentialities for change, and other connected matters. But properly to expound and defend an account of all that would digress too much from the business of this book, and must be set aside for another occasion. I hope, though, I have written enough to give substantial and credible content to the concepts – of things, events, causation and parts – I have been relying on in my tenseless account of time, and especially of change. Now I must move on, and use all this to say in tenseless terms why causes precede their effects, how *earlier* differs from *later*, why we know so much less about the future than the past, and what makes prediction possible and time travel impossible. These questions have attracted much attention, but have mostly been treated rather separately. In fact they are all connected, and the materials needed to answer them are now to hand.

9   The direction of time

The direction of time is the difference between *earlier* and *later*; a difference not easy to pin down. *Earlier* and *later* are not differently related to each other, for each is just the other's converse. That is, if any thing, event or date e is earlier than some other thing, event or date $e^\star$, then $e^\star$ is later than e – and *vice versa*. Nor do they have different formal properties: each is irreflexive, transitive and asymmetrical. That is, no e is either earlier or later than itself; for all e, $e^\star$ and $e^{\star\star}$, if e is earlier (later) than $e^\star$ and $e^\star$ is earlier (later) than $e^{\star\star}$, then e is earlier (later) than $e^{\star\star}$; and if e is earlier (later) than $e^\star$, then $e^\star$ is not earlier (later) than e. (This assumes, what I will later show, that time does not go round in a circle. But even if it did, *earlier* and *later* would still not differ in their formal properties: e.g. each would be reflexive and symmetrical.)

The A series could easily distinguish *earlier* and *later*. To be earlier is to be more past or less future, to be later is to be more future or less past. Specifically, e is earlier than $e^\star$ if e is sometime present when $e^\star$ is future and sometime past when $e^\star$ is present, whereas $e^\star$ is never present when e is future or past when e is present. *Earlier* and *later* are clearly definable by the order in which things, events and dates cease to be future and become first present and then past; and the difference between them is that everything moves from future to past, not *vice versa*. If only the A series existed, that would be the direction of time. But as it doesn't, the difference between *earlier* and *later* must be sought elsewhere.

The tensed and tenseless concepts will still be connected, of course, only the connection has to be defined the other way round. To be more past or less future is to be earlier, and to be more future or less past is to be later. More accurately, since tense is really just a mode of thought, what *earlier* and *later* have to define is the difference between past and future tense beliefs: to be true, past tense beliefs have to be held later than whatever they are about, while future tense beliefs have to be held earlier.

What a tenseless difference between *earlier* and *later* has to explain, therefore, is the different roles past and future tense beliefs play in our thought. Why does perception yield past and present tense beliefs whereas action also needs future tense ones? The question is not easy to answer, but the difficulty is not peculiar to the tenseless view. Anyone using past, present and future to explain *earlier* and *later* has to say why we only perceive the past and only affect the future. The difficulty is not met by making this part of what 'past' and 'future' mean, for then we need to know why past and future do not overlap. That past and future are incompatible is the fact to be explained, not an explanation of it.

I will give an explanation, using the tenseless difference between *earlier* and *later*. But before doing that, I must say what the difference is. Perhaps it is *sui generis*. I have remarked how we can often see that one event is earlier, not later, than another. To revive the old example, seeing a clock hand move clockwise is *inter alia* to see it pass '1' just before, not just after, it passes '2'. Being earlier in this case is a perceptible relation between events, as spatial distance often is between things. It no more needs defining than colour does: we just see it.

This view has the merit of not making our ability to tell time from space, and to detect the direction of time, gratuitously and implausibly theoretical. The difference between something visibly moving and something spread out in space is indeed as visible as the difference between black and white. We need no theoretical physics to reassure us of it, nor could physics deny it. Of course physics can sometimes correct our unaided judgment, as when relativity tells us that some events which look to have a definite temporal order really don't. And instruments based on physics vastly extend our ability to measure short and long times and spatial distances. But even when correcting and extending our temporal and spatial judgments, physics itself relies on our making and distinguishing them unaided in familiar cases. The results of physics experiments must themselves be taken in by people, usually by reading spatial arrays of letters or figures one after the other. Physics, in short, cannot impugn the visible distinction between temporal and spatial order, because its own practice relies on it. All physics can do is explain how we draw the distinction, much as it explains how we tell colours by showing how differently our eyes respond to light of different frequencies.

Similarly for the direction of time. Normally we need no theory to tell us which is the earlier of two events. Even when we use slowed-down "action replays" – the temporal equivalent of microscopes – to make visible very short temporal intervals that we could not see unaided, we must be able to see the temporal order of events in the replay itself (just as we must be able to see spatial patterns in a microscope). We can only ever see temporal relations anywhere because we can sometimes see precedence with the naked eye. Here again, physics relies ultimately on our being able to see one event precede another, not the other way round.

This ability moreover can define 'earlier' and 'later' ostensively, just as colour words like 'black' and 'white' can be ostensively defined. Colours too are related by complementary contrasts – e.g. of intensity and hue – which fail on their own to distinguish complementary colours, just as *earlier* and *later* are not distinguished by their complementary relations. A newly sighted man might know all about complementary colour relations and still not tell black from white, because he does not know what either of them looks like. But to tell him what the difference is, we have only to show him, i.e. point out samples of each shade. Having seen what black and white look like, he will know thereafter which is which; the ostensive definition is all it takes.

Similarly with *earlier* and *later*. Suppose someone knew all the facts listed at the start of this chapter, but still did not know which of these relations was which. To tell him the difference, we have only to point out instances. We could point to a clock's second hand and say that it passes '1' just before, not just after, it passes '2'. That will show him what one event preceding another looks like, and how different it looks from the same event succeeding the other. He should then be able to distinguish these relations in other cases, just as he can distinguish black from white. The ability no doubt improves with practice, and may be extended and corrected by collateral knowledge. But in the end, as with colour, it comes down to being able simply to see the difference. No further definition is needed. The direction of time is a visible fact.

The perception of precedence

Tempting as this analogy with seeing colours is, it must be wrong. Consider how it answers the questions posed above. Why do events usually occur before we perceive them, and our actions precede their consequences? By this analogy these should be contingent facts that we observe to be so but might equally well have observed to be otherwise; and that is not so.

It is true enough that we observe these facts. Suppose, to revive another familiar example, I see you turn on the radio when you hear the clock strike one. I see you hear the clock after it strikes, and hear the radio come on after you turn it on. Similarly in other cases. We generally see events precede their perceptions, and actions precede their consequences. And we can, on the other hand, envisage exceptions to the general rule: precognition and backwards causation – e.g. time travel into the past – are not obviously impossible.

But the rule itself is not contingent. Exceptions could not occur wholesale. Events could not *usually* occur after they are perceived, nor actions usually follow on their consequences. Yet this should be possible if seeing precedence were like seeing colour. For the visual sensation which tells me I am seeing something white could come from things of any kind. It doesn't, as a matter of fact, since natural laws govern the colours of materials; but it could. The laws which say that chalk is white and carbon black could easily have been false. Chalk could generally have been black and carbon white; at least, we can easily conceive so. So if seeing precedence were a matter of having peculiar – in this case peculiarly temporal – sensations, the laws which say that events precede their perceptions and actions their consequences could likewise have been generally false. We should be able to conceive those sensations of temporal order occurring generally the other way round. Yet we can clearly conceive no such thing.

Earlier and *later* can anyway not be phenomenal relations as colours are phenomenal properties, for quite a different reason: namely, that the difference between e preceding $e^\star$ and $e^\star$ preceding e lies in the *relata*, not in the relation. In both cases one event precedes and another follows. In other words, both relations are seen whenever either is, because each is only the converse of the other. So even if their instances did give us different sensations, this would never distinguish them as black is visibly distinguished from white, since both sensations would always occur together.

In fact, neither *earlier* nor *later* gives rise to a peculiar kind of sensation when their instances are perceived. When I see *e* precede *e*★, the only sensations I need have are those that reveal to me the two events themselves. What makes me see them to be in that order is not another sensation, but simply that I see them in that order. To see *e* precede *e*★ is first to see *e* and then to see *e*★. The different order in which I see *e* and *e*★ is what distinguishes my seeing *e* precede *e*★ from my seeing *e*★ precede *e*. But then my perceptions of precedence seem to reduce to mere instances of it, not anything independently intelligible which might explain what precedence is.

Nonetheless we should not lightly let go of the idea that precedence is definable by how it is perceived. It is very striking that seeing *e* precede *e*★ means seeing *e* before seeing *e*★. Perceptions do not usually share the features they are perceptions of. Seeing one thing to be larger than another, for example, does not involve sending correspondingly sized pairs of objects up the optic nerve. Feeling hot water does not mean the skin transmits hot water to the brain. There need be nothing thermal about feeling heat, nothing coloured in colour vision, and nothing (relevantly) spatial about perceiving spatial relations. In no other case need perceptions resemble what they are perceptions of; they need only correlate with it. But perceiving temporal order does demand a corresponding temporal ordering of perceptions. That feature of its perception is unique to time, and clearly not accidental. We may still do well to seek in it the source of time's direction.

Let us look more closely at how precedence is perceived. To see *e* precede *e*★ I must see *e* and see *e*★, and see *e* first, but is that all? Suppose I have forgotten seeing *e* when I see *e*★, i.e. I retain no memory of the previous perception that I could by any means recall to mind. Surely I should not then at any time have seen the order of these two events, because I have never connected them in thought. Yet I did see *e* and see *e*★, and see *e* first. So there must be more to it. For me to see *e* precede *e*★, my seeing *e*★ must include something like a memory-trace of my seeing *e*. It need not be an explicit or a conscious memory, but some trace of the earlier perception must somehow be incorporated in the later one. What it might be, and how it might be embodied, is for neurophysiology to say – except for one obvious fact: the trace is an effect of my seeing *e*.

So unless my seeing $e^\star$ is in some way affected by my having seen e, I shall not thereby see their succession. My seeing e needs to affect my seeing $e^\star$ to make those perceptions parts of a causal mechanism which thereby constitutes a whole event, namely my seeing e precede $e^\star$. The same causal connection would of course have been there had I seen $e^\star$ precede e, only the other way round. My seeing e would have been affected by my seeing $e^\star$. So my seeings of these alternative temporal orders do not just differ in the temporal order in which I see the two events. They differ also in the causal order of those seeings. My seeing of the event I see come first has to be a cause, not an effect, of my seeing the other event.

As for me, so (I take it) for everyone; as for seeing, so for hearing and all the other senses – not human senses only, but any sense able to perceive precedence. And as for e and $e^\star$, so for any events whose succession can be perceived. The perception of precedence demands a corresponding causal order in the perceptions of the events whose succession is thereby perceived. In that simple but central fact lies the source of time's direction.

Causes and effects in the perception of time

Before trading on the fact, I must elaborate, defend and qualify it. (Readers willing to take it on trust may skip this section, which has perforce to be rather laborious.) First, the fact's scope is wider than it seems. I said above that e and $e^\star$ were events. They can also be things, temporal "stages" of things, dates or instants: anything which can be seen to be earlier or later than something else. Perceptions of e and $e^\star$ need to be events, but e and $e^\star$ themselves do not.

Admittedly e and $e^\star$ must somehow cause their perceptions, perception being a causal process. Even so, e and $e^\star$ need not be events, so long as events mediate their perception. Things, for example, are only seen when they change, e.g. by emitting or reflecting photons which then travel to the eye. Similarly for thing-stages, which only cause their own successors. Only when a thing changes, thereby generating outside effects, can that stage of it be perceived. Dates and instants are also not immediately perceptible. Seeing an instant or a date means seeing or hearing a thing or event – a clock or chime of bells – which is made to tell the time.

But if events have to mediate our perception of things, thing-stages and dates, so they do for most events. The perception of an event is almost never an immediate effect of it. An event at any distance can only be seen via a chain of contiguous causes and effects, either of contiguous events or of stages of an unchanging thing, such as a photon, transmitted from event to perceiver. And this means nearly all events, because most events are at a distance, and because we cannot perceive most of those that aren't. We may perhaps taste the immediate causes of sensations on our tongues, but we certainly do not see the immediate causes of our visual sensations. I cannot see photons landing on my retina, let alone what goes on later in the optic nerve.

None of this of course prevents most of our perceptions being immediate in the usual sense. We need not perceive distant things and events by *perceiving* the other things and events that mediate our perceptions. On the contrary, as my not perceiving photons illustrates, we perceive very little of our perceptual processes. Normally I see nothing of what links what I see to my eyes. In that sense, I usually see what I see immediately or, as I shall say (to prevent confusion), *directly*.

Not all perception is direct. Seeing times has to be indirect: I can only see the time by seeing a clock. Similarly, we only see photons and electrons via seeing something else. Even things which can be seen directly need not be. We may see them indirectly, say on television, or when a vapour trail shows me a high flying aircraft. And a thing or event may be directly perceptible in some respects and only indirectly perceptible in others. A man whose voice I can hear directly, for instance, while he is out of sight, is only indirectly perceptible to me as being a man rather than a woman.

In short, facts about things and events are what we directly or indirectly see or hear. Which brings me to my second point, this time a qualification. What I have said about perceiving precedence applies only to its direct perception. In indirect perception the successive events may not be separately perceived, and there can be no order, temporal or causal, in non-existent perceptions. We do not directly see, for instance, one billiard ball hit another before the other moves off. Those events happen too quickly for the eye to follow. To verify the order properly – to show, say, that the balls only interact on contact, or to test allegations of coincidence – we need a slowed-down film of the sequence of events.

Perhaps the succession of events is not perceived even indirectly in the billiard ball case, merely inferred from collateral information.

Perhaps succession can only be perceived indirectly by means, such as action replays, which involve directly perceiving corresponding events, and hence a corresponding temporal order. I would not dispute that claim, since it makes no odds to me; but I doubt it. However, all I need is the causal mechanism of direct perception. Succession often is perceived directly in the way I have described, and indirect perceptions of it get their authority only by agreeing with or consistently extrapolating the results of direct perception. To be right, an action replay must preserve the order which a quicker observer would see directly in the events themselves. That is all I need to assume, and why I hereafter confine myself to the direct perception of succession.

My third point is this. I say my seeing e affects my seeing $e^\star$ when I thereby see e precede $e^\star$. But my seeing $e^\star$ must also be an effect of $e^\star$ itself, since perception is a causal process. How can it be an effect of both? The answer is that my seeing $e^\star$, like most events, has many causes, which severally explain its various properties. There is nothing mysterious or problematic in that. I remarked in chapter 8 that a long piece of music could also be loud, despite length and loudness being distinct and separable properties. But if a musical event is both long and loud, the cause of its length may well differ from the cause of its volume. Similarly with my seeing $e^\star$: $e^\star$ causes that event to be my coming to believe that $e^\star$ has happened; my seeing e previously causes it also to be my coming to believe that e preceded $e^\star$. These are distinct beliefs, whose acquisitions are distinct properties of events, just as length and loudness are. But that does not prevent one and the same event being both. Only, if it is, it must differ somehow from my coming to believe that $e^\star$ has happened *without* coming to believe that e preceded it. And the cause of this difference is my previously seeing e.

This difference might in theory have some other cause, unlikely though that is in practice; and that possibility raises the fourth of the points I have to make. Perhaps my seeing $e^\star$ could make me believe that e preceded it without my ever having seen e; and that belief might of course be true. But it would be true then only by co-incidence, not as a result of my perceiving that order of events, because e would *ex hypothesi* not have been perceived at all. In short, succession in events is not perceived if the events themselves are not perceived. Now I dare say that is obvious; but what else perception calls for here is less so, and I should say what I at least will mean by it. So far I have gone along with the usual ambivalence in our use of 'see', 'hear', etc. as to whether our seeing or hearing something implies that it is so. On the one hand, I implied earlier that we might see a succession that failed to exist because the same events would have been seen in the opposite order in other reference frames. On the other hand, I have assumed that seeing e implies that e affects that seeing, and hence that e exists. But I have not said just how far a perception of something can fail the requirements of veridical perception – truth, suitable causation, etc. – without ceasing to be a perception of that thing. That is a nice question, to which I have no general answer. Here, however, apart from my having to perceive first e and then $e^\star$, I think all my perception of e's and $e^\star$'s succession needs is the right causal connection between the perceptions of those events. That seems to me enough to make the consequent belief that e preceded $e^\star$ the product of direct perception, whether the belief is true or false. For even if it is false, its falsity will not result from any defect in my sense of time. It will only be for relativistic reasons, or because e.g. e was so much nearer than $e^\star$ that, although it happened later, light or sound from e arrived first. So even when these perceptions are wrong, they are still direct perceptions of precedence; and they remain so even if the beliefs they generate are later corrected by collateral information.

At least these perceptions will do for me. Whatever meets these conditions, I will call a direct perception of precedence. For what matters, of course, is the fact, not the title. So long as what I call direct perceptions of precedence exist, with the features and authority I say they have, it makes no odds if others would restrict the word 'perception' to veridical instances or, on the other hand, apply it even more loosely than I do.

Fifthly, one feature of what I call perceptions of precedence is that they are changes in the perceiver. This is implicit in what I have already said, but it should be made explicit. To start with, perceptions of anything have to be events, because they have independently identifiable causes and effects – in this case for instance the effect my seeing e has on my seeing $e^\star$. So my seeing something at some time cannot just be one of my temporal stages, i.e. it takes more than my having some special property at that time: some event has to happen. Moreover, the event has to be a change in me, since whatever else perception is (e.g. a visual, aural or other sensation), it is also getting, losing or reinforcing a belief. But beliefs are instantaneously possessed properties of believers, in whom consequently their getting, reinforcement and loss are changes. So I change whenever I perceive something, presumably by some spatial part of me, such as my brain, changing. It is not for me to say, in neurophysiological terms, what sorts of changes perceptions of various kinds are. But I can say that, given my other properties at the time, a perception must be such a change as will make me behave as the acquisition of that belief makes me behave. When, for example, already wanting to hear the one o'clock news, I see from my watch that it now is one o'clock, then whatever that perception is, it must be a change in me such as will *inter alia* cause me to get up and turn on the radio.

Lastly, I must show briefly that the causal mechanism of perceptions of precedence satisfies the assumptions made about causation in chapter 8. The first of these was that causation is *inter alia* how agents perceive the world and act in it: that perception is an effect of what is perceived, and the intended upshot of successful action is an effect of the action itself. Now I have noted in this section that we need not perceive every cause of our perceptions, and in particular I need not perceive my having seen e when that event causes me later to see e precede $e^\star$. But I may do. Sometimes I will recall *seeing e* (as well as recalling e itself) when I see $e^\star$ and thereby see also that e preceded it. Then my seeing $e^\star$ will also be a memory of seeing e, which is a kind of perception of that earlier experience – and linked to it as effect to cause in just the way prescribed in chapter 8.

Causation here is also connected to action as in chapter 8 I said it is. Although seeing e is no action, it may be the intended effect of one, e.g. of looking hopefully to see e happening. Seeing e precede $e^\star$ may well be a further intended effect of the same action; but if so, it can clearly only come about via first seeing e and then $e^\star$. The cause–effect relation between seeing e and seeing $e^\star$ is what makes the latter also the intended upshot of looking to see e precede $e^\star$. It is a perfect example of causation extending the range of intentional action from cause to effect.

The other conditions on causation were that causes are contiguous to their immediate effects, and make their effects more likely than in the circumstances they would otherwise have been. These conditions too are satisfied. Unless I see $e^\star$ immediately after seeing e, there will be some intermediate causal link between the two perceptions. Either a suitable sequence of causally related events will occur between them, or some trace of my seeing *e* will be embodied in an unchanging part of my brain, which will then so respond to the effects of, say, photons arriving from *e** as to make my perception of that event also a perception of *e* preceding it. And whether or not there is such a chain of intermediate causes and effects, that outcome will clearly be far more likely in the circumstances than it would have been had I not seen *e* at all.

Perceived succession and successive perceptions

I hope I have made the causal link clear and credible between my seeing *e* and my seeing *e** when I thereby see *e* to be earlier than *e**. I have elaborated and defended it at length because my tenseless account of the direction of time depends on it: the difference between *earlier* and *later* does after all depend on how we tell the difference. It does so via the causal order of our perceptions of *e* and *e**. The crucial fact is that I see *e* precede *e** only when my seeing of *e** is suitably affected by my seeing *e*; if the causal link runs the other way, I will see *e** precede *e*. It follows, as we shall see, that to be affected is to be later, to be the cause, earlier. The direction of time is the direction of causation. This criterion, of course, is nothing new. I showed in chapter 4 how relativity uses it to distinguish time from space. But it is not usually derived from how we perceive precedence. And before deriving it, I should say why I think the derivation necessary. Why not define time's direction immediately as the direction of causation?

Now I have made causation the mechanism of perception and action, and have said that events could not usually occur after being perceived, nor actions usually after their consequences. So I do think causes must mostly precede their effects. But that fact seems to me to need explaining: it is evident, but by no means self-evident. And it is not evident at all that causes *never* occur after their effects. 'Effect' does not *mean* the later of two causally connected events or thing-stages; nor does 'later' *mean* the temporal relation an effect has to its cause. If causal and temporal relations were as simply linked as that, then observing either would settle immediately whether the other held, which it does not. I know, for example, that hearing people speak is an effect, not a cause, of their speaking, but this knowledge does not immediately rule out my occasionally hearing what people say before they say it. Conversely, as I have insisted throughout this chapter, we often see the temporal order of events; but we do not thereby automatically see which (if either) affects the other. When I see e precede $e^\star$, my seeing $e^\star$ is affected by my seeing e, but $e^\star$ itself need not be affected by e. $e^\star$ need not even be later than e – my perception might be wrong – and even if it is, e and $e^\star$ could still be causally independent of each other. And if they can be independent, why can they not be causally linked the wrong way round? Nothing said so far prevents e being affected by $e^\star$, even when e is perceptibly the earlier event.

Nor can causes be defined to be always or generally earlier than their effects. The central question would then simply have to be rephrased: why do perception and action generally depend as they do on causation so defined? Putting the question that way is no help at all. I prefer therefore to put it properly, with causation understood – as it is – to be the mechanism of perception and action: why do we generally perceive only what is past and act only on the future?

But in the direct perception of precedence, causation rightly conceived *does* settle the temporal order of events – not of the events perceived, but of our perceptions of them. I see directly that e precedes $e^\star$ only when my seeing e affects my seeing $e^\star$; and *seeing directly that e precedes $e^\star$ entails seeing e before seeing $e^\star$*. The causal order of my perceptions of e and $e^\star$ in these circumstances fixes their temporal order.

The causal test for the direction of time here really is beyond dispute. Without it, the causal and temporal orders of my seeing e and my seeing $e^\star$ would in this case only contingently coincide. But the causal order is what decides whether I perceive e to precede $e^\star$ or *vice versa*. So unless that order also decides which of the two events I see first, it will be merely contingent that I first see the event which – rightly or wrongly – I see to *be* first. The temporal order in which we perceive events could conceivably differ from the order we thereby directly perceive them to have. That, I maintain, is not conceivable.

I can, however, conceive of two misconceptions that might make readers resist this modest proposal, and which I should therefore remove before making it less modest. One is that I am crediting people with infallible awareness of the succession of their own perceptions, which flouts the neurotic conviction of many philosophers that no one is infallibly aware of anything. I do not, I confess, share the conviction, but I am not flouting it here. For one thing, what we are normally aware of is the temporal order of e and $e^\star$, not of our perceptions of them, and there is nothing infallible about that: e and $e^\star$ need not occur in the order I see them in. But even if I could perceive my own perceptions, my perception of their succession still need not be infallible. Suppose e and $e^\star$ are themselves among my own seeings of other events. No doubt my perceptions of e and $e^\star$ could hardly come in a different order from e and $e^\star$ themselves, since there are no relativistic effects in this case and I presumably take about as long to become conscious of e as of $e^\star$. Still, these are only contingent facts about the causal mechanism of consciousness. It *could* conceivably take so much longer for me to perceive e (the first of my seeings) that I actually perceive it only after perceiving my later seeing $e^\star$. So in principle people could mistake the temporal order even of their own perceptions. The fallibility axiom, for what it is worth, is consistent with everything I say.

Anyway, I have said nothing about conscious awareness in saying how precedence is perceived. On the contrary, I have gone out of my way to discredit the idea that perceiving precedence involves being conscious of temporal sensations. Not so: it involves no more than getting beliefs about temporal order by the causal mechanism I have been discussing. Whether or not I am conscious of this mechanism, or of the beliefs it engenders, is immaterial. I have used my consciously seeing one event succeed another as an example of it, but I have not traded on the consciousness involved in human sight. The causal mechanism I have described must obviously occur in all senses, including those of animals wholly unconscious of how they see and hear things. I will even grant beliefs to animals without language or concepts to express them in, including beliefs about succession – which animals can surely get if they can get beliefs at all. If a dog can see anything, it can surely see a cat moving, which means seeing it successively occupy a number of different spatial positions. And it is just as certain in this as in the human case that the order in which a dog sights a cat in different places must be the same as the order the dog thereby directly sees the cat to occupy them in.

The other misconception I must forestall is that I have begged the question against backward causation, i.e. against some events preceding their own causes. Now I make no bones of my intention to prove that to be impossible, and to use my account of time's direction to do so. But I have not done so yet, and readily admit that occasional backward causation is at least conceivable. So I may not yet assume without argument something which backward causation would immediately refute. But my modest proposal may well be opened to that objection by the following train of thought. Imagine I am travelling backward in time, which is conceivable if backward causation is, since all it means is that all causal processes inside me run backwards, i.e. every effect within my body comes before its causes instead of after them. In particular, therefore, my perceptual processes will run backward. Suppose then that while travelling I see *e* precede *e*★, which implies on my account that my seeing *e* affects my seeing *e*★, but not *vice versa*. But if my seeing *e*★ is an effect of my seeing *e*, it follows here that it occurs earlier, not later. That is, I actually see *e*★ *before* I see *e*, despite my directly seeing those events to occur the other way round. In short, when travelling backward in time, the temporal order in which I perceive events differs from the order in which I thereby perceive them to occur. So if backward causation, and therefore backward time travel, is possible, seeing *e* precede *e*★ does not entail seeing *e* before *e*★. Assuming that it does seems therefore to beg a question that has yet to be settled.

This train of thought cannot be stopped by distinguishing perceptions from other events and tying temporal to causal order only for perceptions. Any such distinction would be quite *ad hoc*: I can see no reason to think perceptions are alone incapable of backward causation. And anyway I see no relevant distinction between perceptions and other events. For the fact is that *any* kind of event could be a perception. It is not being of some special kind – e.g. electrical or chemical or organic – that makes an event a perception. Perception is simply a causal process of acquiring belief, a process from which no kind of event can be excluded *a priori*. It is an entirely empirical question what events occur in the working of our own sense organs, and anyway I am not interested only in human perception. My proposal is to apply to all perceptions of precedence, by all conceivable perceivers, among all sorts of events, things and dates, and it must be defensible as such. I assume therefore that any thing, however large, small or otherwise exotic, which is capable of behaviour complex enough to reveal states of desire and belief, is apt to acquire beliefs by perception; and depending on how it is made up, its perceptions can be events of any kind. So any event, of any kind, whose effects occur before it does will seemingly provide a counterexample to my proposal.

In fact, however, my proposal does not beg the question against backward causation. To see why not, we must look more closely at backward time travel, and observe in particular that it always involves alternative measures of the temporal separation of events. Think of Dr Who taking ten minutes in his time machine, *Tardis*, to travel back a century. His getting in and getting out are events both in the outside world he travels in and in the world-line of *Tardis* itself, and they must be supposed to have two equally good temporal separations: a hundred years one way in the outside world and ten minutes the other way inside the time machine. These measures we may suppose supplied by standard clocks, exactly the same both inside and outside *Tardis*. The reason they give startlingly different measures of the temporal separation of the same events is, of course, that their causal processes run at different rates and in opposite directions. But seen from inside *Tardis*, its clocks, like all other causal processes, run exactly as usual. The clock hands move clockwise, and people breathe and speak as usual all at the normal rate. Everyone and everything behave absolutely normally throughout the ten minute trip: a film of any of it would be quite indistinguishable from a film taken of the same events in the world outside. In short, all the usual distinctions of time and tense, of earlier and later, can be drawn in *Tardis* – only because the causal processes used to draw them all run counter to the same processes in the world outside, so will the distinctions themselves. If *Tardis*'s clocks all run backward, so does *Tardis* time. So if during the trip I see e precede $e^\star$, it will still follow in *Tardis*, as it does elsewhere, that I see e before I see $e^\star$.

Backward time travel need not divorce the temporal and causal orders of any events, and *a fortiori* not of those involved in perceiving precedence. Nor therefore need backward causation in general. Any effect preceding its cause may for present purposes be thought of as contained in a miniature *Tardis*, defining its own locally reversed time direction to match its reversed causation. I admit this is not the most natural way to describe these cases – as the very title 'backward causation' proves – but it will do for the time being. Pending their disproof in chapter 10, it will reconcile them temporarily to a causal criterion for time's direction, and so to my own much more modest proposal.

Causation and the direction of time

So much for possible misconceptions. I will now make my proposal less modest, exploiting my admission in the last section that any event could be a perception. Consequently, any causally ordered pair of events could make up a perception of precedence. Most do not; but not because they are of a kind inherently incapable of being perceptions, since there are no such kinds. They simply happen not to be suitably embedded in a network of other events, namely changes in things so interrelated as to be parts of a sense organ in a believer of some sort. Still, we can always envisage them so embedded, with – in particular – the same causal and temporal orders as they actually have. They would then constitute a perception of precedence, so their causal and temporal orders would have to coincide. But *ex hypothesi* these orders are their actual ones; so their causal and temporal orders have to coincide anyway. The local temporal order of all pairs of events is fixed by their causal order.

When neither of two events affects the other, and would not unless they were located elsewhere in spacetime, then of course they could not as they stand constitute a perception of precedence, and I therefore give them no temporal order. So I can accommodate relativity's denying absolute temporal order to pairs of events too far apart to affect each other, and their having a definite temporal order in any one reference frame. For two events may both affect a distant observer even if they cannot affect each other. In particular, both may be seen, and seen to have the same temporal order by all observers at rest relative to each other.

My modest proposal is not restricted to events. It also settles the succession of things and of their temporal stages. I said earlier that things are seen only when they change; but that is not quite true. A thing can also be seen in its beginning and ending, which although not changes in it are still events, able to cause perceptions. They could also *be* perceptions, which could constitute between them a perception of precedence. They are certainly causally related: we saw in chapter 8 that a thing's temporal stages are related as cause to effect; so therefore are its first and last stages, and hence its beginning and ending. Now if the two events did constitute a perception of precedence, the earlier one, i.e. the beginning, would have to be whichever of them affected the other. So that in any case must be the answer. The direction of time from a thing's start to its finish is the direction of causation between those two events.

As for time's direction along one world-line, so for its direction between two or more world-lines. Chapter 8 showed how things can contain a succession of spatial parts. If the beginning of one part and the end of another are causally related, they could constitute the whole thing perceiving some succession. But any two causally related ends of world-lines could constitute a perception of precedence in some larger whole, so the effect must anyway be the later of the two events. Thus when the end of one thing causes the start of another, as when splitting an atom creates new particles, the new thing must start life after the other's demise. Conversely, when the start of one thing causes the end of another, as when a mother dies in giving birth, the two things' dates must overlap. And where as two things stand no causal link is possible between the end of one and the start of the other, their dates will overlap in some reference frames and not in others: their temporal order will be indeterminate.

Finally, my proposal applies also to the temporal stages of things. These are mostly identified by date – e.g. London at the end of 1981 – so their temporal order is built into their identity; but this need not be so. A stage of some thing could for instance be identified by its being a certain distance from something moving past it. It is then an open question which is the earlier of two such stages, and I should be able to get their temporal from their causal order. So I can, though not directly, since perceptions have to be events: thing stages, not being events, cannot themselves be perceptions. But we can always consider instead two events coincident in spacetime with the two stages. Since both are stages of the same thing, one will be among the causes of the other, so the event coincident with it can affect the other event via intermediate stages of the thing itself. So it is the earlier of the two events, and its coincident stage therefore the earlier of the two stages. All along the world-line of even an unchanging thing, as well as from one temporal end of it to the other, the direction of time is the direction of causation.

I conclude that time's direction is always the direction of causation, because of how precedence is directly perceived. That is my tenseless account of how *earlier* differs from *later*. If it is right, it should answer the various questions set for it in the course of this chapter.

First, why could effects not usually precede their causes? The answer to that is not as immediate as it looks. That is, it is not that effects never precede their causes, and so could not usually do so. Recall that I have not yet ruled out backward causation, merely redescribed it as a local reversal of both causation and time. Why then, if such local reversals could occur, could they not predominate? The reason is that if we had rival time directions to choose between, we should take "the" direction of time to be the one predominant in our vicinity. It is basically a matter of majority vote. *Tardis* only travels back in our time because there are fewer people in it than outside it. If most of us were inside, we should take the rest of the world to be travelling backward in our *Tardis* time.

Fortunately, there are no rival time directions to choose between. That will be shown in chapter 10, but I shall anticipate the result in order to simplify the other questions I have to answer. Specifically, I will say why we never perceive the future and act on the past, not why we rarely do so. I shall not thereby beg the question to be answered in chapter 10, since no argument used there depends on this simplification. And that being so, there is no merit in answering complicated questions which never arise rather than simple ones which do.

The answer to these simple questions is as follows. Causation is *inter alia* the means both of perception and action: all my results have been derived on that understanding of it. Every perception is therefore an effect of whatever is thereby perceived, and therefore always starts later than it does. So if a temporally token-reflexive belief about what is perceived, generated in the perceiver by the perception, is to be true, its truth conditions cannot require what is perceived to be later than the perception itself. That is, perception cannot be the acquisition of true future tense belief about what is directly perceived. Indeed, it can only be the acquisition of present tense belief about it provided the A series interval involved is long enough to encompass both what is perceived and its perception. Whereas I can see something of what is happening on the sun *today*, for example, I cannot see what is happening there *this minute*, because it takes sunlight more than a minute to get here. Still, this restriction on perception of the present is not very serious. We get most of our perceptions by seeing things and events quite close by, and light covers terrestrial distances in much shorter times than we normally need to discriminate. For most practical purposes we can see what is going on now.

That is why perception tells us directly only about the past and the present. The reason we act only on the future is this. Causation is the means we act by, i.e. if the intended upshot of an action is something other than the action itself, it must be among the action's intended effects. That means the action must precede it. Actions however themselves need to be caused, *inter alia* (as we saw in chapter 5) by the agent acquiring token-reflexive beliefs like the belief that it is now one o'clock. But I need more than that present tense belief to make me press a switch in order to turn on the radio for the one o'clock news. I must also believe that the news coming on will be an upshot, i.e. an effect, of my pressing the switch, which means believing that the switch is to be pressed before the news comes on. And I need to believe all this before I act, or I shall have no cause to act in good time. So a tenseless belief about the temporal order of action and upshot would not be enough. I need a belief, about the radio being more likely to come on if the switch is pressed, whose truth will in the circumstances make it sensible to press the switch. Which means a belief that is only true before the event it is about takes place, viz. a future tense belief. And as for this case, so for all action done to bring about something other than itself. Its causation demands not only past and present tense beliefs, but also future tense beliefs about what the alternative upshots would be of acting and not acting.

That is my tenseless explanation of why perception relates peculiarly to the past and action to the future, i.e. of the different roles past and future tense beliefs play in our thought. Past tense belief is the typical product of perception because its truth conditions are satisfied only by earlier events, which events perceived, being causes of perception, have to be. Future tense beliefs are needed to cause timely action because their truth conditions are satisfied only by later events, which intended upshots of action, being effects of it, have to be.

But why can I not act on what I have already perceived? That is the last and hardest of the questions I have to answer. All my other answers depend for their force on the answer to this one, and so does the direction of time itself. For if we could generally act on what we have perceived, the distinction between past and future, as the distinct realms respectively of perception and action, would disappear. And so therefore, on my tenseless account, would the direction of time. Indeed it would disappear on any causal theory of time's direction, whether derived from the perception of precedence or not. Causation being the means both of action and perception, being able to act on what we have perceived requires – as we shall see – that one event could, albeit indirectly, be at once both a cause and an effect of another event. If that were to happen, the two events would have no causal order, any more than they do in special relativity when too far apart to affect each other; and as in that case, the causal criterion would then fail to give them a temporal order. And if pairs of events were in general causally related both ways if at all, the causal criterion would be unable to give time any direction whatever. If the difference between *earlier* and *later* is only the difference between cause and effect, it will come to nothing if every effect also affects its own cause.

I do not take this fact to indicate a deficiency in the causal criterion. On the contrary, the right moral to draw from a lack of causal order may well be that then there is no temporal order. That is the moral drawn by special relativity of certain causally unrelated events, and it is the moral I would draw of events causally related in both directions. Where perceiving events does not show them immune to being acted on thereafter, time really has no direction. However, I shall not argue the case for thus describing that fantastic situation. The real problem is not how to describe it, but to say why it is fantastic. That is the problem I propose to solve in the next and final chapter.

10 Prediction, time travel and backward causation

Prediction

To disprove backward causation, I must first draw out some consequences of it, starting with its consequences for prediction. Where we can affect what we have perceived, we can perceive as we act some effects of our action. And once effects have been perceived they cannot be predicted. Yet it is of the essence of action that agents can as they act predict their action's effects. This should be obvious, but is apt to be obscured by some common misconceptions of prediction. To remove them, and so to set the stage for later argument, I must first discuss at some length prediction's relation to perception.

When I say an event is predictable, I do not mean there is reason to predict it. In that common sense of 'predictable', the effects of action are often unpredictable. But that sense, though common, is wrong. Prediction does not need reasons. I can pick my winners with a pin, but I still expect my bookmaker to admit I have predicted them and pay me my winnings.

What then is prediction? Reasons apart, it is supposed to be saying in advance that something will happen: that a war or an election will take place, that a car will crash or a marriage survive. If things do so fall out, the prediction is successful; if not, not. Prediction, however, is not really confined to the future. One can also predict the present and the past. Suppose I accuse Fred, who claims only to have seen the film, of having read *War and Peace*, and his annotated copy bears me out. I call that a successful prediction, even though his reading preceded my prediction of it. To talk of prediction here I fear flouts usage: 'postdiction' and 'retrodiction' are the unlovely terms prescribed for these cases. I shall do without them. They are superfluous and, what is worse, misleading; they mark the wrong distinction. They suggest that the point of predicting something is to do so before it happens, whereas the real point is to do so before it is definitely known to happen.

That prediction anticipates conclusive knowledge of a fact, rather than the fact itself, is shown by our talk of predicting laws of nature, kinds of elementary particles and the existence of mathematical proofs. These are not events which happen after they are predicted. They are not events at all, and if they exist, they do so as much before as after their prediction. Yet talk of predicting them makes perfectly clear sense. Here it is quite clear what needs to come after a prediction, namely more decisive evidence for or against its truth. And that, I submit, is all prediction ever needs.

One might try to rescue usage by denying that such general predictions say all they seem to. That is, perhaps what they predict is not the law or proof itself but the forthcoming evidence for it. But this clearly is not so. The law, or proof or natural kind, really is what is predicted. For one thing, someone making such a prediction may have no idea when or where – or even whether – more evidence will be found, nor what form it will take. When Dirac predicted the existence of magnetic monopoles, he did not thereby predict the observation decades later which those who made it took to verify his prediction. And even when future evidence is foreseen, it still is not the point. Eddington went abroad to test general relativity's prediction of how much light is, and always has been, bent by nearby massive bodies; not merely to test the prediction, footling in itself, that during a coming eclipse he would see a little shift in the position of a star near the sun.

I will therefore put past, present and timeless matters along with future ones within the purview of prediction. That I admit is not good English, but good English here does not conduce to good philosophy. Still, even in my sense of it, prediction does fundamentally as well as usually concern future events, namely the future evidence which settles its success or failure. And the significance of this evidence being future rather than present or past is its not being available to us now.

For prediction to be possible, we must know less about the future than about the past. Otherwise, just as we can now call to mind knowledge acquired earlier, so we could now call to mind knowledge yet to be acquired, including our future knowledge of past, present and timeless matters. And if we could do that, prediction as I mean it would be unknown. For there is no prediction in any serious sense, even of a future state of affairs, once our knowledge of it is as conclusive as it can be. If I know, for example, when Fred was born, I thereby know the dates of all his birthdays, future as well as past. I can predict that he will live to see future birthdays – that does remain to be seen – but I cannot seriously predict their dates. In the trivial dictionary sense I can: I can state in advance the date of his next birthday. But I need not wait to see if I am right; and if I do wait, there will be nothing relevant for me to see. A birthday, as opposed to celebrations of it, is not a perceptible event. It is just a little piece of chronological ageing, which we saw in chapter 8 has no effects, and *a fortiori* has none to be perceived by.

If Eddington had known as conclusively as I know the date of Fred's next birthday what the upshot would be of his expedition, he could likewise have made no serious prediction about it that he either need or could have tested. There would have been nothing relevant there for him to go and see. But of course there was something there for him to see. As it happens, it was more or less what he predicted. But in any case, its previous inaccessibility to him was what gave his voyage point and made his previous statements about its upshot predictions.

Predictions and reliable perception

The acquisition of evidence that settles the success or failure of prediction is perception. Eddington's prediction was verified by his seeing a star shift its position near the sun. The test, albeit inconclusive, of Dirac's prediction of magnetic monopoles was the indirect perception of a cosmic ray. The prediction even of a mathematical proof is settled by some qualified person hearing a token of it or seeing one written down.

Predictions are made because the perceptions which would settle them cannot be had in advance. We cannot perceive the upshot of an action, undertaken as Eddington's was to check a prediction, before the upshot occurs. But the upshot of such an action is itself a perception, the seeing for instance of a star during an eclipse. Not only therefore must the eclipse not be visible before it happens, the seeing of it must not be seen in advance. If we could now perceive the perceptions we are going to have, we should in effect be having them now. They would never be news, and consequently never be perceptions. For perceptions to occur at all, they too, like the events they are perceptions of, can in advance be no more than predictable.

In short, perception itself is only possible because prediction is, and prediction depends on the impossibility of perceiving beforehand what the effect of an action will be – or, put the other way round, the impossibility of affecting what we have perceived. Where that is possible, the prediction and perception of future events are alike prevented.

I must emphasise that perceptions need not be incorrigible to be able to settle predictions. The memories and records of what Eddington saw are not proof against subsequent correction, and even mathematicians are not immune to having mistakes uncovered later in their work. But what corrects a perception is another perception settling the truth of a prediction of a future event, namely the prediction that action undertaken to check the first perception's truth will have the effect of confirming it. Perception remains the final arbiter.

I admitted in chapter 9 that perception need not be veridical to be perception, and that now turns out to be just as well. One perception could hardly correct another if both had to be true to be perceptions. But perceptions can be more or less reliable, i.e. more or less likely to deliver the truth, and when using one perception to check another we naturally try to make the later one the more reliable of the two. If it were not the more reliable, it would be perverse to use it to correct its predecessor.

Since the authority of perceptions depends on their reliability, I must say something about what that is. For reasons painfully familiar to philosophers, I shall only say when our perceptions *are* reliable, not when we know they are, and what I say even about that will perforce be very sketchy. I make no claims to treat the subject as fully as it needs, merely as fully as is needed here. And here it suffices to say that the reliability of a perception has nothing to do with the perceiver having some introspectible justification for the belief it delivers. It is merely a matter of the perception being of a kind that delivers true belief in a high proportion of similar cases. In the simple cases which concern me, of the perceptions that settle predictions, it is a matter of being appropriately caused.

I have said already that causation is the mechanism of perception, and specifically that events perceived must affect events that are perceptions of them, whether or not the perceptions are veridical. It now remains to say how causation serves also to fix how reliable perception is. But first I must forestall an obvious objection to invoking causation at all in the case of false perceptions. Suppose I perceive an event and my perception is false because there *is* no such event as the one I perceive. How can a non-existent event be a cause of a perception? Well, nonentities of course cannot be causes, but that fact presents fewer problems here than it appears to. My having misperceived an event does not mean I have perceived what does not exist. Suppose for instance I see (what I take to be) a swallow flying past which is in fact a swift. My perception is wrong, and I see no flying swallow. The event I saw was not the non-existent flying of a swallow; it was the actual flying of a swift. That is the event which had (via my eyes) to make me acquire this admittedly false belief so that the belief could be a product of perception.

There may be cases of false perception, when belief is acquired by events affecting my senses, in which the event I misperceive is not among them. But I need not go into such cases in order to discuss the reliability of perception. In all the perceptions I need consider, the event perceived can be taken to exist and to affect the perception, even if in fact it is not *as* perceived. When for brevity I talk of seeing events which do not occur, this must be understood as shorthand for misperceiving events which do.

Granted then that the perceived event is a cause of its perception, what else causal is needed to make its perception reliable? So far I have only required causes to make their effects more likely than in the circumstances they would otherwise have been, and I am not going to strengthen that requirement for perception *per se*. Provided the other conditions on perception are met, I reckon I see an event even if it does not occur, so long as that perception would in the circumstances have been made somewhat more likely by its occurrence. It may be that even for perception the increase in probability should be substantial; but since it makes no odds to the ensuing argument, I shall leave that question open. For reliable perception, however, the increase of probability clearly must be substantial. For really reliable perception, an event must in the perceptual circumstances make me almost certain to see it as it is.

Reliability is a property of perceptual situations. Good lighting enables normally sighted people to recognise colours rightly almost every time; suitably sited thermometers provide reliable visible displays of temperature; and so on. Now when these perceptual techniques work, their working is no accident. Perceptual situations embody special cases of statistical laws, showing how events of various kinds make the corresponding beliefs they cause in suitably made and placed perceivers more or less probably true. The higher the probability, the more reliable the situation, ideally of course with a probability 1 of getting true beliefs.

The prediction and testing of the laws which make our perceptions more or less reliable is part of the business of science, a special case of predicting and testing laws in general. Nor is there any vicious circularity in the fact that predicted laws of reliable perception must, if we are to have reason to rely on them, themselves be tested by reliable perceptions. We do not have to know *a priori* that the perceptions we use to test the reliability of our perceptions are reliable. They merely have to *be* reliable; and if some are, we shall be able to verify the fact *a posteriori*, and use them to correct others.

This in brief is how causation makes perceptions reliable. They are reliable to the extent that statistical laws, governing the reactions of perceivers to the effects of events on their senses, make the beliefs thereby generated in them about those events likely to be true. And to the extent that perceptions are reliable, they are authoritative.

What I mean by the authority of perception is the authority it has in settling the fate of predictions, and specifically its authority over any reason there may have been for making the prediction. I cannot too strongly emphasise how absolute the authority of even moderately reliable perceptions is in this respect. Suppose you predict, what I hope you believe, that this copy of this book will not explode in the next five minutes. There are, I trust, solid and sufficient grounds for expecting it not to; sufficient for you – rightly – not to think it worth increasing them by e.g. dumping the book in water, despite the fact that your life may depend on your prediction's truth.

But what right have you to be so confident – or would you have even if you had dumped the book in water? For however much evidence you gather in support of your prediction, it will be as nothing if in two minutes' time you see the flash and feel the blast as the book explodes. You would not, I take it, as you pick yourself up off the floor, use the present grounds of your prediction, strong as they are, to defend its truth against the testimony of your burned face and lacerated limbs. And if the book does survive the interim, it will be your future perception of that fact, not your present grounds for expecting it, which will then persuade you of your prediction's success. So why should you now place so much faith in what will then be so negligible a part of your evidence for the truth of this prediction?

This in my view is the heart of Hume's notorious problem of induction, of saying how we can know that a prediction will succeed, or estimate at least its chances of success. I take the problem to be deep, difficult and not yet solved. Fortunately my business here is not to try and solve it, but to say how it arises: to say why future events can only be predicted, not yet perceived.

The generality of predictions

The answer of course will be that backward causation, which the perception of future events would require, is impossible. But before proving that, one or two minor matters need to be disposed of. The first is the so-called "generality of predictions", a thesis which says that predictions about wholly future things and events have to be general.

I gave an instance of this thesis in chapter 2, namely George III's difficulty in referring to Elizabeth II in the way she can certainly refer to him. The question there was whether this showed she did not exist to be referred to in the future of his world. I suggested not, since the difficulty could be explained in other ways. Now we know it must be, it is time to look at the matter more generally and more closely.

The thesis is that singular predictions about wholly future things and events are impossible. A singular prediction is one about a specific thing or event, as opposed to a general prediction of there being or not being one or more things or events of some kind. That there will be twenty-seven murders in London in May 2079 is a prediction that is general about murders and people and singular about London. That a certain Fred will be one of the victims appears to be a singular prediction about that Fred. The singularity of such a prediction is, however, sometimes denied, usually on the grounds that its apparent subject, Fred, being as yet unconceived, does not yet exist; and so, like all mere possibilities, lacks a definite identity. Only his existence could pick one particular Fred out of all the similar people there might be in London in 2079, and that existence is not yet available. Therefore the prediction cannot be about any one future Fred rather than any other, and must just be that there will in that month be a murder of some Cockney Fred or other.

Suppose there is, suppose it is a Fred Smith; still we cannot say now that the prediction is specifically about him, since it would succeed just as well were he to shoot a Fred Jones – or even another Fred Smith – instead of getting shot himself. Any murdered Fred would do; so the prediction is really general, and not singular as it appears to be.

Not all singular predictions are supposed to be impossible. Once a Fred Smith comes to exist, we can predict of him that he will be murdered, just as we can later see whether or not he is. That prediction really is singular about Fred: no other murdered Fred would satisfy it. But then Fred in this case is not future at the time the prediction is made. His murder is future, but the prediction is only general about the murder. It says only that there will be such an event. It does not try to give the event a particular identity; any of the many possible ways Fred could be murdered that month will do. So even in this case, the rule survives that predictions of later things and events are not singular.

Whether this rule is right or not, I obviously cannot accept the reason I have cited for it. Futurity, we have seen, is no property of anything, and can therefore deprive no real event, thing or person of anything. In particular, it cannot deprive people of definite existence and identity. Any actual future Fred is as much marked off by existence from his innumerable possible variants as is any past or present Fred. Provided our prediction is detailed enough to pick out just one of the actual Freds, his mere futurity could not prevent it being a singular prediction about that very man. However, it is undeniably hard to believe in singular predictions about things and events too far ahead. The generality of predictions thesis has an appeal independent of the appeal of real tenses. Can it be given a tenseless basis?

I indicated in chapter 2 what the tenseless explanation might be in the case of George III and Elizabeth II. Let me now elaborate it somewhat, varying the example. Bertrand Russell could have written about Leibniz, as in fact he did. It is not so easy to conceive of Leibniz writing specifically about Russell, however interested and prescient he might have been. Now, as I said apropos of George III, too much should not be made of this. Given that there is no backward causation, Russell was necessarily wholly imperceptible to anyone of or before Leibniz's time. It is hardly credible therefore that Leibniz could have known enough to pick Russell out from all his contemporaries; and that fact alone may well suffice to explain why we believe that Leibniz could not have referred to him.

Suppose, however, for the sake of argument, that Leibniz could have known enough to pick out Russell: what then? It is admittedly hard to assess the consequences of incredible suppositions; but I can conceive that even then Leibniz's predictions would not have been singular. That would be so if, as some philosophers have suggested, the act of referring to a person (or thing or event) has to be among the direct or indirect effects of his or her life. The idea roughly is that what makes Leibniz the subject of Russell's work is not just that Russell knew a lot, but that his knowledge of e.g. the relevant texts can be traced back causally, through their successive printings, to Leibniz's own activities in writing them. If that sort of causal connection is necessary for referring to things and events, then indeed Leibniz could not without backward causation have referred to Russell, however much he knew. Since no effects of Russell's life preceded it, none in particular could link Russell to Leibniz in the way Leibniz's writing is linked to Russell. Leibniz would be confined to general predictions about twentieth-century philosophy; Russell's work might as a matter of fact have verified them, but the work of anyone else answering to Leibniz's descriptions of Russell would have done just as well.

How much truth there is in causal accounts of reference I am not sure, and the topic is anyway too large to tackle here. Here it is pertinent only to remark that, on such accounts, the lack of backward causation would limit, as well as create, possibilities for singular prediction. The intuition that they are somewhat limited has undoubtedly encouraged the thought that future entities must therefore be less real, substantial or definite than past and present ones are. But that, we now see, not only cannot be the explanation, it need not be. The intuition behind the generality of predictions thesis may be sound, but its proper application is to assessing theories about how we can refer to things and events far off in space and time, not to bolstering the myth that the business of prediction is to speak of what has not yet come to be.

The flow of time

The next minor matter to be disposed of is the flow of time. Several aspects of it have been dealt with already. The unanimity of our travel, with its mysteriously fixed and constant rate, was dealt with first, as a trivial by-product of the way our tensed beliefs' truth conditions depend on when we have them. Then our awareness of the flow of time was identified at the end of chapter 7 with the changes of tense we consequently need to keep making in our beliefs about things and events in order to keep them true. And now that the difference between *earlier* and *later*, which these explanations took for granted, has itself been explained in chapter 9, I can complete my tenseless account of the flow of time by explaining its direction. That is, I can say why it takes us forward into the future rather than back into the past (ignoring any counteracting effects of simultaneous backward time travel, since that will turn out to be impossible in any case).

According to chapter 9, going forward in time means going toward the upshots of our actions and away from the things and events we recall having perceived. We see now that this also means going toward what we predict, i.e. toward the experience of settling by perception a prediction's fate. So what I have to explain is why the flow of time takes us that way, instead of taking us toward what we recall perceiving and away from the predictable upshots of our actions. Why do we perceive predictions to precede rather than follow the perceptions that supersede them – why does the knowledge gained by perception grow rather than diminish?

The answer lies in the causal machinery of recollection. Recollecting something is in effect perceiving it again via the original perception of it. Being a species of perception, recollection has its own causal mechanism, the mechanism of memory. Suppose I remember seeing an event e. My seeing e must have left a trace in my mind, like the trace which enables me to see later that e preceded another event $e^\star$. That perception of $e^\star$ succeeding e indeed *is* a recollection of e, though of course not necessarily a conscious one. Direct perceptions of precedence inevitably involve recalling what is thereby perceived to be the earlier event (or thing, or whatever e and $e^\star$ are).

But now suppose I also directly see $e^{\star\star}$ succeed $e^\star$. This will happen when I see $e^{\star\star}$, suitably affected by my seeing $e^\star$. So, by our causal criterion, it happens after I see $e^\star$ and *a fortiori* after I thereby see $e^\star$ succeed e. It may therefore also be so affected by that earlier perception as to incorporate a *recollection* of it, i.e. of my having seen e succeeded by $e^\star$. Similarly, my seeing yet another event e*** succeed e** may incorporate recollections of my having first seen e* and then e** succeed e. And so on. In short, as other events are successively seen to succeed each other, so e may thereby be seen to have been succeeded by increasing numbers of successive events. That is, the temporal distance of my successive perceptions from e will if anything be seen successively to increase rather than to decrease. And this I take to be how the flow of time appears to take us away from things and events we recall perceiving, namely by accumulating recollections of the things and events we perceive successively to succeed them.

The way the flow of time takes us towards the intended or predicted upshots of our actions is a special case of the same process. Seeing whether an action of mine is successful means seeing whether it actually has the upshot I recall intending it to have when I did it. Since causation is by definition the mechanism of both action and perception, our causal criterion fixes the temporal order of events in this sequence as follows: first the intention, then the action, then the upshot and finally the perception of the upshot. My accumulating recollections of events will therefore include recollections of members of such sequences, acquired in this order, the order in which the flow of time will consequently appear to take me through them.

Similarly for the rather simpler special case of checking a prediction. Seeing whether a prediction of mine is successful means seeing whether some event actually is as I recall having predicted it would be. The event in this case may not be the upshot of an action of mine, but my seeing it will be, if only the upshot of my looking to see it. Again, the temporal order of the relevant sequence of events will be fixed as follows by their causal order: prediction, action, perception. Each member of this sequence is a change in me, an event which I may recollect simultaneously with a later but not with an earlier member. So this too is the order in which the flow of time will appear to take me through them.

As for the sequence of events involved in one action, so for sequences of actions, including causal sequences constituting larger actions, like the sequence of steps that takes me out of a room. As I see the intended upshot of each attempted step, that action is added to my accumulating store of recollectable past events, and so the flow of time takes me successively through the perceived sequence from each step to its causal and therefore temporal descendant.

Forward time travel

So much for our perception of the flow of time, which we see to be nothing more than an accumulation of memories. The fact that a memory is an effect, not a cause, of what is remembered is the real reason the flow of time takes us into the future rather than the past. However, the flow of time is only one kind of future-bound time travel; and while we are on the subject we had better dispose of the other kind too.

Real forward time travel, unlike the flow of time, is more than psychological, and it is not restricted as the flow of time is to a tautological rate of seven days a week. An example of it would be someone taking only ten minutes to reach the end of the next century; and that is an objectively possible achievement. Admittedly, in most science fiction it is also *de rigeur* for future-bound time travellers to disappear during the intervening decades, and I know no way of doing that. But disappearing for the duration is only a melodramatic embellishment, by no means essential to the end result. All we really need is a sufficient slowing down of processes of change and decay so that they take a century to reach the point they would otherwise have reached in ten minutes; and there are two ways at least of doing that.

One way is provided for in special relativity, and works for anything. Just send a spaceship off very fast, turning it round so as to bring it back after a hundred earth years. The spaceship and everything in it will then have aged less than similar things and processes on earth, the discrepancy increasing with the spaceship's speed. Send it off at a speed close enough to the speed of light, and on its return its contents will have aged no more than ten minutes. Clocks, people, processes of every kind – all will return having reached the stage they would have reached on earth ten minutes after take-off.

Peripatetic space travel costs a lot at the speeds needed to arrest ageing much, but there is a cheaper alternative. It will not work for everything, but it will work for people and other organisms, which is what matters most. It works by exploiting the fact that organic processes (like most other chemical reactions) slow down at low temperatures. So we could in principle travel into the future by freezing ourselves for the duration and then thawing out again. (The technique has actually been sold to some gullible Californians, who unfortunately did not survive it.) To a more modest degree hibernation also involves slowing down bodily processes, and so far it is probably the only honestly marketable mode of time travel. Rip van Winkle was a time traveller, therefore, and so in its humble way is every hibernating animal.

All in all, real forward time travel is neither a problematic nor an especially remarkable phenomenon. It is really only an overly grand description of processes slowing down or stopping. Describing a stopped watch as having turned literally into a time machine does rather doll up the situation; and a repairer advertising cures for cases of forward time travel in watches and clocks would be more derided than enriched – as I shall be if I waste more ink on so trifling a topic.

Backward time travel

Travel into the past is altogether more problematic. Going forward a century is relatively easy; the problem is getting back. Still, at first sight, the problem does not look insoluble. If forward time travel is slowing processes down, presumably backward time travel is reversing them – and many natural processes are reversible. Why not, at least in principle, processes of perception, memory, action and physiological ageing?

But reversing natural processes is not enough. If it were, making a clock's hands go anti-clockwise would produce backward time travel; or – an example once proposed in physics – making an electron's charge positive instead of negative, to make it move toward negative charges instead of away from them. Backward time travel indeed entails such reversals, but there is more to it than that. To see what, consider the differences between an ordinary clock C, the same clock going backward in time (C'), and a clock altered to make its hands go round the wrong way (C'').

Suppose for simplicity that the clocks' second hands move discontinuously once a second and that the seconds are numbered, and consider one particular circuit of the hand on each clock from '1' to '60'. The clockwork in C and C' is the same: that is, it makes each movement of the hand affect its movement to the next higher numeral, but not conversely. For example, bending the hand as it passes '2' on either C or C' will make it bent as it passes '3', but not as it passes '1'. On the doctored clock C'', the causal order of the corresponding events is reversed. Bending the hand as it passes '2' will make it bent as it passes '1', but not as it passes '3'. From the clocks' own viewpoints, C and C' are going clockwise, C'' anti-clockwise.

Let e_1 be the event of C's hand passing '1', e_2 be it passing '2', etc., and let e_1', e_2', etc. and e_1'', e_2'', etc. be the corresponding events on C' and C''. Then the differences between the three clocks from the point of view of outside time are that

e_1 precedes e_2, affects it and is unaffected by it,
e_1' succeeds e_2', affects it and is unaffected by it, and
e_1'' succeeds e_2'', is affected by it and does not affect it.

Similarly for the differences between a normal electron (C), an electron travelling backward in time (C') and a positron (C''), as the reader may readily verify – e.g. by imagining the particles moving freely along straight lines numbered '1', '2', etc. at intervals away from a fixed negative charge, and letting e_N, e_N' and e_N'' be each particle respectively passing any numeral 'N' on a particular occasion. What these cases show is that we must distinguish sharply between reversing the temporal order of *types* of events and reversing the order of particular event *tokens*. e_1, e_1' and e_1'' are all token events of one type, namely a clock hand's passing a numeral '1', while e_2, e_2' and e_2'' are all of another type, namely hands passing a numeral '2'. What matters for backward time travel is that the temporal order of a pair of these *tokens* be reversed, i.e. that by the standards of the outside world their causal order be reversed. Of what *types* these tokens are is immaterial, and so therefore is what type normally succeeds what when causation is not reversed. It is irrelevant to time travel that clock hands normally go round clockwise and that electrons outnumber positrons. A positron is not an electron going backward in time, any more than an anti-clockwise clock is an ordinary clock time-travelling – or, come to that, than an ordinary clock is a time-travelling anti-clockwise clock.

Reversing natural processes means reversing the temporal order of types of events, not of tokens of those types. It means clocks going anti-clockwise, spherical radiation collapsing to a point, the universe contracting, high entropy systems spontaneously losing entropy, oaks growing down into acorns, and so on. Bringing this about means getting a token event of one type to be a cause of an event of another type which would normally affect and so precede it, instead of being affected by and so succeeding it. Sometimes this is easy, as it is to make a clock run anti-clockwise, or to reflect outgoing spherical radiation back onto its source; sometimes it is hard, as it is to reverse the expansion of the universe or make oaks shrink into acorns. But neither implies anything about backward causation, nor therefore about backward time travel. If *Tardis* can transport ordinary clocks back in time, it can just as easily transport oak trees, which by the standards of the outside world would then appear to be shrinking into acorns because the causal and therefore the temporal orders of particular token events would all have been reversed. The question is whether *that* is possible, not whether the type of process, acorns growing into oaks, can be reversed either within *Tardis* or without it.

But what is backward causation, if not a local reversal of some type of causal process? I cannot suppose it literally to be *e* affecting *e*★ while being later than *e*★, having made causal order the test of temporal order. Backward causation can only be a local reversal of both temporal and causal order. But if that is not a region of spacetime full of positrons, in which clocks run anti-clockwise, entropy spontaneously decreases, oak trees become acorns, etc., what is it? Take two pairs of events, *e* affecting *e*★ on *Tardis* while it travels back in time, and *e*★★ affecting *e*★★★ outside it. I say that, locally, *e* precedes *e*★ and *e*★★ precedes *e*★★★. What makes the causal and thus the temporal orders of these two pairs of events opposed to each other? How do they differ from two pairs of events whose causal and temporal orders are the same?

I get the answer to this question from the indubitable proposition that to arrive is to have travelled. If Dr Who's *Tardis* sets off in 1984 and arrives later in 1884, it has travelled back in time. Dr Who set off in 1984 before he arrived in 1884 because his nineteenth-century appearance is affected by his twentieth-century departure, not *vice versa*. His wearing his scarf as he emerges from the time machine is an effect, not a cause, of his putting it on as he set off, as is his 1884 recollection of having done so. By leaving it off in 1984 he would have caused himself to lack both the scarf and the memory in 1884, but not conversely – at least, not so far as causation inside *Tardis* goes.

If the trip is instantaneous, these effects of his 1984 activities will be immediate; if not, they will be mediated by a causal chain of events or thing stages inside *Tardis*. But mediated or not, the causal order of his entering and leaving the machine is what makes the latter event later than the former. And what makes it also a century earlier, and hence a case of backward time travel, is that the very same events are also causally linked the other way round by causal chains in the outside world. Just as his 1984 activities affect the nineteenth century, so his 1884 arrival will eventually affect the twentieth, including his own subsequent departure from it. The memorable drawings and photographs of his arrival in *The Illustrated London News*, for instance, which made scarves fashionable among time travellers for the next two centuries, and were so helpful to *Tardis*'s twentieth-century designers. . . .

One could I suppose object that the 1884 arrival, if sufficiently unobtrusive, might not have affected twentieth-century events, and *a fortiori* not Dr Who's departure, so that the two events need not be causally related both ways round. But being unobtrusive does not mean lacking effects, it only means not being perceived. And while *Tardis*'s arrival might well not be seen, it can hardly be invisible. It must have produced the effects of an incursion of an old police box (*Tardis*'s outward guise) with a man emerging from it – displacement of air, reflection of light, etc. If 1884 saw no such effects, it saw no such incursion: we saw in chapter 8 that real events must be contiguous in spacetime to their immediate effects. Then those effects themselves must have effects, and so on forward through the twentieth century; for whether or not there are earlier effects, there must also be enough later ones to make up the pre-dominant causal order outside *Tardis* that our own calendar depends on. And in that order, Dr Who's departure must itself be located to have the absolutely later earthly date, 1984, which *ex hypothesi* it has. Some chain of causes and effects must run through the outside world from *Tardis*'s arrival to its departure. So the events will be causally related both ways round.

Although the forward chain of causes and effects – forward, we saw in chapter 9, simply because predominant – need contain no perceptions of *Tardis*'s 1884 arrival, it could. Dr Who in 1984 could know of it and be consciously affected by it. Suppose in particular then that e is his setting off in 1984, e^* his emerging from *Tardis* in 1884, e^{**} the appearance of a copy of *The Illustrated London News* report of e^*, and e^{***} his reading that report in 1984 to check before setting off that he is properly dressed.

Here e^* clearly affects e^{***} and hence e itself. Whether Dr Who sets off with a scarf will depend on, as well as – inside *Tardis* – determine, whether he emerges with one, is so photographed, sees it in the photograph and dresses accordingly. (He had better dress accordingly, or the tale will be self-contradictory; and although I mean to show it to be impossible, I don't expect to do so that easily.) So via these intermediate effects, his emerging with a scarf in 1884 makes him at least more likely to set off with one in 1984 than in the circumstances he would otherwise have been. $e^\star$ thus meets one at least of the conditions for affecting e laid down in chapter 8, and the reader may easily verify that it meets the others. In this case $e^\star$ affects e as evidently as e affects $e^\star$.

But so it does in any case, whether Dr Who knows it or not. Causation depends not just on what is known to happen, nor even just on what happens. It depends on what else would have happened, or been more or less likely to have happened, if in the circumstances the alleged cause had been different or had not occurred at all. Whether causation can be defined in terms of such so-called "counterfactual conditionals" is a moot point, one of the controversies I indicated in chapter 8 my intention to evade. But it undeniably entails some such counterfactual conditionals, and is often the only credible basis for believing them. I assumed as much in supposing that without causation the coincidence of Dr Who's 1884 and 1984 appearances would be incredible. And by the same token, we must suppose some causal connection between features of $e^\star$ and some feature of e, however remote, obscure and unknown the chain of intermediate causes and effects. In any circumstances, some difference in *Tardis*'s arrival is bound to make more likely some difference in its departure. $e^\star$ will always affect e somehow – which is why, as sci-fi addicts know, backward time-travellers have always to take care, like Dr Who in his choice of scarf, not to inject contradiction into their authors' tales. The risk of contradiction may be more readily avoided when the traveller knows what the causal mechanism is; but it will be there in any case.

What makes Dr Who's trip a case of backward causation, I conclude, is that both e and $e^\star$, his departure and his arrival, directly or indirectly affect each other in some way. That is the only way I can conceive backward causation and backward time travel occurring: it requires a closed chain of causes and effects. For the causal orders of e and $e^\star$ and of $e^{\star\star}$ and $e^{\star\star\star}$ to be opposite, they must one way or another form a loop – here, e affecting $e^\star$, which affects $e^{\star\star}$, which affects $e^{\star\star\star}$, which affects e. Unless they form such a loop, I see no basis for saying that the causal and hence the temporal orders of two pairs of events oppose each other; nor therefore that there is any local reversal of causation and hence of time.

However, two pairs of events forming part of a loop of causes and effects does not automatically oppose their causal and therefore their temporal orders. For one thing, the loop might contain all the events in the universe, with no local reversals of order at all and therefore no locally backward causation. And even in a local loop, something else is needed to determine where it leaves and rejoins the predominant mainstream of forward causation. What, for example, in the loop $e \rightarrow e^{\star} \rightarrow e^{\star\star} \rightarrow e^{\star\star\star} \rightarrow e$, makes $e \rightarrow e^{\star}$ the link opposed in causal and temporal order to the rest, which have all the same order? I am not sure. But then I do not need to be. I am trying to show backward causation to be impossible, and for that purpose I need not say what would suffice for it. All I need is one impossible prerequisite, namely its needing a causal loop. It makes no odds to me if showing that to be impossible disposes of other things as well. None of them is indispensable: no one will go to the stake over and over again for a cyclical universe.

Causal loops

I will prove the impossibility of causal loops by extending an argument of Dummett's (1964). His example has a chief belatedly dancing to secure brave behaviour among his tribesmen. I shall use a simpler example and one less redolent of racial patronage, since belief in backward causation is as common among white physicists as it is in Africa; but the first part of the ensuing argument is essentially the same as his.

Suppose some agents say they can affect the past, whether by travelling back into it or otherwise. What the effects are is immaterial, so long as some perceiver could detect them; we may as well use effects of human action to illustrate the case. So suppose some people claim at any time t_1 the ability to ignite a fire an hour earlier (at t_0) by putting a match to it an hour later (at t_2). As things are, we know they can't; but I shall ignore that and try to verify their claim, making any contingent assumption that would help them to succeed.

We saw in chapter 8 that causes have *inter alia* to make their effects more likely than in the circumstances they would otherwise have been. Here that means the fire must be more likely to ignite at t_0 if a match is put to it at t_2 than it would be otherwise. (We may take it that no match is applied at any other time, nor is any other cause of fire different in the two cases.) Whether this is so cannot of course be tested in a single case, where any of the four possible combinations – ignition & match, ignition & no match, unlit fire & match, unlit fire & no match – might coincidentally occur. So I will suppose as many fires as are needed to pass the most stringent statistical tests anyone could reasonably demand for a significant positive correlation between matches and lighting.

Then our test is as follows. We can see by t_1 which fires ignited at t_0 and which did not: assume about equal numbers of each. We now ask half the self-styled igniters of each group to put matches to their fires at t_2 and the rest to refrain. They try to comply (or we should have no test), we note at t_2 whether they do, and then we assess the results.

One of three things can happen. One is that the igniters do as we tell them, there is no correlation between matches and ignitions, and so their causal claim is disproved. So that must not happen. There must be some non-coincidental correlation, and this could occur in one of two ways.

First, some people with lit fires apply matches who were asked not to, or some with unlit fires who were asked to apply matches don't. There might of course be other causes of this behaviour – people forgetting what they were told, not doing it anyway, becoming paralysed, losing their matches. Since correlations resulting from accidents of that kind prove nothing, we take the obvious physical and psychological precautions against them. We supply enough matches, train people in their use, keep them fit, remind them of what they are to do, say we will reward those who do it – and shoot the rest. And once more we take care to have enough cases for any remaining correlation to be an incredible coincidence, i.e. to be explainable only by a causal connection between fires igniting and matches being put to them.

The trouble now is that the causal connection is the wrong way round. Somehow fires igniting at t_0 make their igniters more likely to apply matches at t_2 than unlit fires do. People's activities at t_2 are somehow constrained, albeit only statistically, by what happens to fires at t_0. Now some constraint we know is inevitable, since we are dealing with a causal loop: ignitions must somehow affect what people do with matches at t_2. But that need not matter. An ignition can affect *how* a match is applied, for example, so long as it does not make it more likely to *be* applied. But if it does not do that, then since we have already removed every other impediment to people doing what at t_1 they were told to do, that is what they will all do. *Ex hypothesi*, however, what we told them to do did not, so far as we could see, correlate at all with fires igniting at t_0. (If it had, the resultant correlation of matches with ignitions would again have proved nothing.) So, as already remarked, if the igniters do as they are told, their claim to affect the past will be refuted. Unless we were wrong at t_1 about some of the ignitions at t_0.

This is the third possible outcome, and the only way a correlation can occur which shows backward rather than forward causation. Either some fires we thought unlit, which we told people to put matches to, had in fact ignited, or some we thought lit, which we told people not to put matches to, had in fact not ignited. Such mistakes might occur for all sorts of reasons: we might mix up our records, a trick of the light might make an unlit fire look lit, or a fire might ignite and then go out between t_0 and t_1, leaving no trace visible of its ignition. But correlations attributable to those causes are again clearly irrelevant, so again we try to preclude them. We set cameras to record what happens at t_0 and t_2, use thermometers to detect temperature rises – in short, we exploit any or all of the effects of ignition to create as reliable and permanent a record as possible of its happening (or not) at t_0 in each case. Yet if the correlation we are looking for is to survive, these precautions will have to fail. There will have to be some fires whose igniting (or not) at t_0 we can by no means whatever reliably perceive until after we can see two hours later whether a match has been put to them.

Now how can that be? I have just said that perception can exploit any effect of ignition or its absence to record the fact. That assertion did not derive merely from the particular methods cited or the others one could readily devise. Recall from chapter 9 that any event may be made a perception of one of its causes by being embedded in a network of other events constituting the acquisition of a belief about that cause. That is what makes perceptions out of otherwise unremarkable chemical and electrical events in our brains. In effect, it is what our use of instruments like thermometers does to the effects on them of rises in temperature: it makes them parts of human perceptions of those temperature rises. And even if for some reason the events in this case could not be made perceptible to people, they could still be made perceptible to perceivers of some kind, who could do the experiment for us and report the result. Indeed the experiment needs no perceivers at all in the usual sense. All it needs are cameras, thermometers and clocks to make the observations, a mini-computer to analyse them statistically, switch on the right pre-recorded instruction for each igniter, and print out the final verdict. The whole experiment could be automated, to test not only this but *any* claim to be able to affect the past. And one would think that *some* immediate effect of any event would be made so likely by its occurrence that a machine could always be built so as to detect it reliably virtually as soon as it occurs.

But in this case that must not be so. The reliability of our seeing a fire ignite at t_0 must be significantly increased by our subsequently seeing a match put to it at t_2. Is that a credible possibility? I think not, for the following reasons. First, what perceptions of events depend on are their effects, not their causes. I may see something indirectly via seeing an effect of it, but not via seeing a cause. The effects of events are also what determine how reliable perceptions of them are. The reliability of a perception depends entirely on how much more likely the cause (the event perceived) makes the effect (the perception). That probability may depend on the perception going via certain intermediate effects of the perceived event, but it does not depend on how likely its causes made the event itself. The probability that a photograph is accurate does not depend on the probability of the events photographed.

It is true that an unreliable photograph will be less conclusive when it shows unlikely events. Blurred photographs of Cambridge crocodiles, for instance, are rightly given less credence than blurred photographs of Cambridge people, even when there is no question of fraud or camera malfunction. But this is not because crocodiles photograph less reliably than people. Since crocodiles reflect photons much as people do, we may take it that they raise the probability of crocodile-shaped images in cameras as much as people raise the probability of people-shaped images. Only not enough for blurred photographs to raise the initially much lower probability of Cambridge crocodiles to the point where we should believe in them and consequently accept the photographs as veridical. So despite their equal reliability, a much lower proportion of blurred Cambridge crocodile photographs should be believed; the correlation between blurred crocodile pictures and crocodiles in Cambridge is rightly taken to be much lower than that between blurred pictures of people and people.

But we only take the correlation to be lower for crocodiles because we have other reasons for thinking Cambridge crocodiles unlikely. Without such reasons we should take the correlations to be equal, the photographs being equally reliable. The difference in the correlations, therefore, is not *evidence* for thinking Cambridge to be short on crocodiles; it is only our natural reaction to what evidence we do have.

As for Cambridge crocodiles, so for our belatedly ignited fires. If we had some other reason to think that putting a match to a fire at t_2 made it more likely to have ignited at t_0, we might use that information to correct an unreliable perception at t_1 that the fire had not ignited – thus generating the correlation we need to save the igniters' causal claims. But a correlation generated in this way does not itself provide any evidence for the claim; it merely signifies that we believe it. What we need is some other reason to use perceptions of events at t_2 to correct earlier perceptions of events at t_0 and so to generate the necessary correlation. Now *prima facie* the only reason for using one perception to correct another is that it is a more reliable perception of the same thing. Seeing whether a match is applied at t_2 must be supposed to be a more reliable, if indirect, way of perceiving whether a fire ignites at t_0 than was available hitherto. To be that, however, applying the match would by definition have to be an effect of the ignition, mediating our perception of it. What any correlation would then show is the extent to which the ignition increases the probability of the match being applied, not the other way round. But we need it the other way round.

What we really need, therefore, is some reason to make these corrections *because* applying the match is a cause, as well as an effect, of ignition; so that some at least of the resulting correlation between them can be attributed to backward causation. That means treating seeing the match applied not as a way of perceiving the ignition, but as a perception of one of its causes, a possible means of bringing the ignition about. Now seeing the cause of an event does give reason to believe in it. With normal forward causation it is the usual basis for predicting events; and if a cause makes an event probable enough, seeing the cause may give the strongest possible grounds for predicting the event. Suppose for example I see a man through the viewfinder of my instant camera as I press the button, having just checked that it is all in order, correctly loaded, focused and exposed. I have seen what are virtually 100% sufficient causes of a man's image appearing shortly afterwards on the film. My perception of those causes gives me every reason to expect the corresponding image to appear.

But suppose it doesn't. Suppose I see instead an image of a crocodile. Must I weigh the authority of that perception against the grounds I had for predicting the image of a man, like a jury working out which of two conflicting tales I am to believe? Might I decide in the end to correct my perception by the grounds I had for the contrary prediction: to say that although I can clearly see a crocodile's image, the strong reasons I had for predicting a man's image make me now conclude *without impugning my eyesight* that the image is visibly human?

Of course not. We saw in the first section of this chapter that provided a perception is at all reliable, it transcends without question the strongest grounds on which prediction can be based. Even if the grounds are the most reliable perception possible of the most nearly sufficient cause of an event, they will not suffice to correct any but the most grossly unreliable contrary perception. And even then, as we have just seen in the case of the Cambridge crocodiles, the correction will not itself impugn the perception's reliability, nor will it serve to verify the efficacy of the alleged cause on whose perception it is based. On the contrary, without independent evidence of that perceived cause's ability to raise the predicted event's probability, we have no reason to think it a cause and so to make the correction at all. But getting that evidence means being able to establish a significant correlation between *reliable* perceptions of the cause and its supposed effect; and reliable perceptions of events cannot be corrected by predictions of them based on perceptions of even well-established causes.

As for normal causes, so for backward ones. Only if applying matches later can be independently shown to make ignitions more likely could seeing the later event, construed as a cause of the earlier one, be used to correct even a very unreliable perception of a fire not igniting. But the increased probability of ignition could only be shown by correlating reliable perceptions of it with reliable perceptions of its alleged cause; but then reliable perceptions of whether ignition occurs cannot be corrected by perceptions of its causes anyway. Yet unless the perceptions are corrected, we have already seen that they will show no relevant correlation at all, and hence show that applying matches later is *not* a cause of fires lighting earlier. In short, backward causation cannot be saved even by rigging the experiment in its favour under the pretext of correcting unreliable results.

The only way the experiment can fail to disprove backward causation is if a fire's igniting or not at t_0 cannot be perceived at all, reliably or unreliably, until after it is seen at t_2 whether a match has been put to it. Since, as we saw in chapter 9, any effect of an event can be a perception of it, this means the fire's igniting or otherwise must have no effects before t_2. But we saw in chapter 8 that real events must have spatiotemporally contiguous effects. Events are wherever in spacetime their immediate effects are, that being the real import of the maxim 'No action at a distance'. So if there really is no way whatever of perceiving the ignition of a fire before t_2, it cannot have ignited before t_2. And if the same goes for the fire not igniting, the fire itself must not exist before that time, since real fires have at any given time either to ignite or not.

So even this way of saving backward causation fails, for now the alleged effect does not in fact precede its alleged cause. In short, no non-coincidental correlation in this experiment can possibly show anything but causation in the normal forward sense. Yet causation, repeated often enough, must show itself in some positive correlation of cause with effect. Since backward causation never can, I conclude that it cannot exist.

Objections to the argument

I foresee three objections to the above argument, which I should answer in anticipation. One will accuse me of begging the question in favour of forward causation, the other two of setting too stringent standards for locating events in spacetime and for causal connections.

First, I have assumed that the effects of events can be perceived afterwards but not beforehand. When backward causation is in question, does not that discriminate unreasonably against it? Since perception for me is by definition a causal process, why is there not backward perception if there is backward causation? In particular, why in the above experiment can putting matches to fires at t_2 not be seen in advance by backward perception, thus enabling their alleged effects to occur before them after all?

To the general question, my reply is that the causal criterion for the direction of time entitles me to take forward causation for granted. What makes most causation forward, we have seen, is that it *is* most. Backward causation is merely causation running against the grain by completing a loop of causes and effects. Having a later cause does not deprive an event of its own normal later effects, and I beg no relevant question by crediting it with them. Dr Who's arrival needs effects in and after 1884 in order to have that temporal location. That in itself does nothing to prevent it also having later causes.

To the particular question, my reply is threefold. First, tests of backward causation cannot all be rescued this way. Unless we may generally infer that perceived events precede their perceptions, we should have no idea when anything happens, nor *a fortiori* what precedes what. (This is why our ability to perceive succession depends on there being a predominant direction to causation.) Still, while backward causation is in question, I must allow occasional exceptions, even though invoking them just to rescue otherwise unsuccessful verifications of backward causation itself begs the question at issue. However, even apart from that, the invocation would not work, because it would vitiate the test in two other ways as well.

For a start, it would be self-defeating. If we can perceive events before they happen, we can no longer infer, merely because we see fires light before matches are put to them, that this really is the temporal order of those events. The second point is more serious still. The whole reason for telling igniters at t_1 what to do at t_2, regardless of what ignitions have by then been seen to occur at t_0, is that it shows the igniters to be unconstrained by those earlier events in their application of matches. It shows that because we know our instructions are not constrained and we make the igniters follow our instructions. But if we have already seen what they will do at t_2, our instructions are useless. Either we must tell them to do what we have already seen them do, or they will have to ignore us. (Or a contradiction will ensue. I am assuming for simplicity that these backward perceptions are completely reliable. Extending the argument to the general statistical case is trivial but tedious; interested readers can work it out for themselves.) Either way we no longer know that the correlations are not produced by events at t_0 affecting actions at t_2 rather than the other way round. The test ceases to show anything whatever about backward causation.

So much for the first objection. Taking events in the test to be perceptible only after they occur does not beg the question against backward causation: it is a necessary condition of the test's being relevant at all. Which brings me to the second objection. Why assume that events must be perceptible *immediately* after they occur? Might not backward causation or time travel affect events whose perceptible effects occur only after their own later causes? Have I in short not set too severe a restriction on when events occur?

To these questions my reply is in two parts. First, I admit that removing this restriction would make backward causation possible. Consider for example an event identical with my birth except for being five years earlier – call it my "prebirth". Prebirths admittedly cause less stir at the time than births do, because their first effects only occur five years later; but once events are allowed to lack contiguous effects, they can hardly be jibbed at on that score. And prebirths are unquestionably affected by later events. Whether a prebirth is of a boy or a girl, for instance, will not be settled until more than four years afterwards.

Secondly, however, it is perfectly obvious that there are no such events as prebirths. They are on a par with all the other kinds of bogus events which had to be disposed of in chapter 8 by requiring events to have contiguous effects. That requirement is not now being imposed *ad hoc* to prevent backward causation: it was needed anyway, in quite other contexts, to mark off real from phoney events. Of course I cannot stop people admitting phoney events and then claiming the ability to affect events after they happen. But then I should not trouble to dispute so useless a conception of backward causation. It suffices me that people can do nothing that will be perceptible or otherwise effective before they have done it.

The third objection I foresee is to my demanding some positive correlation between causes and effects. I foresee of course no objection to the modesty of the correlation, which makes it as easy as it can be to establish a causal connection. If causes need induce no increase in their alleged effects' probabilities, they need certainly not induce the greater increases (up to 1) that many philosophers demand. The objection will rather be either to demanding any increase at all, or to making it show up in a statistical correlation.

To the latter objection I reply by recalling my intention in chapter 8 to evade controversy about what sort of probability is needed to make sense of its role in causation, beyond its having to be objective and more than merely inductive. In particular, I need not identify the probability of effects with the frequency resulting from a statistical test of causation. Indeed I cannot, since I do not take causation to relate only types or classes of events. On the contrary, to make sense of backward causation I have had to make causation relate token events. So if causes have to increase the probability of their effects, they must be able to do it in a single case. One match must be able to make an earlier ignition more likely than it would otherwise have been, even if no other fire is ever belatedly ignited.

What these single case probabilities are, however, I need not say; it suffices that they must exist. For on any interpretation of probability, a single case probability implies that enough such cases would, with overwhelmingly high probability, exhibit a closely similar statistical frequency. And that is all I need. I have shown that enough such cases would show no increased frequency, and hence that there is no increased probability of the effect even in one single case. Whatever objective probability is, so long as it is not merely inductive, a later event cannot increase the probability of an earlier one in the way backward causation requires.

As to why backward causation requires an increased probability of the earlier effect, I explained in chapter 8 why causes in general must make their effects more probable. They must do it to make sense of causation being the mechanism of action and perception; and unless it is so, I cannot tell what it might be nor why it should concern us. If backward causation would not enable events to be seen before they happened or acted on afterwards, I see no reason to care whether it is possible or not. But if it would enable those achievements, then later causes must at least increase the probability their effects would otherwise have. Which we have seen they cannot do.

Lastly, I hope it is clear that the peculiar features of my illustration are quite incidental to the argument. In the nature of the case I could not analyse an actual instance of backward causation, and it seemed better to use a memorable fiction than to retire to abstract symbols.

But I did say that the alleged effect could be an event of any kind perceptible somehow to some kind of perceiver, and that this amounts merely to its having some real effects. Since I have already, on independent grounds, required all real events to have contiguous effects, this means that all possible effects of backward causation are covered.

Nor is the alleged cause restricted to actions, as it may appear to be. Picturesqueness apart, the agent's role in the argument is merely to help exclude the possibility of relevant forward causation by the alleged effect – by making the agent either freely decide not to correlate his actions with their alleged effects, or follow our deliberately non-correlated instructions. If backward causation cannot show up in such a case, *a fortiori* it cannot show up when the alleged cause is not an action and so cannot be guaranteed free of relevant forward causation. The argument applies therefore to both causes and effects of all conceivable kinds. Backward causation is completely impossible.

And not only backward causation. The argument turns only on the causal loop in the illustration, from fires igniting to perceptions of that, to matches being applied and so back to the ignitions. Whether the loops involve merely local reversals of causation, or whether the first link takes in the whole subsequent history of a cyclical universe, is immaterial. I could no more see what I will do in a telescope picking up light reflected from it all round the cycle than I could in any other way.

Cyclical universes are as impossible as backward causation, for the same reason. Chapter 8's modest constraints on causation cannot be met by every link in a closed chain of causes and effects. That is why effects cannot in turn affect their causes, and why in particular we cannot act on what we have perceived, or perceive what we will act on. It is why we know perforce much less about the future than about the past, but can still affect and predict it, while we are perforce impotent to alter the past we have perceived. It completes therefore the true and tenseless explanation of the direction and the flow of time, and hence of all the apparent differences between past, present and future. I hope it will lay for good and all the ghost of tense that has so haunted the philosophy of time.

But that is only a prediction.

Bibliography

The following is a fairly full list of recent or important works in English on the aspects of time dealt with in the book. It also includes a selection of works on other topics discussed. Where two dates are given, the first is that of first publication, the second of the republished or translated version listed.

AARONSON, B. S. 1971. Time, time stance, and existence. *Studium Generale*, **24**, 369–87.

ACKRILL, J. L. 1963. *Aristotle's Categories and De Interpretatione*. Oxford.

ALEXANDER, H. G., ed. 1956. *The Leibniz–Clarke Correspondence*. Manchester.

ALTHAM, J. E. J. 1973. The causal theory of names. *Arist. Soc. Suppl. Vol.* **47**, 209–25.

ANDERSON, J. 1973. The ghosts of times past. *Foundations of Language* **9**, 481–91.

ANSCOMBE, G. E. M. 1957. *Intention*. Oxford.

1964. Aristotle and the sea-battle. *Problems of Space and Time*, ed. J. J. C. Smart, pp. 43–57. New York.

AUGUSTINE (ST.). *Confessions*, ed. A. C. Outler. 1955. London.

AUGUSTYNEK, Z. 1976. Past, present and future in relativity. *Studia Logica* **35**, 45–53.

AUNE, B. 1977. *Action and Reason*. Dordrecht.

AYER, A. J. 1954. Statements about the past. *Philosophical Essays*, pp. 167–90. London.

1956. *The Problem of Knowledge*. London.

1963. Fatalism. *The Concept of a Person*, pp. 235–68. London.

BAKER, L. R. 1975. Temporal becoming: the argument from physics. *Phil. Forum* **6**, 218–33.

1979. On the mind-dependence of temporal becoming. *Phil. Phenomenon. Res.* **39**, 341–57.

BAR-HILLEL, Y. 1954. Indexical expressions. *Mind* **63**, 359–79.

BARRETT, W. 1967. The flow of time. *The Philosophy of Time*, ed. R. M. Gale, pp. 354–76. New York.

BAUERLE, R. 1978. Fugitive propositions again. *Analysis* **38**, 78–80.

BEARDSLEY, M. 1975. Actions and events: the problem of individuation. *Amer. Phil. Quart.* **12**, 263–76.

BEAUCHAMP, T. L. and ROBINSON, D. N. 1975. On von Wright's argument for backward causation. *Ratio* **17**, 99–103.

DE BEAUREGARD, O. C. 1971. No paradox in the theory of time anisotropy. *Studium Generale* **24**, 10–18.

BERGER, G. 1972. Temporally symmetric causal relations in Minkowski space–time. *Synthese* **24**, 58–71.

1974. Elementary causal structures in Newtonian and Minkowskian space–time. *Theoria* **40**, 191–201.

BERGSON, H. L. 1889. *Time and Free Will*, tr. F. L. Pogson. 1910. London.

1922. *Duration and Simultaneity*, tr. L. Jacobson. 1965. New York.

BLACK, M. 1956. Why cannot an effect precede its cause? *Analysis* **16**, 49–58.

BLOKHINTSEV, S. 1973. *Space and Time in the Microworld*. Dordrecht.

BOROWSKI, E. J. 1975. Diachronic identity as relative identity. *Phil. Quart.* **25**, 271–6.

BOSSERT, P. J. 1976. Hume and Husserl on time and time-consciousness. *J. Brit. Soc. Phenomen.* **7**, 44–52.

BRADLEY, F. H. 1920. *Appearance and Reality*, 2nd edn. Oxford.

BRADLEY, R. D. 1959. Must the future be what it is going to be? *Mind* **68**, 193–208.

BRAITHWAITE, R. B. 1928. Time and change. *Arist. Soc. Suppl. Vol.* **8**, 162–74.

1933. The nature of believing. *Knowledge and Belief*, ed. A. P. Griffiths, pp. 28–40. 1967. London.

BRAUDE, S. 1973. Tensed sentences and free repeatability. *Phil. Rev.* **82**, 188–214.

BRIER, B. 1972. An atemporal view of causality. *J. Crit. Anal.* **4**, 8–16.

1973. Magicians, alarm clocks and backward causation. *Southern J. Phil.* **11**, 359–64.

BROAD, C. D. 1923. *Scientific Thought*. London.

1938. *An Examination of Mc Taggart's Philosophy*. Cambridge.

1955. Kant's mathematical antimonies. *Proc. Arist. Soc.* **55**, 1–22.

BROCKELMAN, P. 1977. Action and time. *Man and World* **10**, 317–33.

BULL, R. 1970. An approach to tense-logic. *Theoria* **36**, 282–300.

BURGESS, J. P. 1979. Logic and time. *J. Symb. Log.* **44**, 566–82.

CAHN, S. M. 1967. *Fate, Logic and Time*. New Haven.

1974. Statements of future contingencies. *Mind* **81**, 574.

CAPEK, M. 1961. *The Philosophical Impact of Contemporary Physics*. Princeton.

1971. The fiction of instants. *Studium Generale* **24**, 31–43.

CHANDLER, H. S. 1970. Depending continuants. *Noûs* **4**, 279–84.

CHAPMAN, T. 1975. Prior's criticism of the Barcan formula. *Notre Dame J. Form. Log.* **16**, 116–18.

CHAPPELL, V. C. 1961. Whitehead's theory of becoming. *J. Phil.* **58**, 516–28.

CHISHOLM, R. M. 1970. Events and propositions. *Noûs* **4**, 15–24.

1976. *Person and Object*. London.

CHRISTENSEN, F. 1974. McTaggart's paradox and the nature of time. *Phil. Quart.* **24**, 289–99.

CLARK, M. 1978. Time-slices of particular continuants as basic individuals. *Phil. Stud.* **33**, 403–8.

CLEUGH, M. F. 1937. *Time*. London.

COBURN, R. 1976. The persistence of bodies. *Amer. Phil. Quart.* **13**, 173–84.

COHEN, L. J. 1951. Tense, usage and propositions. *Analysis* **11**, 80–7.

DAVIDSON, D. 1967a. The logical form of action sentences. *The Logic of Decision and Action*, ed. N. Rescher, pp. 81–120. Pittsburgh.

　　1967b. Causal relations. *J. Phil.* **64**, 691–703.

　　1967c. Truth and meaning. *Synthese* **7**, 304–23.

　　1970a. Events as particulars. *Noûs* **4**, 25–32.

　　1970b. The individuation of events. *Essays in Honor of Carl G. Hempel*, ed. N. Rescher, pp. 216–34. Dordrecht.

　　1971. Mental events. *Experience and Theory*, eds L. Foster and J. Swanson, pp. 79–101. Boston.

　　1976. Psychology as philosophy. *The Philosophy of Mind*, ed. J. Glover, pp. 101–10. Oxford.

DAVIES, P. C. W. 1977. *Space and Time in the Modern Universe*. Cambridge.

DENBIGH, K. G. 1975. *An Inventive Universe*. London.

DICKASON, A. 1976. Aristotle, the sea fight, and the cloud. *J. Hist. Phil.* **14**, 11–22.

DINGLE, H. 1979. Time in philosophy and in physics. *Philosophy* **54**, 99–104.

DOMOTER, Z. 1972. Causal models and space–time geometries. *Synthese* **24**, 5–27.

DUMMETT, M. 1960. A defence of McTaggart's proof of the unreality of time. *Truth and Other Enigmas*, pp. 351–7. 1978. London.

　　1964. Bringing about the past. *Truth and Other Enigmas*, pp. 333–50. 1978. London.

　　1969. The reality of the past. *Truth and Other Enigmas*, pp. 358–74. 1978. London.

　　1973. *Frege*. London.

DWYER, L. 1975. Time travel and changing the past. *Phil. Stud.* **27**, 341–50.

　　1977. How to affect, but not change, the past. *Southern J. Phil.* **15**, 383–5.

　　1978. Time travel and some alleged logical asymmetries between past and future. *Can. J. Phil.* **8**, 15–38.

EARMAN, J. 1970. Space–time, or how to solve philosophical problems and dissolve philosophical puzzles without really trying. *J. Phil.* **67**, 259–77.

　　1972a. Implications of causal propagation outside the null cone. *Austral. J. Phil.* **50**, 222–37.

　　1972b. Notes on the causal theory of time. *Synthese* **24**, 74–85.

　　1972c. Some aspects of general relativity and geometrodynamics. *J. Phil.* **69**, 634–47.

　　1974. An attempt to add a little direction to 'the problem of the direction of time'. *Phil. Sci.* **41**, 15–47.

1975. What is physicalism? *J. Phil.* **72**, 565–7.

1977. How to talk about the topology of time. *Noûs* **11**, 211–26.

EDDINGTON, A. S. 1920. *Space, Time and Gravitation.* Cambridge.

EINSTEIN, A. 1917. The foundation of the general theory of relativity. *The Principle of Relativity*, A. Einstein *et al.*, tr. W. Perrett and G. B. Jeffery, pp. 109–64. 1923. London.

EVANS, G. 1973. The causal theory of names. *Arist. Soc. Suppl. Vol.* **47**, 187–208.

FARRELL, B. A. 1973. Temporal precedence. *Proc. Arist. Soc.* **73**, 193–216.

FELDMAN, R. H. AND WIERENGA, E. 1979. Thalberg on the irreducibility of events. *Analysis* **39**, 11–16.

FERRE, F. 1972. Grünbaum on temporal becoming: a critique. *Internat. Phil. Quart.* **12**, 426–45.

FEYNMAN, R. P. 1949. The theory of positrons. *Physical Rev.* **76**, 749–759.

FIELDS, H. 1979. On the status of 'the direction of time'. *Method. Sci.* **12**, 213–35.

FINDLAY, J. N. 1941. Time: a treatment of some puzzles. *Logic and Language*, 1st series, ed. A. G. N. Flew, pp. 37–54. 1955. Oxford.

1956. An examination of tenses. *Contemporary British Philosophy*, 3rd series, ed. H. D. Lewis, pp. 165–87. London.

1975. Husserl's analysis of inner time-consciousness. *Monist* **59**, 3–20.

1978. Time and eternity. *Rev. Metaphys.* **32**, 3–14.

FISHER, J., ed. 1973. *The Magic of Lewis Carroll.* London.

FITZGERALD, P. 1968. Is the future partly unreal? *Rev. Metaphys.* **21**, 421–46.

1969. The truth about tomorrow's sea fight. *J. Phil.* **66**, 307–29.

1970. Tachyons, backwards causation and freedom. *Boston Studies in the Philosophy of Science*, vol. 8, eds R. C. Buck and R. S. Cohen, pp. 415–36. Dordrecht.

1974. On retrocausality. *Philosophia* **4**, 513–51.

FLEW, A. 1954. Can an effect precede its cause? *Arist. Soc. Suppl. Vol.* **38**, 27–62.

1956. Effects before their causes? – addenda and corrigenda. *Analysis* **16**, 104–10.

1973. Magicians, alarm clocks, and backward causation. *Southern J. Phil.* **11**, 365–6.

FODOR, J. A. 1974. Special sciences (or: the disunity of science as a working hypothesis). *Synthese* **28**, 97–115.

FRANK, P. 1938. *Interpretations and Misinterpretations of Modern Physics.* Paris.

FREEMAN, E. AND SELLARS, W., eds 1971. *Basic Issues in the Philosophy of Time.* La Salle, Illinois.

FREEMAN, K. 1953. *Pre-Socratic Philosophers*, 3rd edn. Oxford.

FREUNDLICH, Y. 1973. 'Becoming' and the asymmetries of time. *Phil. Sci.* **40**, 496–517.

FRIEDMAN, M. 1981. *Foundations of Space–Time Theories.* Princeton.

GALE, R. M. 1962. Tensed statements. *Phil. Quart.* **12**, 53–9.
  1963. A reply to Smart, Mayo and Thalberg on 'Tensed statements'.
  Phil. Quart. **13**, 351–6.
  ed. 1967. *The Philosophy of Time.* New York.
  1968. *The Language of Time.* London.
  1971. Has the present any duration? *Noûs* **5**, 39–48.
GEACH, P. T. 1955. Form and existence. *Proc. Arist. Soc.* **55**, 251–72.
  1965. Some problems about time. *Logic Matters,* pp. 302–18. 1972.
  Oxford.
  1979. *Truth, Love and Immortality.* London.
GLYMOUR, C. 1972. Topology, cosmology and convention. *Synthese* **24**,
  195–218.
GOCHET, P. 1977. Model theory and the pragmatics of indexicals. *Dialec-*
  tica **31**, 389–408.
GÖDEL, K. 1949. A remark about the relationship between relativity
  theory and idealistic philosophy. *Albert Einstein: Philosopher–Scientist,*
  ed. P. A. Schilpp, pp. 557–62. La Salle, Illinois.
GODFREY-SMITH, W. 1977. Beginning and ceasing to exist. *Phil. Stud.* **32**,
  393–402.
  1978a. The generality of predictions. *Amer. Phil. Quart.* **15**, 15–25.
  1978b. Prior and particulars. *Philosophy* **53**, 335–42.
  1979. Special relativity and the present. *Phil. Stud.* **36**, 233–44.
  1980. Travelling in time. *Analysis* **40**, 72–3.
GOLD, T. 1962. The arrow of time. *Amer. J. Phys.* **30**, 403–10.
  ed. 1967. *The Nature of Time.* New York.
  1970. *A Theory of Human Action.* Englewood Cliffs, New Jersey.
GOLDMAN, A. 1971. The individuation of action. *J. Phil.* **68**, 761–74.
GOODMAN, N. 1951. *The Structure of Appearance.* Cambridge, Mass.
  1965. *Fact, Fiction and Forecast,* 2nd edn. New York.
GOTSHALK, D. W. 1930. McTaggart on time. *Mind* **39**, 26–42.
GRAHAM, G. 1977. Persons and time. *Southern J. Phil.* **15**, 309–15.
GRANDY, R. E. 1975. Stuff and things. *Synthese* **31**, 479–85.
  1980. Ramsey, reliability and knowledge. *Prospects for Pragmatism,* ed.
  D. H. Mellor, pp. 197–210. Cambridge.
GRICE, H. P. 1957. Meaning. *Phil. Rev.* **66**, 377–88.
GRÜNBAUM, A. 1957. The philosophical retention of absolute space in
  Einstein's general theory of relativity. *Phil. Rev.* **66**, 525–34.
  1962. Carnap's views on the foundations of geometry. *The Philosophy of*
  Rudolf Carnap, ed. P. A. Schilpp, pp. 599–684. La Salle, Illinois.
  1964a. Popper on irreversibility. *The Critical Approach to Science and*
  Philosophy, ed. M. Bunge, pp. 316–31. New York.
  1964b. The nature of time. *Frontiers of Science and Philosophy,* ed. R. G.
  Colodny, pp. 147–88. London.
  1967a. The anisotropy of time. *The Nature of Time,* ed. T. Gold,
  pp. 149–86. New York.
  1967b. The status of temporal becoming. *The Philosophy of Time,* ed.
  R. M. Gale, pp. 322–54. New York.

1968. *Modern Science and Zeno's Paradoxes.* London.
1969. The meaning of time. *Essays in Honor of C. G. Hempel,* ed. N. Rescher, pp. 147–77. Dordrecht.
1971. The meaning of time. *Basic Issues in the Philosophy of Time,* eds E. Freeman and W. Sellars, pp. 195–230. La Salle, Illinois.
1973. *Philosophical Problems of Space and Time,* 2nd edn. Dordrecht.
HAACK, S. 1974. On a theological argument for fatalism. *Phil. Quart.* **24,** 156–9.
HAMILTON, W. B. 1975. Existential time: a re-examination. *Southern J. Phil.* **13,** 297–307.
HARRISON, C. 1972. On the structure of space–time. *Synthese* **24,** 180–93.
HARRISON, J. 1971. Dr Who and the philosophers. *Arist. Soc. Suppl. Vol.* **45,** 1–24.
HARRISON, R. 1973. Lost times. *Analysis* **33,** 65–71.
HAWKING, S. W. AND ELLIS, G. F. R. 1973. *The Large-Scale Structure of Space–Time.* Cambridge.
HEDMAN, C. G. 1972. On when there must be a time difference between cause and effect. *Phil. Sci.* **39,** 507–11.
HELLMAN, G. P. and THOMPSON, F. W. 1975. Physicalism: ontology, determination, and reduction. *J. Phil.* **72,** 551–64.
HELM, P. 1974. Divine foreknowledge and facts. *Can. J. Phil.* **4,** 305–15.
1975a. Timelessness and foreknowledge. *Mind* **84,** 516–27.
1975b. Are 'Cambridge' changes non-events? *Analysis* **35,** 140–4.
1978. Detecting change. *Ratio* **19,** 34–8.
HINCKFUSS, I. C. 1975. *The Existence of Space and Time.* Oxford.
HINTIKKA, J. 1967. *Time and Necessity.* Oxford.
HIRSCH, E. 1976. Physical identity. *Phil. Rev.* **85,** 357–89.
HOLDCROFT, D. 1973. Escaping Taylor's fate. *Ratio* **15,** 303–14.
HOLLIS, M. 1967. Time and spaces. *Mind* **76,** 524–36.
HORGAN, T. 1978. The case against events. *Phil. Rev.* **83,** 28–47.
HORNSBY, J. 1979. Actions and identities. *Analysis* **39,** 195–201.
HORWICH, P. 1975. On some alleged paradoxes of time travel. *J. Phil.* **72,** 432–44.
1978. On the existence of time, space and space–time. *Noûs* **12,** 397–419.
HOY, R. C. 1975. The role of genidentity in the causal theory of time. *Phil. Sci.* **42,** 11–19.
1976. Science and temporal experience: a critical defence. *Phil. Res. Arch.* **2,** no. 1196.
1978. Becoming and persons. *Phil. Stud.* **34,** 269–80.
HUME, D. 1739. *A Treatise of Human Nature.* London.
HUSSERL, E. 1928. *The Phenomenology of Internal Time-Consciousness,* tr. J. S. Churchill. 1964. Bloomington, Indiana.
JAMMER, M. 1974. *The Philosophy of Quantum Mechanics.* New York.
JEFFREY, R. C. 1965. *The Logic of Decision.* New York.
1980a. Coming true. *Intention and Intentionality,* eds C. Diamond and J. Teichman, pp. 251–60. London.

1980b. How is it reasonable to base preferences on estimates of chance? *Science, Belief and Behaviour*, ed. D. H. Mellor, pp. 179–87. Cambridge.

JOBE, E. K. 1976. Temporal predication and identity. *Austral. J. Phil.* **54**, 65–71.

KAMP, H. 1971. Formal properties of 'now'. *Theoria* **37**, 227–73.

KANT, I. 1781. *Critique of Pure Reason*, tr. N. K. Smith, 1929. London.

KHATCHADOURIAN, H. 1973. Do ordinary spatial and temporal expressions designate relations? *Phil. Phenomen. Res.* **34**, 82–94.

KIM, J. 1976. Events as property exemplifications. *Action Theory*, eds M. Brand and D. Walton, pp. 159–77. Dordrecht.

KING-FARLOW, J. 1974. The positive McTaggart on time. *Philosophy* **49**, 169–78.

KNEALE, M. 1969. Eternity and sempiternity. *Proc. Arist. Soc.* **69**, 222–238.

KNEALE, W. C. 1957. What can we see? *Observation and Interpretation in the Philosophy of Physics*, ed. S. Körner, pp. 151–9. London.

LACEY, H. M. 1968. The causal theory of time, a critique of Grünbaum's version. *Phil. Sci.* **35**, 322–54.

1971. Quine on the logic and ontology of time. *Austral. J. Phil.* **49**, 47–67.

LAYCOCK, H. 1975. Theories of matter. *Synthese* **31**, 411–42.

LEE, H. N. 1972. Time and continuity. *Southern J. Phil.* **10**, 295–9.

LEHRER, K. AND TAYLOR, R. 1965. Time, truth and modalities. *Mind* **74**, 390–8.

LEWIS, D. K. 1976. The paradoxes of time travel. *Amer. Phil. Quart.* **13**, 145–52.

1979. Counterfactual dependence and time's arrow. *Noûs* **13**, 455–76.

LICHTBLAU, D. E. 1976. Prior and the Barcan formula. *Notre Dame J. Form. Log.* **17**, 602–24.

LLOYD, G. 1978. Time and existence. *Philosophy* **53**, 215–28.

LUCAS, J. R. 1973. *A Treatise on Time and Space*. London.

LYCAN, W. G. 1974. Eternal sentences again. *Phil. Stud.* **26**, 411–18.

MABBOTT, J. D. 1951. Our direct experience of time. *Mind* **60**, 153–67.

MACKIE, J. L. 1966. The direction of causation. *Phil. Rev.* **75**, 441–66.

1974. *The Cement of the Universe*. Oxford.

MALAMENT, D. 1977. Causal theories of time and the conventionality of simultaneity. *Noûs* **11**, 293–300.

MARGOLIS, J. 1963. Statements about the past and future. *Phil. Rev.* **72**, 84–7.

MARTIN, R. M. 1971. *Logic, Language and Metaphysics*. New York.

MASSEY, G. J. 1969. Tense logic – why bother? *Noûs* **3**, 17–32.

MATTHEWS, G. 1979. Time's arrow and the structure of spacetime. *Phil. Sci.* **46**, 82–97.

MAYO, B. 1961. Objects, events and complementarity. *Phil. Rev.* **70**, 340–61.

1962. The open future. *Mind* **71**, 1–14.

McArthur, R. P. 1974. Factuality and modality in the future tense. *Noûs* **8**, 283–8.

1975. Tense and temporally neutral paraphrase. *Austral. J. Phil.* **53**, 27–35.

1976. *Tense Logic.* Dordrecht.

McArthur, R. P. and Slattery, M. P. 1974. Peter Damian and undoing the past. *Phil. Stud.* **25**, 137–41.

McCall, S. 1966. Temporal flux. *Amer. Phil. Quart.* **3**, 270–81.

1971. Time and the physical modalities. *Basic Issues in the Philosophy of Time*, eds E. Freeman and W. Sellars, pp. 102–22. La Salle, Illinois.

McGilvray, J. A. 1973. The function of tenses. *Noûs* **7**, 164–78.

1979. A defense of physical becoming. *Erkenntnis* **14**, 275–99.

McGinn, C. 1978. Mental states, natural kinds and psychophysical laws. *Arist. Soc. Suppl. Vol.* **52**, 195–220.

McKim, V. R. and Davis, C. C. 1976. Temporal modalities and the future. *Notre Dame J. Form. Log.* **17**, 233–8.

McTaggart, J. McT. E. 1908. The unreality of time. *Mind* **18**, 457–84.

1927. *The Nature of Existence*, vol. 2. Cambridge.

Mehlberg, H. 1961. Physical laws and time's arrow. *Current Issues in the Philosophy of Science*, eds H. Feigl and G. Maxwell, pp. 105–38. New York.

Meiland, J. W. 1974. A two-dimensional passage model of time for time travel. *Phil. Stud.* **26**, 153–73.

Mellor, D. H. 1974a. In defense of dispositions. *Phil. Rev.* **83**, 157–81.

1974b. Special relativity and present truth. *Analysis* **34**, 74–8.

1979. The possibility of prediction. *Proc. Brit. Acad.* **65**, 207–23.

1980a. Consciousness and degrees of belief. *Prospects for Pragmatism*, ed. D. H. Mellor, pp. 139–73. Cambridge.

1980b. The self from time to time. *Analysis* **40**, 59–62.

1980c. On things and causes in spacetime. *Brit. J. Phil. Sci.* **31**, 282–8.

1981a. McTaggart, fixity and coming true. *Reduction, Time and Reality*, ed. R. Healey, pp. 79–97. Cambridge.

1981b. 'Thank goodness that's over'. *Ratio* **23**, 20–30.

1982. The reduction of society. *Philosophy* **57**.

Michael, F. S. 1976. What is the master argument of Diodorus Cronus? *Amer. Phil. Quart.* **13**, 229–35.

Miller, B. 1973. Change in a four-dimensionalist universe. *Phil. Papers* **2**, 84–8.

Mink, L. O. 1960. Time, McTaggart and Pickwickian language. *Phil. Quart.* **10**, 252–63.

Minkowski, H. 1908. Space and time. *The Principle of Relativity*, A. Einstein *et al.*, tr. W. Perrett and G. B. Jeffery, pp. 73–91. 1923. London.

Moore, G. E. 1942. A reply to my critics. *The Philosophy of G. E. Moore*, ed. P. A. Schilpp, pp. 535–677. La Salle, Illinois.

Moravcsik, J. 1965. Strawson and ontological priority. *Analytical Philosophy*, 2nd series, ed. R. J. Butler, pp. 106–19. Oxford.

MORRISON, R. P. 1978. Kant, Husserl and Heidegger on time and the unity of 'consciousness'. *Phil. Phenomen. Res.* **39**, 182–98.

MOTT, P. 1973. Dates, tenseless verbs and token-reflexivity. *Mind* **82**, 73–85.

MUNDLE, W. C. K. 1959. Broad's views about time. *The Philosophy of C. D. Broad*, ed. P. A. Schilpp, pp. 353–74. La Salle, Illinois.

MUNITZ, M. K. 1957. *Space, Time and Creation*. New York.

NERLICH, G. 1979a. Time and the direction of conditionship. *Austral. J. Phil.* **57**, 3–14.

1979b. How to make things have happened. *Can. J. Phil.* **9**, 1–21.

1979c. What can geometry explain? *Brit. J. Phil. Sci.* **30**, 69–83.

NEWTON, R. G. 1970. Particles that travel faster than light? *Science* **167**, 1569–74.

NEWTON-SMITH, W. 1980. *The Structure of Time*. London.

NORTH, J. 1970. The time coordinate in Einstein's restricted theory of relativity. *Studium Generale* **23**, 203–23.

NUSENOFF, R. E. 1976. Two-dimensional time. *Phil. Stud.* **29**, 337–41.

OAKLANDER, L. N. 1976. Propositions, facts, and becoming. *Phil. Stud.* **29**, 397–402.

1977. The 'timelessness' of time. *Phil. Phenomen. Res.* **38**, 228–33.

ODEGARD, D. 1978. Phenomenal time. *Ratio* **20**, 116–22.

O'NEILL, J., ed. 1973. *Modes of Individualism and Collectivism*. London.

OTTEN, J. 1977. Moving back and forth in time. *Auslegung* **5**, 5–17.

PARK, D. 1971. The myth of the passage of time. *Studium Generale* **24**, 19–30.

PEARS, D. F. 1951. Time, truth and inference. *Essays in Conceptual Analysis*, ed. A. G. N. Flew, pp. 228–52. 1966. London.

1957. Priority of causes. *Analysis* **17**, 54–63.

PERRY, J. 1979. The problem of the essential indexical. *Noûs* **13**, 3–21.

PIKE, N. 1965. Divine omniscience and voluntary action. *Phil. Rev.* **74**, 27–46.

POLAKOW, A. 1979. The irreducibility of B-relations to A-determinations. *Mind* **88**, 430–6.

1981. *Tense and Performance*. Amsterdam.

POPPEL, E. 1971. Oscillations as a possible basis of time perception. *Studium Generale* **24**, 85–107.

POPPER, K. R. 1957. *The Poverty of Historicism*. London.

1978. On the possibility of an infinite past. *Brit. J. Phil. Sci.* **29**, 47–48.

PRIOR, A. N. 1957. *Time and Modality*. Oxford.

1958. Time after time. *Mind* **67**, 244–6.

1959. Thank goodness that's over. *Philosophy* **34**, 12–17.

1967. *Past, Present and Future*. Oxford.

1968. *Papers on Time and Tense*. Oxford.

1970. The notion of the present. *Studium Generale* **23**, 245–8.

PUTNAM, H. 1962. It ain't necessarily so. *Mathematics, Matter and Method*, pp. 237–49. 1975. Cambridge.

1967. Time and physical geometry. *Mathematics, Matter and Method*, pp. 198–205. 1975. Cambridge.

1973. Reductionism and the nature of psychology. *Cognition* 2, 131–45.

QUINE, W. V. 1960. *Word and Object*. Cambridge, Mass.

QUINN, P. L. 1979. Existence throughout an interval of time, and existence at an instant of time. *Ratio* 21, 1–12.

QUINTON, A. M. 1962. Spaces and times. *Philosophy* 37, 130–47.

1973. *The Nature of Things*. London.

1976. Social objects. *Proc. Arist. Soc.* 76, 1–27.

RAMSEY, F. P. 1929a. General propositions and causality. *Foundations*, ed. D. H. Mellor, pp. 17–39. 1978. London.

1929b. Knowledge. *Foundations*, ed. D. H. Mellor, pp. 126–7. 1978. London.

REICHENBACH, H. 1928. *The Philosophy of Space and Time*, tr. M. Reichenbach and J. Freund. 1958. New York.

1947. *Elements of Symbolic Logic*. New York.

1949. The philosophical significance of the theory of relativity. *Albert Einstein: Philosopher–Scientist*, ed. P. A. Schilpp, pp. 287–311. La Salle, Illinois.

1957. *The Direction of Time*. Berkeley.

RESCHER, N. 1967. Truth and necessity in temporal perspective. *The Philosophy of Time*, ed. R. M. Gale, pp. 183–220. New York.

ROMNEY, G. 1978. Temporal points of view. *Proc. Arist. Soc.* 78, 237–52.

ROSENBERG, A. 1974. On Kim's account of events and event-identity. *J. Phil.* 71, 327–36.

1975. Propter hoc, ergo post hoc. *Amer. Phil. Quart.* 12, 245–54.

ROSENBERG, J. F. 1972. One way of understanding time. *Philosophia* 2, 283–301.

ROSENTHAL, D. M. 1976. The necessity of foreknowledge. *Midwest Stud. Phil.* 1, 22–5.

RUCH, R. S. 1979. Present-moment living. *The Humanist* 39, 32–5.

RUSSELL, B. 1900. *A Critical Exposition of the Philosophy of Leibniz*. Cambridge.

1903. *The Principles of Mathematics*. Cambridge.

1915. On the experience of time. *Monist* 25, 212–33.

1922. *Our Knowledge of the External World*. London.

1927. *An Outline of Philosophy*. London.

RYLE, G. 1954. *Dilemmas*. Cambridge.

1957. Predicting and inferring. *Observation and Interpretation in the Philosophy of Physics*, ed. S. Körner, pp. 165–70. London.

SALMON, W. C. 1975. *Space, Time and Motion*. Encino, California.

1977. The philosophical significance of the one-way speed of light. *Noûs* 11, 253–92.

SANFORD, D. H. 1976. The direction of causation and the direction of conditionship. *J. Phil.* 73, 193–207.

SCHLESINGER, G. 1963. *Method in the Physical Sciences*. London.

1975. The similarities between time and space. *Mind* 84, 161–76.

1978a. The reduction of B-statements. *Phil. Quart.* **28**, 162–5.
1978b. Comparing space and time once more. *Mind* **87**, 264–6.
1980. *Aspects of Time.* Indianapolis.
SCHLICK, M. 1920. *Space and Time in Contemporary Physics,* tr. H. L. Brose. Oxford.
1949. *Philosophy of Nature,* tr. A. von Zeppelin. New York.
SCHRÖDINGER, E. 1950. Irreversibility. *Proc. Roy. Irish Acad.* **51**, 189–95.
SCRIVEN, M. 1957. Randomness and causal disorder. *Analysis* **17**, 5–9.
SELLARS, W. 1962. Time and the world order. *Minnesota Studies in the Philosophy of Science,* vol. 3, eds H. Feigl and G. Maxwell, pp. 527–616. Minneapolis.
1973. Actions and events. *Noûs* **7**, 174–202.
SHEA, W. R. 1975. McTaggart and the neo-positivist entropists. *Philosophy* **50**, 346–51.
SHER, G. 1974. On event identity. *Austral. J. Phil.* **52**, 39–47.
SHOEMAKER, S. 1969. Time without change. *J. Phil.* **66**, 363–81.
SHORTER, J. M. 1977. On coinciding in space and time. *Philosophy* **52**, 399–408.
SKILLEN, A. 1965. The myth of temporal division. *Analysis* **25**, 44–7.
SKLAR, L. 1974. *Space, Time and Spacetime.* Berkeley.
SLOTE, M. A. 1978. Time in counterfactuals. *Phil. Rev.* **87**, 3–27.
SMART, J. J. C. 1949. The river of time. *Essays in Conceptual Analysis,* ed. A. G. N. Flew, pp. 213–27. 1966. London.
1962. 'Tensed statements': a comment. *Phil. Quart.* **12**, 264–5.
1963. *Philosophy and Scientific Realism.* London.
ed. 1964. *Problems of Space and Time.* New York.
1967. Time. *The Encyclopedia of Philosophy,* vol. 8, ed. P. Edwards, pp. 126–34. New York.
1971. Causal theories of time. *Basic Issues in the Philosophy of Time,* eds E. Freeman and W. Sellars, pp. 61–77. La Salle, Illinois.
SMITH, T. P. 1973. On the applicability of a criterion of change. *Ratio* **15**, 325–33.
SOSA, E. 1979. The status of becoming: what is happening now? *J. Phil.* **76**, 26–42.
STEIN, H. 1968. On Einstein–Minkowski space–time. *J. Phil.* **65**, 5–23.
1970. On the paradoxical time-structures of Gödel. *Phil. Sci.* **37**, 589–601.
STENNER, A. J. 1974. Toward a theory of event identity. *Phil. Sci.* **41**, 65–83.
STRANG, C. 1960. Aristotle and the sea battle. *Mind* **69**, 447–65.
STRAWSON, P. F. 1959. *Individuals.* London.
STREVELER, P. A. 1973. The problem of future contingents. *New Scholasticism* **47**, 233–47.
SUPPES, P. 1973. *Space, Time and Geometry.* Dordrecht.
SWARTZ, N. 1973. Is there an Ozma-problem for time? *Analysis* **33**, 77–82.
SWINBURNE, R. G. 1965. Conditions for bitemporality. *Analysis* **26**, 47–50.
1968. *Space and Time.* London.

TARSKI, A. 1956. *Logic, Semantics, Metamathematics*, tr. J. H. Woodger. Oxford.

TAYLOR, R. 1955. Spatial and temporal analogies and the concept of identity. *J. Phil.* **52**, 599–612.

1957. The problem of future contingents. *Phil. Rev.* **66**, 1–46.

1959. Moving about in time. *Phil. Quart.* **9**, 289–301.

THALBERG, I. 1963. Tenses and now. *Phil. Quart.* **13**, 298–310.

1977. *Perception, Emotion and Action*. Oxford.

1978. The irreducibility of events. *Analysis* **38**, 1–9.

1980. Can we get rid of events? *Analysis* **40**, 25–31.

THEOBALD, D. W. 1976. On the recurrence of things past. *Mind* **85**, 107–11.

THOM, P. 1975. Time-travel and non-fatal suicide. *Phil. Stud.* **27**, 211–16.

THOMASON, R. H. 1970. Indeterminist time and truth-value gaps. *Theoria* **36**, 264–81.

TRAVIS, C. 1973. Causes, events and ontology. *Philosophia* **3**, 201–44.

VAN FRAASSEN, B. 1970. *An Introduction to the Philosophy of Space and Time.* New York.

1972. Earman on the causal theory of time. *Synthese* **24**, 87–95.

VENDLER, Z. 1957. Verbs and times. *Phil. Rev.* **66**, 143–60.

VON WRIGHT, G. H. 1968. *Time, Change and Contradiction.* Cambridge.

WATERLOW, S. 1974. Backwards causation and continuing. *Mind* **83**, 372–87.

WATLING, J. 1974. Are causes events or facts? *Proc. Arist. Soc.* **74**, 161–170.

WEINGARD, R. 1972. On traveling backward in time. *Synthese* **24**, 117–31.

1977. Space–time and the direction of time. *Noûs* **11**, 119–31.

1979. General relativity and the conceivability of time travel. *Phil. Sci.* **46**, 328–32.

WERTH, L. F. 1978. Normalising the paranormal. *Amer. Phil. Quart.* **15**, 47–56.

WEYL, H. 1919. *Space, Time and Matter*, tr. H. L. Brose. 1922. London.

WHEELER, J. A. 1962. Curved empty space–time as the building material of the physical world. *Logic, Methodology and Philosophy of Science*, ed. E. Nagel *et al.*, pp. 361–74. Stanford.

WHITEHEAD, A. N. 1920. *An Enquiry Concerning the Principles of Natural Knowledge.* Cambridge.

1929. *Process and Reality.* Cambridge.

WHITROW, G. J. 1961. *The Natural Philosophy of Time.* London.

1972. *What is Time?* London.

WIENER, N. 1961. *Cybernetics.* New York.

WIERENGA, E. 1976. Chisholm on states of affairs. *Austral. J. Phil.* **54**, 148–52.

WIGGINS, D. 1980. *Sameness and Substance.* Oxford.

WIGNER, E. P. 1965. Violations of symmetry in physics. *Sci. Amer.* **213**, 28–42.

WILKERSON, T. E. 1973. Time and time again. *Philosophy* **48**, 173–7.

WILLIAMS, C. E. 1974. 'Now', extensional interchangeability, and the passage of time. *Phil. Forum* **5**, 405–23.

1976. Meaning, reference and tense. *Analysis* **36**, 132–6.

WILLIAMS, C. J. F. 1978. True tomorrow, never true today. *Phil. Quart.* **28**, 285–99.

WILLIAMS, D. C. 1951. The myth of passage. *J. Phil.* **48**, 457–72.

WILSON, N. L. 1955. Space, time and individuals. *J. Phil.* **52**, 589–98.

1974. Facts, events and their identity conditions. *Phil. Stud.* **25**, 303–21.

WOODHOUSE, M. B. 1976. The reversibility of absolute time. *Phil. Stud.* **29**, 465–8.

WOODS, M. 1976. Existence and tense. *Truth and Meaning*, eds G. Evans and J. McDowell, pp. 248–62. Oxford.

ZEMAN, J., ed. 1971. *Time in Science and Philosophy*. Amsterdam.

ZENZEN, M. 1977. Popper, Grünbaum and *de facto* irreversibility. *Brit. J. Phil. Sci.* **28**, 313–24.

ZWART, P. J. 1972. The flow of time. *Synthese* **24**, 133–57.

Index